CW01508127

Spinoza's Heresy

Spinoza's Heresy

Immortality and the Jewish Mind

Steven Nadler

CLARENDON PRESS · OXFORD

OXFORD
UNIVERSITY PRESS

Great Clarendon Street, Oxford OX2 6DP

Oxford University Press is a department of the University of Oxford.
It furthers the University's objective of excellence in research, scholarship,
and education by publishing worldwide in

Oxford New York

Athens Auckland Bangkok Bogotá Buenos Aires Cape Town
Chennai Dar es Salaam Delhi Florence Hong Kong Istanbul Karachi
Kolkata Kuala Lumpur Madrid Melbourne Mexico City Mumbai Nairobi
Paris São Paulo Shanghai Singapore Taipei Tokyo Toronto Warsaw

with associated companies in Berlin Ibadan

Oxford is a registered trade mark of Oxford University Press
in the UK and in certain other countries

Published in the United States
By Oxford University Press Inc., New York

© Steven Nadler 2001

The moral rights of the author have been asserted

Database right Oxford University Press (maker)

First published 2001

All rights reserved. No part of this publication may be reproduced,
stored in a retrieval system, or transmitted, in any form or by any means,
without the prior permission in writing of Oxford University Press,
or as expressly permitted by law, or under terms agreed with the appropriate
reprographics rights organization. Enquiries concerning reproduction
outside the scope of the above should be sent to the Rights Department,
Oxford University Press, at the address above

You must not circulate this book in any other binding or cover
and you must impose this same condition on any acquirer

British Library Cataloguing in Publication Data

Data available

Library of Congress Cataloging in Publication Data

Nadler, Steven M., 1958–
Spinoza's heresy : immortality and the Jewish mind / Steven Nadler.
p. cm.
Includes bibliographical references and index.
1. Spinoza, Benedictus de, 1632–1677—Views on immortality.
2. Immortality—Judaism. 3. Future life—Judaism. 4. Portugees-Israelietische Gemeente te
Amsterdam—Membership. 5. Philosophy, Jewish. 6. Philosophy, Medieval. I. Title.

B3999.I4 N33 2002 199′.492—dc21 2001036731

ISBN 0-19-924707-2

1 3 5 7 9 10 8 6 4 2

Typeset in 10/13.5pt Calisto MT,
by Graphicraft Limited, Hong Kong
Printed in Great Britain by
Biddles Ltd., Guildford & Kings Lynn

For
Samuel Nadler ז"ל
and
Louis Hertz ז"ל

Preface

Despite Spinoza's firm recommendation of the life of reason as the path to true happiness and his warning against allowing ourselves to be 'tossed about' by the passions, by the constantly changing emotions that, as passively affective responses to the world around us, alternately sway us this way and that, it is easy to become passionate about —even obsessed with—Spinoza's philosophy. His is a rich and multifaceted system, one that rewards long and careful study. He also basically got it all right.

This book is, in a sense, a sequel to my biography of Spinoza (*Spinoza: A Life*, Cambridge University Press, 1999); it is probably also a prequel to further projects. My goal in this work is to look more closely at his *cherem*, or expulsion, from the Portuguese Jewish congregation in Amsterdam, and to situate his views on one of the issues that reportedly occasioned that extreme punishment within a broad Jewish context.

In the biography I purposefully avoided engaging any scholarly debates over the interpretation of his philosophy or the understanding of the events of his all too brief career. That book was written for a general audience interested in the life, times, and thought of one of history's most fascinating and radical thinkers, and it did not seem appropriate or useful to the purpose at hand to get bogged down in deep philosophical detail or academic polemic. Thus, when discussing what may have been the reasons behind Spinoza's *cherem*, I opted to maintain an appearance of neutrality and evenhandedness. I laid out the numerous hypotheses that scholars have offered to explain his expulsion from the synagogue, made some cursory remarks of my own about what seemed to be the likely causes for the event, and then moved on. It was not the right occasion to argue at length for or against any particular interpretation of the *cherem* or to show in detail how and why certain issues would have mattered to the parties involved.

This present book is both more focused and broader in scope than the biography. It is more focused in that the question that frames the discussion is simply: Why was Spinoza excommunicated? More particularly, I am interested in exploring why this particular seventeenth-century Jewish community felt it necessary to ban, with a writ of *cherem* harsher than any that it had ever used before or would ever use again, a remarkably intelligent and promising member of one of its more prominent families. Even more particularly, I want especially to try to understand why one of the issues that is alleged to have played a role in the decision to excommunicate Spinoza—his denial of the immortality of the soul—*did* play such a role. Given the nature of the question of immortality and the tradition of Jewish thinking on this issue, it seems an unlikely candidate for the cause of such a vitriolic ban.

The book's scope is broader than that of the biography, however, in that Spinoza's philosophical thinking on the human being, and in particular on the human mind—its nature, its well-being, and its eternity—is considered in the larger context of both the Jewish religious and textual tradition and medieval Jewish philosophy. I hope to show how Spinoza's denial of the immortality of the soul is not only an outgrowth of his own highly idiosyncratic but well-reasoned metaphysical principles, but also the culmination—indeed, the logical and natural conclusion—of a certain intellectualist trend in Jewish rationalism.

Because of the attention given to the Jewish context, some readers may feel compelled to complain that I ignore the many other important philosophical and cultural influences on Spinoza, especially Descartes and other early modern thinkers, but also the radical and iconoclastic figures that populated the contemporary (and volatile) Dutch intellectual scene. My response to this is simple: It is not my intention to deny or even minimize the role that Descartes, Hobbes, and others (moderns and ancients) played in Spinoza's intellectual development. Rather, I aim only to place Spinoza's thought on one particular issue within a different philosophical and religious tradition.

It is a tradition that is too often neglected in philosophical scholarship on Spinoza; rare is the book written on him by a philosopher that considers with any depth his relationship to and standing within Jewish philosophy. And yet, if one does not pay attention to this context, much of what he has to say cannot make any sense; indeed, I believe that the many scholars who profess not to understand—or, worse, who dismiss as incoherent—what Spinoza is claiming about the eternity of the mind are not taking seriously the Jewish philosophical tradition in which his thought on this question needs to be placed.

While it is true that the Cartesian context is the truly important one when it comes to understanding Spinoza's metaphysics and epistemology—essentially, Parts One and Two of the *Ethics*—this is not the case with respect to his moral philosophy, and particularly his account of virtue, human happiness, and the eternity of the mind. Cartesian philosophy may have laid the 'first principles' for the conclusions that Spinoza draws in Parts Four and Five of the *Ethics*, but the doctrines that we find embedded in the propositions of those parts are a response to a far different tradition, one that has as its most prominent members the medieval Jewish philosophers Maimonides and Gersonides. So if Descartes and others seem to be slighted in this study of Spinoza's approach to the problem of immortality, then I plead *nolo contendere*: they simply did not, I believe, play the most important role in Spinoza's thinking on this question.

Other readers may complain, however, that I have left out of this book a good deal of important Jewish material, that I have been overly selective in my choice of Jewish texts and thinkers that are relevant to the question of immortality. I have indeed been very selective in this regard. But I must stress that I do not intend for this book to be a broad, general, and exhaustive survey of Jewish views on immortality and the afterlife. The Jewish opinions I do discuss (some briefly, others at greater length) are presented only in order to provide some religious background as well as the immediately relevant philosophical context for what *is* my (admittedly narrower) main project: understanding both Spinoza's approach to the problem of immortality and the role this issue played in his community's decision to ban him.

I would, finally, like to offer in this Preface three remarks to serve as a *caveat lector*. First, while this work may be regarded as a sequel to the biography, I do not presume any familiarity with that book. Therefore, in a number of places in this study I briefly summarize some of the material from the biography when it provides necessary background or is relevant to my argument. This is particularly the case with Chapter 1, where I introduce the reader to the procedure of *cherem*, both in Judaism generally and in Amsterdam, and to Spinoza's *cherem* in particular. I hope readers of the biography will forgive this repetition of material that I have presented more fully in that book.

Second, I resort to summary overviews of various elements of Spinoza's philosophy when it is necessary to do so in order to approach intelligibly the specific problem of his views on the nature of the human being, his happiness, and the eternity of the mind. The reader should not expect a detailed defense of every aspect of my reading of Spinoza's philosophy, as potentially contentious as it may be. There are innumerable books and articles devoted to Spinoza's philosophy as a whole, as well as to the theses and arguments of his metaphysics and epistemology. By contrast, there are relatively few studies of his doctrine of the eternity of the mind (especially considered as a denial of the immortality of the soul), and even fewer of the Jewish context for this aspect of his thought. I hope the reader will forgive my ignoring some interesting and important debates over the finer points of Spinoza's philosophy in order that I might be able to get right to the heart of the issue that fascinates me here: Spinoza's rejection of personal immortality, its relationship both to his own philosophical project and to Jewish philosophical and religious tradition, and the role this issue played in the decision by the Amsterdam Sephardic Jews to expel him from their community.

Finally, while I hope this book is of interest and use to specialists in Spinoza's philosophy, I also want to engage the general reader, academic or otherwise—especially the person who, after reading the biography, wants to learn a little more about Spinoza's views and why they would have led to his harsh banning, and about his place in the history of Jewish thought. This lay reader will not be as interested as the specialist may be in the various ways in which some propositions, demonstrations, scholia, and corollaries of the *Ethics* (especially those early in the book that do not immediately appear in Spinoza's account of the eternity of the mind) can be read as either supportive of or inconsistent with my reading of his doctrines. I am afraid that, for the sake of accessibility and readability—two virtues not often found in specialized Spinoza scholarship—I use a fairly broad brush, leaving some technical loose ends dangling. I try to address many of these questions in the notes, but surely some will remain unanswered. I make no apologies, however, for concentrating on the forest rather than on the trees (and the branches and the twigs); if only more historians of philosophy would do the same.

Acknowledgements

A number of people were very helpful to me in providing comments on various draft versions of this work. I would like to take this opportunity to thank Lenn Goodman, Kenneth Katz, Larry Kohn, Michael Morgan, David Novak, Tamar Rudavsky, Donald Rutherford, and David Sorkin for their suggestions, criticisms, encouragement, and advice. I am extremely grateful—and very lucky—to have such generous friends and colleagues.

During the writing of the book I was able to benefit from the opportunity to present material from its central chapters to audiences at Princeton University, the University of Toronto, Washington University in St Louis, Rutgers University, Hebrew University (Jerusalem), and Ohio State University. I am grateful to my hosts for the invitations, and to the members of the audiences for the useful discussions that followed my presentations. Part of Chapter 6 was also presented to a conference entitled 'Spinoza and Judaism' at the University of Wisconsin–Madison, and the comments I received there from an eclectic gathering of specialists on Spinoza and Jewish Studies were invaluable.

I want also to thank the Koret Foundation and the National Foundation for Jewish Culture, who awarded *Spinoza: A Life* the 2000 Koret Jewish Book Award for biography. The support from that award was important, in many ways, to my being able to complete this book.

Finally, I am, once again and as ever, full of gratitude and love to my wife, Jane, who still takes my breath away; and my children, Rose and Ben, to whom I was always impatient to return after getting some writing in, for yet another game of roughhouse.

Contents

Abbreviations

For references to the writings of Spinoza, I have used the following abbreviations:

C	*The Collected Works of Spinoza*, trans. E. M. Curley, vol. i
G	*Spinoza Opera*, ed. Carl Gebhardt, 5 vols.
S	*Theological–Political Treatise*, trans. Samuel Shirley
TTP	*Tractatus Theologico-Politicus*

Citations for the *Ethics* incorporate the standard indications of part and proposition, as well as (when relevant) scholium. Thus, Ip15s1 is Part One, proposition 15, scholium 1. (c: corollary; d: demonstration.)

Cherem in Amsterdam 1

It is a splendid mystery.

In 1656 Bento de Spinoza was 23 years old. He was the middle son in a prominent family of moderate means in Amsterdam's Sephardic Jewish community. As a boy, he had undoubtedly been one of the star pupils in the congregation's Talmud Torah school. He was intellectually gifted, and this could not have gone unremarked by the congregation's rabbis. Perhaps Baruch—as he would have been called in the classroom and in the synagogue (the Portuguese and the Hebrew both mean 'blessed')—was, as he made progress through his studies, being groomed for a career as a rabbi. But he never made it into the upper levels of the curriculum, those which included advanced study of Talmud. At the age of 17 he was forced to cut short his formal studies. His elder brother, Isaac, had died, and the young man was needed in the family's importing business. Just a few years later, by late 1654, with his father dead, he was running the firm with his younger brother, Gabriel (or Abraham). He had joined the ranks of 'Portuguese [read: Jewish] merchants' in Amsterdam. During the next eleven months, as required by Jewish law, he daily recited Kaddish, the prayer of mourning, for his father, Miguel. He also continued to pay his dues to the congregation.

And then, on July 27, 1656 (the sixth of Av 5416 by the Jewish calendar), the following proclamation was read in Hebrew from in front of the ark of the Torah in the crowded synagogue on the Houtgracht:

The *Senhores* of the *ma'amad* [the congregation's lay governing board] having long known of the evil opinions and acts of Baruch de Spinoza, they have endeavored by various means and promises, to turn him from his evil ways. But having failed to make him mend his wicked ways, and, on the contrary, daily receiving more and more serious information about the abominable heresies which he practiced and taught and about his monstrous deeds, and having for this numerous trustworthy witnesses who have deposed and borne witness to this effect in the presence of the said Espinoza, they became convinced of the truth of this matter; and after all of this has been investigated in the presence of the honorable *chachamim* ['wise men', or rabbis] they have decided, with their consent, that the said Espinoza should be excommunicated and expelled from the people of Israel. By decree of the angels and by the command of the holy men, we excommunicate, expel, curse and damn Baruch de Espinoza, with the consent of God, Blessed be He, and with the consent of the entire holy congregation, and in front of these holy scrolls with the 613 precepts which are written therein; cursing him with the excommunication with which Joshua banned Jericho and with the curse which Elisha cursed the boys and with all the castigations which are written in the Book of the Law. Cursed be he by day and cursed be he by night; cursed be he when he lies down and cursed be he when he rises up. Cursed be he when he goes out and cursed be he when he comes in. The Lord will not spare him, but then the anger of the Lord and his jealousy shall smoke against that man, and all the curses that are written in this book shall lie upon him, and the Lord shall blot out his name from under heaven. And the Lord shall separate him unto evil out of all the tribes of Israel, according to all the curses of the covenant that are written in this book of the law. But you that cleave unto the Lord your God are alive every one of you this day.

The document concludes with the warning that 'no one should communicate with him, neither in writing, nor accord him any favor nor stay with him under the same roof nor [come] within four cubits in his vicinity; nor shall he read any treatise composed or written by him'. A Portuguese version of the proclamation was later entered into the community's record books.[1]

It was the harshest writ of *cherem*, or expulsion, ever pronounced upon a member of the Portuguese Jewish community of Amsterdam.[2] The community's lay governors, the self-electing *parnassim*, dug deep into their books to find just the right words for the occasion. The text used for the *cherem* had been brought back to Amsterdam from Venice by Rabbi Saul Levi Mortera almost forty years earlier. In 1619 Mortera was sent on an embassy to Venice, the city of his birth and upbringing, because the Amsterdam leaders were hoping that the *parnassim* of that older and more established Sephardic community could help resolve a rancorous dispute over property and prerogative within one of the city's congregations.[3] The Venetians, desirous of an amicable reconciliation and seeking (in vain, it turned out) to forestall a schism, nonetheless recommended that recalcitrant parties be threatened with a *cherem*. Mortera received the appropriate text from Venice's chief rabbi, his former teacher, Leon Modena. Modena, in turn, had adapted it from the late thirteenth-century compendium of Jewish law and customs, the *Kol Bo* ('All is Within').[4] Mortera's Venetian mentor, a man possessed of both immense learning and a seriously flawed character, was not one to be trifled with.[5] He cobbled together a document full of curses and imprecations, one *maldicion* after another; their sheer quantity makes the *cherem* actually used for Spinoza decades later seem mild by comparison. It was a text that the Amsterdam Jews seem to have kept in reserve, perhaps to be used only when the case which called for a ban was a particularly serious one. As far as we know, Modena's elaborate composition was brought out in the seventeenth century only for the banning of Spinoza.[6]

Therein lies the puzzle.

We do not know for certain why Spinoza was punished with such extreme prejudice. That the punishment came from his own community—from the congregation that had nurtured and educated him, and that held his family in such high esteem[7]—only adds to the enigma. Neither the *cherem* itself nor any document from the period tells us exactly what his 'evil opinions and acts' (*más opinioins e obras*) were supposed to have been, nor what 'abominable heresies' (*horrendas heregias*) or 'monstrous deeds' (*ynormes obras*) he is alleged to have practiced and taught. He had not yet published anything, nor (as far as we know) even composed any treatise. Spinoza never refers to this period of his life in his extant letters, and thus does not himself offer his correspondents (or us) any clues as to why he was expelled.[8] All we know with certainty is that Spinoza received, from the *parnassim* composing the community's leadership in 1656, a *cherem* like no other in the period. It was never rescinded.

Although it is a convenient and common label, to call what Spinoza received in 1656 an 'excommunication' is not quite right. A religion that has no 'communion' to begin with, no formal set of obligatory sacraments and rites from which one can be excluded, cannot 'excommunicate' its members. Judaism, in its structures of power and prerogative, is not like the Catholic Church. Its lack of centralized authority and theological dogma make it difficult to take the terms of sanction operating in Catholicism and apply them meaningfully to the Jewish experience. Moreover, Spinoza was excluded not by ecclesiastic authorities, but by a community. What he was deprived of was more than just the right to partake in certain liturgical ceremonies. It went, in fact, right to the heart of what it means to be Jewish.

The use of the *cherem* by a Jewish community to punish, threaten, or coerce its rebellious members goes back at least to the first and second centuries, the Tannaitic period, when the sages of the Mishnah, the Tannaim, were struggling over the establishment of Jewish law. Originally, in its biblical use, the term *cherem* designated something or someone that is separated off from ordinary things and with which common use or contact is forbidden.[9] It can also refer to the destruction of some person or thing. The reason for the separation may be that the object or person is sacred or holy, and thus must not be handled; or—and this would be the grounds for destruction—it may be that it is polluted or an abomination to God. The Torah, for example, declares that anyone who sacrifices to any god other than the Israelite God is *cherem* (Exodus 22: 20). He is to be destroyed, and the idols he worshipped burned. Deuteronomy (7: 1–2) declares that the nations occupying the land that God has promised to the Israelites are *cherem*, and thus must be destroyed. On the other hand, something that has been devoted and consecrated to the Lord (*cherem l'adonai*) is 'most holy [*kodesh kodashim*] to the Lord' (Leviticus 27: 29), and thus cannot be sold or redeemed. There are also in the Hebrew Bible occasions when a separation or destruction is used to threaten or punish those who would disobey a command. The people of Israel are ordered to destroy (*tacharemu*) the population of Yavesh-gil'ad because it failed to heed the call to battle against the tribe of Benjamin (Judges 21: 5–11). In the period after the return from exile in Babylonia in the sixth century BCE Ezra declared that anyone who does not obey the proclamation to gather in Jerusalem within three days 'will lose [*yacharam*] all of his property and he will be separated from the congregation of the exiles' (Ezra 10: 7–8).

Among the rabbis of the Mishnah, whose deliberations, sayings, and disputes form the core of the Talmud, *cherem* (or, more properly, *niddui*) functioned as a form of punitive exclusion. A person who has violated some law or commandment is punished by being declared *menuddeh*, or 'defiled'. He (or, in some cases, she) is therefore to be isolated from the rest of the community and treated with contempt. *Niddui* seems also originally to have indicated more particularly some kind of expulsion from the ranks of the Pharisees or scholars. Thus, the Talmud tells of Rabbi Eliezer, who fell into dispute with some other rabbis over the ritual cleanliness of an oven constructed in a certain manner. Rabbi Eliezer insisted that *halachah*, or accepted legal tradition, was on his side and that the oven was *tahor*, or clean; his disputants, who made up a majority, remained unconvinced. Even God was unable to intervene successfully on Rabbi Eliezer's behalf. 'On that day, they brought all of the objects that Rabbi Eliezer had declared clean and they burned them in fire. Then they took a vote and excommunicated him.'[10]

Over time the term *cherem* often came to be used to refer to a more serious form of punishment than a *niddui*. In his *Mishneh Torah*, an exhaustive and monumental codification of Jewish law, the twelfth-century rabbi and philosopher Moses ben Maimon (more commonly known as Maimonides) discusses the case of a *chacham*, or wise man, who has sinned. At first, a *niddui* is pronounced upon him. If, after thirty days, the learned *menuddeh* has not reformed his ways, he is given another thirty days. During the time that he is under a *niddui*, he is to act and be treated as someone who is in mourning: he cannot cut his hair, he cannot wash his clothes or even his body, and no one may come within four cubits of his vicinity. If he should die while the *niddui* is still in effect, then it is not permitted to accompany his coffin to burial. If, after the sixty days under *niddui*, the sinner is still unrepentant, he is given a *cherem*. It is now forbidden to engage in business with him; he may not sell or purchase anything, nor negotiate or bargain. He is also forbidden to teach others and to be taught by someone else (although he is permitted to teach himself, 'lest he forget his learning').[11]

Among the offenses for which one should be given a *niddui* were, according to Maimonides, showing disrespect for rabbinical authority or personally insulting a rabbi, using a Gentile court of law to recover money that would not be recoverable under Jewish law, performing work on the afternoon before Passover eve, hindering someone else from performing a *mitzvah* (or commandment), violating any of the laws surrounding the preparation and consumption of kosher meat, intentional masturbation, not taking sufficient precautions when owning dogs or other potentially dangerous things, and mentioning God's name in everyday discourse.[12] Rabbi Joseph Caro, the author of the *Shulchan Arukh* ('The Ordered Table'), a sixteenth-century compendium of Jewish law that has been of particular importance to Sephardic communities around the world, adds a number of other acts for which one would deserve a *niddui*, including breaking an oath, performing work while a corpse lies unburied in town, demanding the performance of the impossible, and the taking over of a teacher's functions by one of his students.[13]

To be put under a *cherem* was of great consequence for an observant Jew. It affected the life of an individual and his family in both the secular and religious spheres, in matters both public and private. The person under a *cherem* was cut off, to one degree or another, from participating in the rituals of the community and thus from performing many of the everyday tasks that make life meaningful for a Jew. The harshness and duration of the punishment usually depended upon the seriousness of the offense. Because of the restrictions on dealing and bargaining, not to mention conversation, the *muchram*, or banned person, was, first of all, isolated from his ordinary business and social contacts. He might also be forbidden from serving as one of the ten men required for a *minyan* (prayer quorum), or from being called to the Torah in synagogue, or from serving in a leadership post of the congregation, or from performing any number of *mitzvot*, deeds that fulfill the moral and legal obligations incumbent upon any Jew. In extreme cases, the punishment extended to the offender's relatives: as long as a person was under a *cherem*, his sons were not to be circumcised, his children were off-limits for marriage, and no member of the family could be given a proper Jewish burial. Clearly, a *cherem* carried a tremendous emotional and spiritual impact. As one historian puts it, 'the excommunicated individual felt himself losing his place in both this world and the next'.[14]

Despite—or perhaps because of—the potentially extraordinary power of the *cherem*, the Sephardim of Amsterdam were not shy about using it. Disregarding Maimonides' admonition to wield this most extreme form of punishment only sparingly, the leaders of the Talmud Torah congregation employed the *cherem* widely for maintaining discipline and enforcing conformity among its members. Part of the reason for this stems, no doubt, from that community's unusual history, a remarkable story in its own right.[15]

There were, in essence, no Jews in Amsterdam before 1600. What there *were* were 'Portuguese merchants', who started arriving in the Netherlands in significant numbers in the final decades of the sixteenth century. Almost all of these immigrants were of 'converso' (or, to use the uglier term employed by their Old Christian neighbors in Iberia, 'marrano', or 'swine') heritage. When given an ultimatum by the Spanish monarchs in 1492 (and, again, by the Portuguese king in 1497), their Jewish ancestors chose conversion over exile. Perhaps most of these 'New Christians' were indeed sincere in their adopted faith. But many undoubtedly were not, and continued to practice some attenuated form of Judaism in secret. When the Iberian Inquisitors, always on the lookout for heretics, started taking a deep (and usually violent) interest in the conversos in their realms, many of them fled. A good number went first, in the mid-1500s, to Antwerp, part of the still-loyal Spanish Netherlands, where they hoped to continue business as usual with less harassment. But, as the end of the century drew near and the rebellious United Provinces of the Netherlands begain to gain the upper hand in their struggle for independence from Habsburg

Spain, the refugees headed north to Amsterdam, which by that time had eclipsed Antwerp as the commercial center of northern Europe. What they found there was not only the opportunity to regain the commercial success that they had left behind in the old country, but also the famed Dutch toleration, which made it possible for them eventually to return openly to Judaism. Article 13 of the Union of Utrecht (which set forth, in 1579, the founding principles of the Dutch Republic) explicitly declares that 'every individual shall remain free in his religion, and no one should be molested or questioned on the subject of divine worship'. It is an extraordinary statement for its time, although its framers seem not to have considered the possibility that it would some day have to accommodate Jews.

Official recognition—as opposed to tacit acquiesence—was slow in coming. But by 1619, as the city of Amsterdam informally granted the Jews the right to practice their religion publicly, there were over 500 ex-conversos in the city's Vlooienburg district. They lived, worked, and worshiped in the wood and brick houses along the Houtgracht, the 'wood canal'. It was by no means a ghetto. The Jews were not confined by law to this part of town, and these hard-working and experienced merchants, the more wealthy of whom lived in large mansions on the more upscale canals, maintained extensive business and social contacts with their Gentile neighbors. (The Dutch clearly appreciated—and the Spanish clearly resented—the contribution that Amsterdam's Jews, with their worldwide mercantile networks, made to the young nation's economy.) Within a relatively short period of time the quarter was home to a thriving and prosperous community, with Amsterdam acquiring the reputation of being a veritable 'Dutch Jerusalem'.

It was also, however, from the standpoint of normative Judaism, a somewhat problematic community. It was founded, after all, by Jews who had only recently returned to the fold. Most of the original members of the community came from families that, in their exclusively Catholic environments, had long been cut off from Jewish texts and practices. They had, at best, a rather tenuous grasp and idiosyncratic understanding of the requirements and expectations of Judaism, and were only now being introduced to orthodoxy and educated in its rigorous demands. The first congregations in Amsterdam, in fact, imported rabbis from Venice and elsewhere to educate their members in Jewish beliefs and traditions. These were eager learners, of course, and lacked no motivation for leading proper Jewish lives. But there had been generations of repression and assimilation. Even those who, in Spain and Portugal, did succeed in secret Judaizing found themselves with a somewhat hybrid religion—one that included, for example, a feast for 'St Esther' on the Purim holiday. It was the remnants of this 'Catholicized' Judaism that the rabbis fought to expunge, while the community's lay leaders took on the difficult task of molding the community at large into a properly Jewish one.[16] And sometimes even the most basic lessons need to be reinforced by robust sanctions.

There were various degrees of punishment of which the governing board of the Talmud Torah congregation could avail itself. It could, first of all, simply issue a warning. But offenders might also be denied admission to the synagogue on Yom Kippur, the Day of Atonement, and the most important holy day of the Jewish calendar; or they could be denied entry to all services in the synagogue. They could be forbidden from being called up to bless the Torah or read from the week's portion, that is, from performing *aliyah*, a great honor and privilege; they could be denied charity from the community's treasury; or they could be prevented from holding some communal office. The *chazzan*, or cantor, Abraham Baruch Franco, was at one time under prolonged punishment by a sentence of flogging, which took place before every new moon for two years. The directors of the community thus recognized, at least tacitly, a wide range of sanctions. But the ultimate punishment was the ban.

In many cases, a ban was directly attached by the community's regulations to violations of specific laws. In fact, there were certain laws for the breaking of which a ban was mandatory: establishing a *minyan*, or prayer quorum, for common prayer outside the congregation; disobeying orders of the governing board (the *ma'amad*), or raising a hand against a fellow Jew with the intention of striking him either within the synagogue or in its vicinity; arriving at synagogue with a weapon (although an exception would be considered for people who were in a quarrel with a Christian and felt that they needed to carry a weapon for protection); circumcising non-Jews without the permission of the *ma'amad*; speaking in the name of the Jewish nation without permission of the *ma'amad*; brokering divorce documents without the permission of the *ma'amad*; dealing in contraband coins; and engaging in common prayer with persons who had never been members of the synagogue or who had rebelliously left the synagogue.[17]

A ban was attached to the violation of certain rules regarding religious and devotional matters, such as attendance at synagogue, the purchase of kosher meat, and the observance of holidays. One could not, for example, buy meat from an Ashkenazic butcher.[18] Then there were ethical regulations: one could be banned for gambling or for lewd behavior in the streets. Social precepts protected by the ban included a rule against marrying in secret, that is, without parental consent and not in the presence of a rabbi. There were also regulations deriving from the political and financial structure of the community. For example, one could be banned for failing to pay one's taxes, or for showing personal disrespect to a member of the *ma'amad*, apparently a not uncommon event.

Other bannable activities included making public statements derisive of other members of the community, especially the rabbis; publicly defaming the Portuguese (but not the Spanish!) ambassador; writing letters to Spain containing any mention of or reference to the Jewish religion, which might jeopardize the recipient—most likely someone of converso descent—by putting them under the suspicion of being a secret Judaizer; printing a book without permission from the *ma'amad*; and removing a book from the congregation's library without permission. Women were forbidden, under the threat of a ban, from cutting the hair of Gentile women, and Jews were forbidden from engaging Gentiles in theological discussions.[19]

It goes without saying that the public expression (orally or in writing) of certain heretical or blasphemous opinions—such as denying the divine origin of the Torah or slighting any precept of God's law or demeaning the reputation of the Jewish people—would also warrant a ban.

In 1639 Isaac de Peralta was banned for disobeying and insulting a member of the *ma'amad*, and then attacking him in the street. Jacob Chamis was banned for a couple of weeks in 1640 when he circumcised a Pole without permission; in his own defense, he claimed that he was not aware that the man was a non-Jew.[20] Joseph Abarbanel was put under a *cherem* in 1677 for buying meat that was kosher, but from an Ashkenazic butcher. Several individuals were given a ban for adultery.[21] In all, between 1622 and 1683, as the historian Yosef Kaplan has discovered, thirty-nine men and one woman were banned by Spinoza's congregation, for periods ranging from one day to eleven years. (The woman, the wife of Jacob Moreno, was banned in 1654 with her husband when they failed to heed the warning that they were causing a scandal in the community by allowing Daniel Castiel to enter their house to visit her when Jacob was not home.) Rarely—as in the case of Spinoza—was the ban never removed. All of this indicates that a ban was not intended by the Jewish community of Amsterdam to be, by definition, a permanent end to all religious and personal relations. It may, on occasion, turn out to have that result, as it did for Spinoza. But it seems usually to have been within the power of the individual being punished to determine how long it would be before he fulfilled the conditions set for his reconciliation with the congregation.

The *cherem*, then, was used in Amsterdam to enforce social, religious, and ethical conduct thought becoming of a proper Jewish community, and to discourage deviancy not just in matters of liturgical practice but also in matters of everyday behavior and the expression of ideas. All of these would be particularly important issues for a community founded by former conversos. The leaders of the Talmud Torah congregation had to work hard to maintain religious cohesion among a community of Jews whose faith and practice were still rather unstable and often tainted by unorthodox beliefs and practices. Moreover, such a community might feel insecure about its Judaism, and thus in compensation might be particularly inclined to resort frequently to the most rigorous means to keep things 'kosher'. The Amsterdam Sephardim did use the sanction of the *cherem* for offenses for which other congregations—such as those of Hamburg and Venice—adopted less extreme measures.[22]

Cherem in Amsterdam

The power to ban an individual had originally been vested by Jewish tradition in a community's rabbinical court, the Beth Din. This would seem natural given the normative role played by the court in interpreting and enforcing Jewish law. But during the Middle Ages there was a good deal of disagreement over this delegation of authority, as prominent and powerful lay members of various communities took on many of the leadership functions that had earlier often been reserved for rabbis. Over the centuries different traditions emerged as Jewish practice and the organization of the community adapted to changing times and circumstances. The ceremony of pronouncing a severe *cherem* was usually held in the synagogue, where a rabbi or *chazzan* read the ban either in front of the Torah in the open ark or from the pulpit. The *shofar* (ram's horn) would be blown, while members of the congregation held candles (sometimes black) that were extinguished after the *cherem* was proclaimed.[23]

There is no evidence that such a powerful symbolic drama was carried out in the case of Spinoza's *cherem*. One of his earliest biographers, Jean Maximilian Lucas—who knew Spinoza personally—claims that, in fact, Spinoza's expulsion ceremony did not follow this procedure:

> When the people have assembled in the synagogue, the ceremony they call *cherem* begins with the lighting of a number of black candles and the opening of the Tabernacle, where the books of the law are stored. Afterwards, the cantor, from a slightly elevated place, intones in a gloomy voice the words of the excommunication, while another cantor blows a horn, and the wax candles are turned upside down so that they fall drop by drop into a vessel filled with blood. At which point the people, animated by a holy terror and a sacred rage at the sight of this black spectacle, respond Amen in a furious voice, which testifies to the good service which they believe they would be rendering to God if they could tear the excommunicant apart, which they would undoubtedly do if they would run into him at that moment or when leaving the synagogue. With respect to this, it should be remarked that the blowing of the horn, the inverting of the candles and the vessel filled with blood are rituals which are observed only in cases of blasphemy. Otherwise they are content simply to proclaim the excommunication, as was done in the case of Spinoza, who was not convicted of blasphemy but only of a lack of respect for Moses and for the law.[24]

The text of the ban could have been read by Rabbi Mortera, as he was the chief rabbi of the congregation at the time. But another early writer, the Lutheran minister Johan Colerus (who had the good fortune to rent the same room in The Hague that Spinoza occupied in the final years of his life), says that some 'Jews of Amsterdam' told him that 'old rabbi Aboab'—Isaac Aboab da Fonseca, a learned kabbalist from Portugal who was the community's first deputy rabbi and who happened to be presiding over the Beth Din at the time—was responsible for this.[25] But even if the task of making the public pronouncement was given to a rabbi, the authority to issue a *cherem* was, among the Amsterdam Sephardim, firmly in the hands of the community's lay leaders, the *parnassim* sitting on the *ma'amad*. The founding regulations of the Talmud Torah congregation leave no question whatsoever on this point: the *ma'amad* has the absolute and sole right to punish members of the community who, in their judgment, have violated certain regulations.[26] They were, of course, permitted and even encouraged to seek the advice of the rabbis before issuing a ban against someone, particularly if the alleged offense involved a matter of *halachah*. But such consultation was not required. The *ma'amad*'s exclusive right to ban members of the community goes virtually unchallenged in the seventeenth century. Only Rabbi Menasseh ben Israel, when he was angry over the treatment he and his family had received at the hands of the *ma'amad* over an incident in 1640, protested that the right of issuing a ban poperly belongs to the rabbis. For his impertinence—and perhaps to make sure that he got the point—he was given a ban, albeit for only a day.[27]

The frequency with which the Amsterdam congregation wielded the ban, either in act or in warning, and the routine way in which its use is written into the community's regulations, should not mislead us into trivializing the event. Spinoza did or said something very wrong. His offense, whatever it may have been, was regarded with the utmost seriousness. The text of his *cherem* exceeds all the others proclaimed on the Houtgracht in its vehemence and fury. There is no other act of banning of the period issued by that community that measures up to the wrath directed at Spinoza when he is expelled from the congregation. The matter-of-fact tone of Isaac de Peralta's *cherem* is more typical:

Taking into consideration that Isaac de Peralta disobeyed that which the aforesaid *ma'amad* had ordered him, and the fact that Peralta responded with negative words concerning this issue; and not content with this, Peralta dared to go out and look for [members of the *ma'amad*] on the street and insult them. The aforesaid *ma'amad*, considering these things and the importance of the case, decided the following: it is agreed upon unanimously that the aforesaid Isaac de Peralta be excommunicated [*posto em Cherem*] because of what he has done. Because he has been declared under punishment of *niddui* [*Menudeh*], no one shall talk or deal with him. Only family and other members of his household may talk with him.[28]

After four days Peralta begged forgiveness and paid a fine of 60 guilders, and the ban was removed. David Curiel was able to remove his *cherem* in 1666 by paying 1,000 guilders to the congregation's charity fund, 'considering the long time that he was outside the community and the pressing needs of the poor'.[29] But there is no mention in Spinoza's *cherem* of any measures that he could take that would serve as a sufficient sign of repentance or of any means by which he could reconcile with the congregation. The time for that had passed.[30] Even the *cherem* of Juan de Prado, Spinoza's friend and fellow excommunicant in 1656 (who was, it would seem from contemporary documents, guilty of similar offenses), while it is just as uncharacteristically long as that of Spinoza and rules out any further reconciliation overtures, is nonetheless relatively reasoned and mild in its tone. Prado will not again be allowed to beg forgiveness and profess the mending of his ways; and the board of governors asks him and his family to move away from Amsterdam, preferably overseas. But there is none of the anger and vehemence that characterizes their condemnation of Spinoza.

Because Daniel de Prado has been convicted by numerous testimonies before the members of the *ma'amad* and the rabbis of having relapsed with great scandal, of having tried once again to seduce other people with his detestable opinions against our Holy Law, the said sirs of the *ma'amad*, with the advice of the rabbis, have unanimously decided that the said Daniel de Prado should be put under *cherem* and separated from the nation. Under pain of this same *cherem*, they also ordain that no member of this Holy Community may communicate with him either verbally or in writing, neither within this city nor outside it, with the exception of the members of his family. May God ward off the unhappiness of his people, and peace upon Israel. By order of the sirs of the *ma'amad*.[31]

What philosophers call 'overdetermination'—an apparent abundance of causal factors, each of which would, singly and by itself, be sufficient to explain the phenomenon at hand and that together provide more explanatory power than is, strictly speaking, necessary—is both the historian's nightmare and his field of dreams. The fall of Rome, the Protestant Reformation, the French Revolution, the American Civil War: these are events for which extraordinarily rich (indeed, overrich) causal stories can be told, stories that probably include a number of particular subplots that alone would do the trick of making sense of things. Overdetermination is both the ultimate curse and the supreme gift for historical and biographical narrative.

It leads to endless debates about causes.

It also makes it easy to find a place to start.

Abominations and Heresies 2

Engaging in a search for the reasons behind Spinoza's *cherem* might appear, for a number of very different reasons, pointless. First, such a project seems irremediably speculative. Unlike many of the other *cherem* cases among the Amsterdam Sephardim, neither the writ of *cherem* itself nor any other official document tells us what exactly he has done wrong. There is, in fact, so little confirmed and explicit information to go on that all one can really do is hazard an informed guess. Unless further material shows up—in the form of a long-lost letter or proclamation—there is no direct, concrete evidence that specifies what were the specific reasons for his ban. Second—and this reason is only prima facie inconsistent with the first—such a project seems absurdly unnecessary: Is it not *obvious* why Spinoza was excommunicated? Anyone who has read his major writings, the *Ethics* and the *Theological–Political Treatise*, will wonder what could possibly be the mystery here. If Spinoza was, around the time of his *cherem*, uttering even a small selection of the audacious opinions that appear in these mature treatises, there can be no wonder that he was severely punished by his congregation. Can there truly be any question as to why one of history's boldest and most radical thinkers was banned from his synagogue as a young man?

I am fully sympathetic to the sentiments behind both of these objections. And yet, as I hope to show through an examination of one of the crucial issues that reportedly instigated Spinoza's *cherem*, the inquiry into the reasons behind his ban—as speculative *and* superfluous as it may seem—is a fascinating and informative exercise. There are still some questions that need to be (and can be) answered, questions that should be of interest to anyone who has wondered not only about Spinoza's *cherem*, but also about the traditions of Jewish moral and eschatological thought. Moreover, such an inquiry can both throw new light on Spinoza's philosophical views and clarify his intellectual relationship to Jewish philosophy and religion. What should emerge in the end is not a rigorous causal explanation of his ban. This is most likely not an event for which we will ever have a conclusive and demonstrative understanding. But, I also grant, neither is it the case that to make sense of this event we really need much more beyond a basic familiarity with Spinoza's mature views on God, nature, and religion. Thus, I here fully concede the force of the objections cited above. Rather, the result of such a study should be a better analytical and contextual vision of what Spinoza was up to in his philosophical work, and a deeper understanding of why certain issues mattered, both to him and to his contemporaries in Jewish Amsterdam.[1]

The banning of Baruch Spinoza had a very clear political dimension. In Spinoza's era, in fact, the distinction between the private and the public, the personal and the political, was not very well conceived, much less respected. And there was very little of consequence in the volatile cultural, intellectual, and religious environment of the Dutch 'Golden Age' that was not also political. Sectarian and devotional squabbles, personal vendettas, family rivalries, professional jealousies, even artistic disagreements all ended up spilling over into the arena of politics and power. When the dissenting Arminians (or 'Remonstrants') were expelled from the Dutch Reformed Church in 1618 for doctrinal liberalism; when orthodox *predikanten* fulminated, in the 1640s and 1650s, against moral permissiveness and the laxity in religious observance among the populace; when a controversy arose within the universities over the teaching of Descartes's 'new philosophy'; and in numerous other instances, an initially specific and nominally apolitical controversy invariably ballooned until it involved the body politic at large. In the Dutch Republic—as in the long, retreating interiors of its genre paintings, where the rooms of a house let onto a courtyard that runs into the street—the line between the private and the public was never clearly drawn. Even Rembrandt's decision to move to Amsterdam in the 1630s was, as one scholar has plausibly argued, based on the theological–political persuasions of that city's art patrons and not just their wealth and aesthetic preferences.[2]

The public sphere was comprised of two main political camps: the conservative 'Orangists', who favored a strong centralized government with the Stadholder (a quasi-monarchical post traditionally held by the Prince of Orange) as the head of state and commander-in-chief; and the so-called 'States party faction', which preferred a more devolved federation of autonomous provinces, with true power based in the local regents of each province's municipalities. Their dispute infected, and in turn was exacerbated by, all of the other—sometimes petty, sometimes important—differences that ordinarily characterize a society. Dutch life in the seventeenth century was rife with partisanship; its resemblance to the peaceful landscapes of Ruisdael or the calm social interiors of Vermeer was only superficial.

What was true of the Republic at large was also, albeit to a somewhat lesser degree, true of its 'Portuguese Hebrew nation'. The Jews of Amsterdam were too sophisticated, too conscious of their own not-too-distant history of victimization in the face of sectarianism, not to be well aware of these political tensions and theological divisions running barely beneath the surface of their host country. They were especially alert to the potential dangers they held for the well-being of the community. Whenever the more narrow-minded elements among the Calvinists (and Orangists) gained the upper hand, Jews, Catholics, and dissenting Protestant sects all keenly felt their vulnerability in the face of these reactionary forces. There were, in other words, well-known, sometimes dormant, but always unpredictable limits to the famed Dutch toleration. When the Sephardic Jewish leaders regulated and administered the internal social, moral, and religious life of their community, they always had one eye on the external Dutch political scene.

To be sure, the 1650s were not a particularly threatening time. The Grand Pensionary of the States of Holland—the Republic's chief political officer—was Johan de Witt, perhaps the greatest, and certainly the most astute statesman in Dutch history. De Witt and his liberal supporters had, for the time being, a near monopoly on political power, and the period of the 'True Freedom' was well under way by the end of the decade. The Amsterdam regents, in particular, were very aware of the important contribution their Portuguese residents made to the city's economic life. They were not about to commit, or allow anyone else to commit on their behalf, the enormous mistake made by the Spanish monarchs when they expelled the Jews in 1492. But the winds of Dutch politics were notoriously shifty, subject to sudden and radical changes of direction—what the Dutch call *wetsverzettingen*. In a matter of weeks, or even days, a town's political weather could completely change; its ruling body overthrown and its policies reversed.[3] It happened briefly in Amsterdam in 1650, and—for all anyone knew—it could happen again. The Jews were, no doubt, rather cautious about putting too much confidence in the status quo. Ever conscious of their dependence on the good will of their hosts, this population of former refugees seems to have gone to great lengths to remind and reassure the Dutch that their community was a controlled, well-ordered, and orthodox one. Their use of the ban of *cherem*—which, at first glance, might seem to have been a tool geared simply for maintaining a disciplined Jewish congregation—thus takes on a political dimension, as a public act that was meant to communicate such reassurance to a wider audience.

The regents of Amsterdam must have expected nothing less. When the city granted its Portuguese merchants the right to practice Judaism publicly, in 1619, the town council expressly ordered them to regulate their conduct and ensure that the members of the community kept to a strict observance of Jewish law.[4] As representatives of a religion deeply committed to the text of the 'Old Testament', the Calvinists may simply have desired to have in their midst what they at least perceived to be a living embodiment of the children of Abraham. But this also occurred right after the momentous Synod of Dort, when, after a tumultuous struggle with the theologically more liberal

Remonstrants, the strict Calvinists solidified their control over the Dutch Reformed Church. Thus, the warning to the Jews was, at least in part, an effort to insure that they kept to themselves, at least in religious matters. The recently resettled Sephardim thus found themselves in a precarious situation. They were refugees living in a society torn by religious division. They were tolerated, and even encouraged to practice their religion. But the city of Amsterdam officially and explicitly told them to keep their house clean, to enforce Jewish orthodoxy, and not let their affairs stray into the Dutch arena. This must have left the Jews with a deep sense of insecurity and a very strong desire to be cautious, to insure that they do or permit nothing in their community that would attract the attention of the municipal authorities and bring down upon themselves any unfavorable judgments.

Nearly twenty years later there was still evident among the Sephardim a sensitivity about how they were regarded by the Dutch. In the regulations adopted in 1639 when the three Amsterdam congregations merged into one, Talmud Torah, there is a prohibition against public wedding or funeral processions, lest non-Jews be offended by the display and the Jews be blamed for the ensuing disturbance. There is also, in accordance with the city's wishes, a regulation prohibiting Jews from discussing religious matters with Christians and from attempting to convert them to Judaism, for such activities might 'disturb the liberty we enjoy'.[5] Even in 1670, over fifty years after being granted the right to live openly as Jews in Amsterdam, they are cautious about maintaining an appearance of rectitude and of being a well-ordered society-within-a-society. On November 16 of that year Rabbi Aboab submitted to the congregation's board a request that they should undertake to build a new synagogue—the magnificent one still in use at the end of the Jodenbreestraat. They needed a building that would be large enough to accommodate their expanding population, which at this point had reached over 2,500 individuals. People were, Aboab says in his request, fighting for seats, and the 'unpleasantnesses' were so disturbing services 'that we cannot pay attention to praying to our creator'.[6] At around the same time, the elders of the community brought a petition to the city magistrates, asking them to reauthorize the regulations adopted by the community in 1639. In this routine request they include and explicitly cite the right of the *parnassim* to ban 'unruly and rebellious people'.[7] This seems a tactful but clear reminder to the Amsterdam regents that the same community that is expanding and wants to build a new synagogue has also vested its leaders with strong disciplinary powers, that they had nothing to worry about with a large and active Jewish community in their midst.

The use of the ban, then, in addition to its internal social function in regulating conduct among the congregation's members, was a public[8]—indeed, political—act that was meant to communicate to the Dutch authorities the message that the Jews ran a well-ordered community; that they—in accordance with the conditions laid down by the city when it granted them the right to practice openly—tolerated no breaches in proper Jewish behavior or doctrine. It was the Jewish community's way of saying to the Amsterdam regents (and the more worrisome *predikanten*): 'Look, we *can* keep our house clean.'

In this regard, however, Spinoza's *cherem* would be no different from any of the others issued by the *ma'amad* in the period. If it is true of his punishment, it would be equally true of the punishment of Isaac de Peralta and of Jacob Chamis and of Rabbi Menasseh and of the thirty-five others: there was a broad political dimension to the use of the ban in Jewish Amsterdam in the seventeenth century.

But—and here, once again, is the problem—Spinoza's ban *was* different. In its vehemence and finality, it is unequaled. If the political card is going to be played, and if in Spinoza's case an especially strong message needed to be conveyed to the Dutch, then there must have been something remarkable about that case in the first place.

Now certainly Spinoza's own political opinions—both in his mature writings and, probably, even in his earlier years—might have been viewed with some concern within the leadership of the Jewish community. His ideas on the state and society were profoundly democratic. He was, at least in his theory, a liberal republican for whom ultimate sovereignty lay in the will of the people. Democracy, he insisted, is, of all the possible constitutions, the most consistent with natural right, the least subject to the abuse of power, the most stable, and the most conducive to human liberty. It is, on Spinoza's view, the safest and most reasonable form of political organization.[9] In his political writings he argued strenuously for freedom of thought and speech and for a polity in which the rights of citizens were protected against any abuses of power. On the other hand, neither the city of Amsterdam nor its Portuguese Jewish community nor the Dutch Republic as a whole was a democracy. The leaders of Amsterdam's Sephardim were wealthy merchants who governed the affairs of the community in an autocratic manner. The community was run as an oligarchy, with the more prosperous families constituting a self-perpetuating social and political elite. Moreover, they had a substantial economic stake in the Dutch status quo—an oligarchy as well, run by the regent families, also merchants and professionals—and their own political opinions must have been rather conservative. Some of them may even have been supporters of the Orangist faction in Dutch politics, the party calling for the return of the quasi-monarchical stadholdership. Spinoza's radical democratic persuasions, and his contacts with would-be revolutionaries like his Latin tutor Franciscus van den Enden and social radicals like the Collegiants, a dissenting Reformed movement many of whose members were harshly critical of capitalism, would no doubt have irritated the *parnassim*, not to mention the Amsterdam regents.[10]

But these political considerations can give us only a context, not an answer. There is much more to Spinoza's *cherem*—there *has* to be more—than simply a clash of political persuasions. The Sephardim of Amsterdam were a cosmopolitan community of eclectic background. In general, they certainly would have tolerated a diversity of views on purely political questions. It is hard to believe that anyone would have received a *cherem* because of disagreement, no matter how extreme, on such matters.

The answer cannot lie in the political context alone.[11]

A good place to start the investigation would be the text of the *cherem* itself. It does not say much that is informative about its causes, but it does speak, first, of Spinoza's 'deeds' and the acts that he 'practiced'. Perhaps, after the period of mourning for his father—the eleven months of saying Kaddish would have ended at the beginning of March of 1655—when he was finally on his own and relieved of the pressures of keeping up appearances for the sake of the family (his mother had died when he was only 6), Spinoza began to drift from regular attendance at synagogue and proper observance of Jewish law. Maybe he ceased, in a particularly ostentatious way, to observe the sabbath or to comply with Judaism's rigorous dietary code. These would, of course, have been offensive actions, and, according to the community's bylaws, would have automatically warranted a ban. Maybe this is what his early biographer Lucas means when he (possibly relying on what Spinoza himself told him) reports that Spinoza was convicted 'not of blasphemy, but only of a lack of respect for Moses and the law'.[12] But Spinoza would not have been alone in the community in his lax conformity to orthodox behavior. There must have been numerous members of Talmud Torah who were somewhat less than zealous in the performance of their religious obligations, whose attendance at synagogue was infrequent at best, or who rarely contributed to the charitable societies that formed so important a part of the community. We know that when Abraham Mendez was in London, he did not join a *minyan* there and pray on a regular basis. His punishment, in 1656, was that he could not be called to the Torah for two years. Another man was threatened with a ban for failing to circumcise his sons. As Yosef Kaplan has noted, 'acts of that sort were typical of daily life in the community'.[13] Many of Amsterdam's Sephardim had only a tenuous sense of Jewish identity and a weak commitment to carrying out the *mitzvot*, or commandments of the Torah. Even Rabbi Menasseh was known on occasion, when forgetful of the day, to pick up a pencil on the sabbath. It thus does not seem likely that the origins of the impassioned expulsion of Spinoza lie simply in his departure from the behavioral norms of Judaism. Besides, the *parnassim* knew that many of those norms were impossible to police on a regular basis in the cosmopolitan world in which these Jews operated. Amsterdam's Portuguese merchants were in constant commercial and social contact with their Dutch neighbors and business associates, and there was a certain degree of cultural assimilation. The Jews (as we can see in numerous portraits of the period) dressed like the Dutch, went about town like the Dutch, and furnished their homes like the Dutch. They were also known to visit the city's cafés and eating establishments, where neither the wine nor the food were likely to be kosher.

But perhaps Spinoza went even further. Juan de Prado, the fellow excommunicant with whom we know Spinoza was keeping company immediately after (and probably before) his *cherem*, is said by witnesses to have been mocking Jews on their way to synagogue and openly showing disrespect to the rabbis and the *ma'amad*. He was also caught trying to persuade some of the students in one of the community's schools that it was not forbidden to carry money on the sabbath; it was they who testified before the *parnassim* to Prado's 'scandalous actions'. Along with his friend Daniel Ribera, he was allegedly even plotting to compose a number of 'scandalous and immoral' letters and leave them at the house of Rabbi Mortera.[14] Here, clearly, was a man who was going out of his way to offend.[15]

We have no indication as to whether, in his behavior and actions, Spinoza went as far as his friend Prado to show open disdain for his religion and his congregation. David Franco Mendes, an early chronicler of the community, suggests that he did. Franco Mendes was serving as honorary secretary of the community in 1769—the year he began his 'Memorial of the Establishment and Development of the Portuguese and Spanish Jews in the Famous City of Amsterdam'—and presumably had access to otherwise secret archives. Writing over a century after the fact, by which time the 'Spinoza affair' had passed from current events into the realm of communal mythology, Franco Mendes says that 'his [Spinoza's] perversity even led him to provoke a major scandal in the eyes of the [Jewish] nation, saying in his blasphemies that people should abandon all that is a part of tradition and even encouraging the violation of the Sabbath and festivals'.[16] And yet, given what we know of Spinoza's character, there is something highly implausible in Franco Mendes's account. It does not seem likely that, even as a young man, Spinoza sought to instigate a confrontation, or even to offend. He was not one to court controversy. Far from being a provocateur, Spinoza throughout his life went well out of his way to avoid conflict and the disturbance of the peace. He describes himself as someone 'who absolutely dreads quarrels'.[17] His preference, he insists, is 'to keep silent rather than thrust my opinions on men . . . and incur their hostility'.[18]

Still, if we must continue to search among deeds (*obras*) and actions, there are other avenues. Is it possible that Spinoza's 'sins' were legal and monetary in nature? One scholar believes so, arguing that Spinoza 'had to be removed from the community because financial interests were at stake'.[19] In March of 1656, just four months before his *cherem*, Spinoza stepped outside of the communal legal structure to seek protection from his creditors. He went through the process of having himself declared an orphan (and, thus, a minor) by the municipal authorities of Amsterdam in order to free himself from responsibility for paying debts owed on the estate of his late father. Although Spinoza had recently satisfied some of those creditors himself, and thus apparently taken charge of the estate, he quickly realized that the debts were so great that assuming full responsibility meant only financial ruin. He would also lose what remained of his mother's estate (she had died in 1638), which his father had inherited in trust for him. He thus asked the city magistrates to rule so that they 'discharge him from any such act committed as heir as he, in any way, could have committed regarding the inheritance from his said father . . . and that the said Bento de Spinosa, with his claim on his mother's goods, will be given preference [on the estate] above all other creditors'.[20]

By going directly to the city authorities for protection against debts within the Portuguese Jewish community—the record indicates that the primary creditors on his father's estate were Duarte Rodrigues, Lamego Anthonio, Rodrigues de Morajs, and the curators of the estate of Pedro Henriques—Spinoza was in clear violation of one of the primary regulations instituted by the community governing business dealings among local Jews. The *ascamot*, or regulations, of the Talmud Torah congregation clearly stipulate that 'disputes between Jews concerning business matters are to be arbitrated by the executive committee . . . Only if a compromise is impossible to obtain are the parties free to bring the case before a general non-Jewish court.'[21] There is no indication that Spinoza took the preliminary step of going to the executive committee. So perhaps his Portuguese Jewish creditors, angry over Spinoza's use of Dutch law to avoid what they saw as his obligation to them—and it could have been a significant sum of money—complained to the community's governors and instigated the *cherem*.

But the *ascamot* do not say that a *cherem* is mandatory for violation of this rule, as they do in the case of other types of disobedience (although Maimonides does say that a *cherem* should be issued to someone who uses a Gentile court to recover money that is not recoverable under Jewish law[22]). Moreover, the mundane nature of such an offense argues against it being the real factor behind the uniquely harsh and highly personal ban that Spinoza received. Still, it may be that this legal mess was compounded by other financial factors. There are even relevant documents here, but they call for intepretation.

There were typically three kinds of financial contribution that a member of Talmud Torah gave to the community, twice a year (on Rosh Hashanah, the Jewish New Year, and Pesach, or Passover). First, there was the *imposta*, a tax on business dealings that was assessed according to the total value of an individual's trade for the previous half-year. Then there was the *finta*, a dues-type payment that was demanded of every member and calculated according to one's wealth. Finally, every congregant was expected to pledge a certain amount for the *promesa*, an act of *tzedakah* or charity, a voluntary offering that went into the community fund for the poor.

The community's record books show that in the year preceding his *cherem* the payments Spinoza made to the congregation diminished substantially. This is one of the few documented facts about Spinoza's life before 1661, but its significance is unclear. The first month of 5414 (September 1654), after the death of his father, seems to be when Spinoza initially took over responsibility for making the payments on behalf of his family and their business. In the year that followed, Spinoza made significant contributions to the charity fund, promising 11 guilders and 8 stuivers in September and 43 guilders and 2 stuivers in March (in addition to two *finta* payments of 5 guilders each, and a one-time contribution of 5 guilders to a fund for the Jewish poor in Brazil, most of whom came from Amsterdam).[23] These high sums may represent memorial offerings for his father. They indicate, as well, that Spinoza was still, in mid-1655, an at least nominally active member of the community, keeping up appearances and willing to do his part and satisfy the basic obligations that were expected of every congregant. On Rosh Hashanah of the following year, 5415 (September 1655), he pledged a noticeably smaller *promesa* sum, 4 guilders and 14 stuivers (again accompanied by a 5 guilder *finta* payment). Three months later, on the sabbath of Channukah, he offered six small pieces of gold.[24] In Nisan of that year (March 1656) he pledged a *promesa* of only 12 stuivers, a sum that was never paid.

Was Spinoza banned because of his arrears in membership payments and other financial debts to the community? It hardly seems likely. The community's laws did stipulate a ban for failure to pay communal taxes, but the harsh wording of Spinoza's punishment argues against this relatively common occurrence being the aggravating factor in his case.

Rather than seeing these numbers as representing the *cause* of his *cherem*, they might be better read as a *symptom* of other, more important considerations. It is, in fact, tempting to interpret the payment record as a reflection—indeed, *the* ultimate expression—of a rebellious Spinoza's flagging dedication to the Talmud Torah congregation, even to Judaism itself, and of his strained relations with the leaders of the community.[25] Spinoza was, by 1655 (and probably earlier), most likely experiencing a loss of faith and commitment. He was in his early twenties, and must have already begun formulating, at least in his own mind, his radically naturalistic ideas on God and morality, as well as the foundations of his harsh critique of organized religion (especially Judaism); he began writing down his philosophy only a few years later, and one does not move into this kind of mindset overnight. Such an intellectual and spiritual evolution would explain why, by late 1654, he was off studying Latin, philosophy, and other subjects outside the Jewish community.[26] He may even at this point have moved from the Vlooienburg district to another part of town.[27] Of course, most of this is just speculation—aside from his merchant activities, we do not really know *what* Spinoza was doing and thinking and feeling in this period. But the declining tax and charity payments could at least be seen as the only concrete evidence we have in favor of a plausible and coherent story.

Now there can be no doubt that Spinoza's religious faith and sense of Jewish identity did, in fact, suffer a serious decline by the end of 1655. No account of Spinoza's *cherem* will have any credibility if it does not take such a development into account. However, one should not rest too much of the case for this on the *gabbai*'s (treasurer's) ledger, for its figures may not be a reflection of this emotional and spiritual fact at all. It could be that the true explanation of the *gabbai*'s record on Spinoza is also the most obvious one: the rapid and significant decrease in his payments to the community may simply be the result of a bleak financial situation. The fact that his *imposta* payments dropped from 16 guilders to 6 in half a year, and then to nothing six months later, indicates that business had fallen precipitously, and that either the value or the volume of his trade was way down. The lack of a *finta* payment in March of 1656 is quite possibly just a sign that his personal wealth was too low or his finances too precarious to warrant an assessment. This economic interpretation of Spinoza's payment record[28] is supported by the drastic steps that he took at around the same time to relieve himself of the debts that he inherited with his father's estate. Thus, rather than being the occasion for the community's leaders to exercise some punitive oversight on a congregant's fiscal obligations, or, on the other hand, the direct indication of a loss of faith and commitment, the decline in Spinoza's payments may be nothing but the inevitable result of the failing fortunes and mounting debt of the family business. Indeed, his brother Gabriel, who took over the firm and, thus, responsibility for the payments when Bento left the community, made only nominal *promesa* contributions and no payments for the *finta* or *imposta* for the next ten years.[29]

We are fishing in the wrong waters. It is hard to believe that Spinoza was engaging in such 'monstrous deeds', in acts so 'evil' that—more than anyone else in the community, including the mocking, offensive, would-be corruptor of youth Juan de Prado—he deserved the kind of *cherem* that had never before been issued by the congregation's leaders. By 1656 the worldly *parnassim* must surely have become used to dealing in a more routine way with deviant behavior among Amsterdam's cosmopolitan merchant Jews. No, what really lay behind Spinoza's vicious *cherem* were not actions, but rather, as the proclamation reads, *más opinioins* and *horrendas heregias*: 'evil opinions' and 'abominable heresies'—that is, ideas.[30]

Three relatively reliable sources tell us as much. In Lucas's chronology of the events leading up to the *cherem*, there was much talk in the congregation about Spinoza's opinions; people, especially the rabbis, were curious about what the young man, known for his intelligence, was thinking. As Lucas tells it—and this particular anecdote is not confirmed by any other source—'among those most eager to associate with him there were two young men who, professing to be his most intimate friends, begged him to tell them his real views. They promised him that whatever his opinions were, he had nothing to fear on their part, for their curiosity had no other end than to clear up their own doubts.'[31] They suggested, trying to draw Spinoza out, that if one read Moses and the Prophets closely, then one would be led to the conclusion that the soul is not immortal and that God is material. 'How does it appear to you?', they asked Spinoza. 'Does God have a body? Is the soul immortal?' After some hesitation, Spinoza took the bait.

> I confess, said [Spinoza], that since nothing is to be found in the Bible about the non-material or incorporeal, there is nothing objectionable in believing that God is a body. All the more so since, as the Prophet says, God is great, and it is impossible to comprehend greatness without extension and, therefore, without body. As for spirits, it is certain that Scripture does not say that these are real and permanent substances, but mere phantoms, called angels because God makes use of them to declare his will; they are of such kind that the angels and all other kinds of spirits are invisible only because their matter is very fine and diaphanous, so that it can only be seen as one sees phantoms in a mirror, in a dream, or in the night.

As for the human soul, Spinoza reportedly replied that 'whenever Scripture speaks of it, the word "soul" is used simply to express life, or anything that is living. It would be useless to search for any passage in support of its immortality. As for the contrary view, it may be seen in a hundred places, and nothing is so easy as to prove it.'

Spinoza did not trust the motives behind the curiosity of his 'friends' —with good reason—and he broke off the conversation as soon as he had the opportunity. At first his interlocutors thought he was just teasing them or trying merely to shock them by expressing scandalous ideas. But when they saw that he was serious, they started talking about Spinoza to others. 'They said that the people deceived themselves in believing that this young man might become one of the pillars of the synagogue; that it seemed more likely that he would be its destroyer, as he had nothing but hatred and contempt for the Law of Moses.' Lucas relates that when Spinoza was called before his judges, these same individuals bore witness against him, alleging that he 'scoffed at the Jews as "superstitious people born and bred in ignorance, who do not know what God is, and who nevertheless have the audacity to speak of themselves as His People, to the disparagement of other nations" '.[32]

Then there is the report of Brother Tomas Solano y Robles. Brother Tomas was an Augustinian monk who was in Madrid in 1659, right after a voyage that had taken him through Amsterdam in late 1658. The Spanish Inquisitors were interested in what was going on among the former marranos now living in northern Europe, most of whom had once been in its domain or still had converso relatives back in Iberia. They interviewed the friar, as well as another traveler to the Netherlands, Captain Miguel Pérez de Maltranilla, who had stayed in the same house in Amsterdam, and at the same time, as Brother Tomas. Both men claimed that in Amsterdam they had met Spinoza and Prado, who were apparently keeping each other company after their respective banishments. The two apostates told Brother Tomas that they had been observant of Jewish law but 'changed their mind', and that they were expelled from the synagogue because of their views on God, the soul, and the Law. They had, in the eyes of the congregation, 'reached the point of atheism'.[33] According to Tomas's deposition, they were saying that the soul was not immortal, that the Law was 'not true' (*no hera verdadera*), and that there was no God except in a 'philosophical' sense.[34] Maltranilla confirms that, according to Spinoza and Prado, 'the Law . . . was false [*falsa*]'.[35]

The community poet–historian David Franco Mendes is our final witness on this matter. Although he was writing many years later, his work undoubtedly represents a repository of communal record and memory. He insists, in his brief report on the case, that Spinoza not only violated the sabbath and the laws governing the festivals, but also was filled with 'atheistic' ideas, and was punished accordingly.[36]

'God exists only philosophically', 'The Law is not true', and 'The soul is not immortal'. These are rather vague and indeterminate propositions, particularly the first two. Ordinarily, there is no more telling what is intended by them than what is meant by the notoriously ambiguous charge of 'atheism'. But in Spinoza's case we have some fair basis for knowing what he would have meant, for they are likely just the views that he would at least begin elaborating and arguing for in his written works within five years. To be sure, we cannot be certain that what we find in those writings was exactly what he was saying vive voce within the community. But the report by Lucas and the testimony by Brother Tomas indicate that the metaphysical, moral, and religious doctrines that are to be found in his philosophical masterpiece the *Ethics* (a first draft of which was apparently complete by 1665, but which was later reworked substantially and not published until after his death) and the *Theological–Political Treatise* (begun in 1665 and published anonymously, to great alarm, in 1670) were already in his mind, and not necessarily in only an embryonic form, in the mid-1650s.

Spinoza probably began working seriously on the *Ethics* around mid-1662, only six years after his ban. He was unsatisfied by his first attempt at a systematic presentation of his ideas, the aborted *Short Treatise on God, Man and his Well-Being* (*c.*1661), and now sought a more rigorous and evident mode of exposition. He composed the *Ethics* in order to lay out 'in a geometrical fashion' what he believed were the basic metaphysical truths about God, the world, and the human being; and to demonstrate what important moral principles follow from those. The reduction of God to the most basic principles of nature; the proof that the universe is an absolutely deterministic system, all aspects of which follow necessarily from those most basic principles of nature; the elimination of divine and human freedom; the examination of the ways in which we are ordinarily governed (indeed, 'tossed about') by our passions and emotions; and the investigation of knowledge are all only preliminary steps in what is ultimately a deeply 'moral'—in the broadest sense of the term—project. Spinoza wants to show how we can acheive control over our passions and, thus, well-being (what the Greeks called *eudaimonia*, roughly translated as 'happiness'), peace of mind, even 'salvation' through a rational understanding both of the universe in its most eternal aspects and of our place in it. An important part of this project is the elimination of superstition and an exposition and critique of what has traditionally passed for religion.[37]

The God of Spinoza's philosophy is a far cry from the God of Abraham, Isaac, and Jacob.[38] Spinoza's God is not some just, wise, good, and providential being; it is not a personal being whom one would thank or bless, or to whom one would pray or seek comfort in times of good or bad fortune. It is not a God that would foster a sense of spiritual piety, or sustain the hope of divine reward or the fear of eternal punishment. In the *Ethics* Spinoza strips God of all traditional psychological and moral characteristics. God, he argues, is substance, the ultimate and immanent reality of all things—nothing more. Endowed with the infinite attributes of thought and extension, Spinoza's God is identical with the active, generative aspects of nature. In an infamous phrase that appeared in the Latin but not the more accessible Dutch edition of his works, published right after his death, Spinoza refers to 'Deus sive Natura', 'God or Nature'. 'By God', he says in one of the opening definitions of Part I, 'I understand a being absolutely infinite, i.e., a substance consisting of an infinity of attributes, of which each one expresses an eternal and infinite essence.' God *is* the underlying and infinite causal nature of things.

This definition is meant to preclude any anthropomorphizing of the divine being. Spinoza explicitly tells us that he is writing against 'those who feign a God, like man, consisting of a body and a mind, and subject to passions . . . they wander far from the true knowledge of God'.[39] His contempt for the fallacious inference that allows for the anthropomorphizing of God is obvious:

If will and intellect do pertain to the eternal essence of God, we must of course understand by each of these attributes something different from what men commonly understand. For the intellect and will which would constitute God's essence would have to differ entirely from our intellect and will, and could not agree with them in anything except the name. They would not agree with one another any more than do the dog that is a heavenly constellation and the dog that is a barking animal.[40]

Besides being false, an anthropomorphic conception of God can have only deleterious effects on human freedom, activity, and well-being, as it tends to strengthen passions such as hope and fear. When understood in the philosophically proper manner, 'God' is seen to refer to nothing but an impersonal, infinite, unique, uncaused causal source of everything else that exists.

[Ip16] From the necessity of the divine nature there must follow infinitely many things in infinitely many modes (i.e., everything which can fall under an infinite intellect).

Demonstration: This proposition must be plain to anyone, provided he attends to the fact that the intellect infers from the given definition of any thing a number of properties that really do follow necessarily from it (that is, from the very essence of the thing); and that it infers more properties the more the definition of the thing expresses reality, that is, the more reality the essence of the defined thing involves. But since the divine nature has absolutely infinite attributes, each of which also expresses an essence infinite in its own kind, from its necessity there must follow infinitely many things in infinite modes (i.e., everything which can fall under an infinite intellect).

Corollary 1: From this it follows that God is the efficient cause of all things which can fall under an infinite intellect.

Corollary 2: It follows, second, that God is a cause through himself and not an accidental cause.

Corollary 3: It follows, third, that God is absolutely the first cause.

Such a God obviously cannot be endowed with freedom. All talk of God's purposes, intentions, goals, preferences, or aims is just an anthropomorphizing fiction.

All the prejudices I here undertake to expose depend on this one: that men commonly suppose that all natural things act, as men do, on account of an end; indeed, they maintain as certain that God himself directs all things to some certain end, for they say that God has made all things for man, and man that he might worship God.[41]

God is not some goal-oriented planner who then judges things by how well they conform to his purposes. Things happen only because of Nature and its laws. 'Nature has no end set before it . . . All things proceed by a certain eternal necessity of nature.' To believe otherwise is to fall prey to the same superstitions that lie at the heart of most organized religions.[42]

[People] find—both in themselves and outside themselves—many means that are very helpful in seeking their own advantage, e.g., eyes for seeing, teeth for chewing, plants and animals for food, the sun for light, the sea for supporting fish . . . Hence, they consider all natural things as means to their own advantage. And knowing that they had found these means, not provided them for themselves, they had reason to believe that there was someone else who had prepared those means for their use. For after they considered things as means, they could not believe that the things had made themselves; but from the means they were accustomed to prepare for themselves, they had to infer that there was a ruler, or a number of rulers of nature, endowed with human freedom, who had taken care of all things for them, and made all things for their use.

And since they had never heard anything about the temperament of these rulers, they had to judge it from their own. Hence, they maintained that the Gods direct all things for the use of men in order to bind men to them and be held by men in the highest honor. So it has happened that each of them has thought up from his own temperament different ways of worshipping God, so that God might love them above all the rest, and direct the whole of Nature according to the needs of their blind desire and insatiable greed. Thus this prejudice was changed into superstition, and struck deep roots in their minds.[43]

It follows, as well, that God is not a transcendent creator, that is, a being who spontaneously causes a world distinct from himself to come into being by producing it out of nothing. More importantly to the Jewish mind, Spinoza's conception of God strikes right at the core of the account of creation in Genesis (*Bereshit*, 'In the beginning . . .'), according to which God purposively brings order out of *tohu v'vohu*, chaos. Spinoza's God is the cause of all things, but only because all things follow causally and necessarily from the divine natures—that is, from Nature itself. Or, as he puts it, from God's infinite power or nature 'all things have necessarily flowed, or always followed, by the same necessity and in the same way as from the nature of a triangle it follows, from eternity and to eternity, that its three angles are equal to two right angles'.[44]

To say that for Spinoza 'God exists only philosophically' does not even begin to do justice to the radical nature of his conception of God. Descartes's God, it was often said by his religious critics, is a 'merely philosophical' God—a dispassionate, infinitely powerful cause whose ways are beyond our comprehension, who is not in any way 'close' to human beings with the kind of care often portrayed in biblical writings. And yet even Descartes's God still has will and understanding,[45] and acts with an indifferent, libertarian freedom but nonetheless with reason.[46] Descartes's God has purposes. For Spinoza, on the other hand, God is not even the kind of being of which it is coherent to speak of will or purpose. Spinoza's God is substance, period; along with whatever else follows necessarily from that claim. The moral and psychological spareness of Spinoza's conception of God goes well beyond anything Descartes could have imagined.

Spinoza's God is also not a lawgiver, at least not in the ordinary sense so central to the Judeo-Christian world-view. While there is a 'divine' core in the Mosaic Law, consisting in a simple, supreme moral message ('Love your neighbor'),[47] the Torah and its commandments are not the result of a direct, personal communication from on high. God is not the author of the legal code and historical narratives of Scripture; the Torah is not literally of divine origin. And, once disengaged from a necessarily omniscient and veracious author, the value of Torah as a source of truth is therefore open to question. This is not to deny that the Bible conveys certain important lessons of a political, ethical, and historical nature. On the contrary, therein lies its importance. Rather, its prescriptions and proscriptions are not necessarily to be taken as absolutely binding on all Jews—much less on all peoples—at all times. Or, to use the words of Spinoza's young interrogators and informers, 'the Law is not true'.

It will be said that, although God's law is inscribed in our hearts, Scripture is nevertheless the Word of God, and it is no more permissible to say of Scripture that it is mutilated and contaminated than to say this of God's Word. In reply, I have to say that such objectors are carrying their piety too far, and are turning religion into superstition; indeed, instead of God's Word they are beginning to worship likenesses and images, that is, paper and ink.[48]

The Bible, he argues in the *Theological–Political Treatise*, is a human document. It was the work of a number of authors and editors, all living well after Moses, and the text we have is the result of a long and natural process of historical transmission. Spinoza denies that Moses wrote all, or even most, of the Torah. The references in the Pentateuch to Moses in the third person; the narration of his death and, particularly, of events following his death; and the fact that some places are called by names that they did not bear in the time of Moses all 'make it clear beyond a shadow of doubt' that the writings commonly referred to as 'the Five Books of Moses' were, in fact, written by someone who lived many generations after Moses. Moses did, to be sure, compose some books of history and of law; and remnants of those long lost books can be found in the Pentateuch. But the Torah as we have it, as well as the other books of the Hebrew Bible (such as Joshua, Judges, Samuel, and Kings) were written neither by the individuals whose names they bear nor by any person appearing in them. Spinoza believes that these texts were, in fact, all composed by a single historian living many generations after the events narrated, and that this was most likely Ezra. It was the post-exilic leader who took the many writings that had come down to him and began weaving them into a single (but not seamless) narrative. Ezra's work was later completed and supplemented by the editorial labors of others. What we now possess, then, is nothing but a compilation, and a rather mismanaged, haphazard, and 'mutilated' one at that.

If one merely observes that all the contents of these five books, histories and precepts, are set forth with no distinction or order and with no regard to chronology, and that frequently the same story is repeated, with variations, it will readily be recognised that all these materials were collected indiscriminately and stored together with a view to examining them and arranging them more conveniently at some later time. And not only the contents of these five books but the other histories in the remaining seven books right down to the destruction of the city were compiled in the same way.[49]

As for the books of the Prophets, they are of even later provenance, compiled (or 'heaped together', in Spinoza's view) by a chronicler or scribe perhaps as late as the Second Temple period. Canonization into Scripture occurred only in the second century BCE, when the Pharisees selected a number of texts from a multitude of others. Because the process of transmission was a historical one, involving the conveyance of writings of human origin over a long period of time through numerous scribes, and because the decision to include some books but not others was made by fallible human beings, there are good reasons for believing that a significant portion of the text of the 'Old Testament' is corrupt.

If the Bible is not the handiwork of God, or of Moses acting as God's amanuensis, then the metaphysical doctrines that it seems to imply and the personal and epic stories that it tells are not necessarily true. The purpose of Scripture is to inspire or command obedience to God, not to communicate philosophical, scientific, or theological truth. We should give our fealty to a particular moral message—in the case of Scripture, that message is one of universal love—and not to the words on paper that communicate it.

Finally, among Spinoza's opinions that would surely have given offense to the *parnassim*, there is the question of the 'election' of the Jewish people, an article of the Jewish faith that is grounded in the narratives of the Torah. If the origins and authority of Scripture are now suspect, then so must be its grand claims about the 'vocation' of the Hebrews. It is 'childish', Spinoza insists, for anyone to base their happiness on the uniqueness of their gifts; in the case of the Jews, it would be the uniqueness of their being chosen among all people. The ancient Hebrews, in fact, did not surpass other nations in their wisdom or in their proximity to God. They were neither intellectually nor morally superior to other peoples. 'Inasmuch as God is to all men equally gracious . . . [the Jew] possessed no gift of God above other men, and there was no difference between Jew and Gentile.'[50] The Jews were 'chosen' only with respect to their social organization and political good fortune. God (or Nature) gave them a set of laws and they obeyed those laws, with the natural result that their society was well ordered and their autonomous government persisted for a long time. Their election was thus a temporal and conditional one. Their kingdom, however, is now long gone. Consequently, the ceremonial laws that were so important a part of that kingdom and its rituals are no longer binding. The entire foundation of their validity—in fact, the rational basis for almost all of the commandments of the Torah—has been swept away by time. The only practical commandments that properly belong to true religion are those that are necessary to carry out the moral precept and 'confirm in our hearts the love of our neighbor'. Spinoza concludes that 'at the present time there is nothing whatsoever that the Jews can arrogate to themselves above other nations'.[51]

Denying the providential God of the Hebrew Scriptures, the divine origin of the Torah and the continued validity of its laws, and the election of the Jewish people: these are not sentiments likely to endear one to the rabbis of a Jewish community in the seventeenth century. On the basis of these opinions alone, the Sephardim of Amsterdam would have had good cause to issue a strong *cherem* against Spinoza.[52] And they would have found the authority for such a harsh response in Maimonides, whose halachic rulings were of particular importance to Jews of Iberian origin.

Maimonides insists that the 'truth' of the Torah and the existence of a God who is a free creator, giver of laws, and judge—and not, we can presume, just an 'infinite substance'—are two central and indispensable tenets of the Jewish religion. They are found among the thirteen articles of faith that Maimonides insists are required beliefs for any Jew. The first fundamental principle, he insists, is the existence of God the creator; while the fifth principle stipulates that God is separate from all natural processes, and that only he is a totally free agent. The eighth principle states that the Torah came from God.[53] In the *Mishneh Torah* he proclaims that 'whoever denies the Torah', including anyone who 'says that the Torah is not of divine origin, even if he says it of one verse, or of a single word', will not have a place in the world to come. Such people will be 'separated and destroyed, and for their great wickedness and sinfulness are condemned for ever and ever'.[54] Maimonides is here echoing the words of the *Mishnah*:

> All Israel have a portion in the world to come, for it is written, 'Thy people are all righteous; they shall inherit the land forever, the branch of my planting, the work of my hands, that I may be glorified'. But the following have no portion therein: He who maintains that resurrection is not a Biblical doctrine, *the Torah was not divinely revealed*, and an epikoros [heretic].[55]

The question of the 'truth' of the Law was an issue particularly dear to Amsterdam's Rabbi Mortera. His *magnum opus* was a long defense of the divine origin and 'truth' (*verdade*) of the Torah. Mortera did not start writing his *Tratado da verdade da Lei de Mose* (Treatise on the Truth of the Law of Moses) until 1659—three years after Spinoza's *cherem*—but there is no question that the issues that he addresses in that work (including the 'proof' of the divinity of the Mosaic Law) had been occupying his mind for some time. The topic recurs several times in his earlier sermons. Recalling Maimonides' summation of the Jewish faith in thirteen articles, he reminds his listeners, in one of his homilies, that one of those articles is 'the principle of the divine origin of the Torah', the denial of which will result in a person's losing his share in the world to come.[56]

The leaders of any Jewish congregation in the seventeenth century—in Amsterdam, but also in Hamburg, Venice, Salonika, and elsewhere—would have been most concerned had a member been publicly expressing any one of these opinions, much less all three together. And a community of former refugees, including many recent immigrants, would have been particularly worried if any of those opinions were of a sort such as to give offense to their Gentile hosts. The question of the divine election of the Jewish people may or may not have meant much to the typical member of the Dutch Reformed Church. But the contemporary validity of God's law, the status of Hebrew Scripture as a direct revelation from God, and the existence of a transcendent God who is creator and judge are tenets that are as important to a Calvinist *predikant* as they are to a Jewish rabbi. We can begin to see the details of the political dimension of Spinoza's *cherem*.

There is one charge, however, that appears in both Lucas's account of Spinoza's interrogation by his fellow students and the testimony of Brother Tomas but that, conspicuously, we have not yet touched upon. According to both narratives, Spinoza was claiming that 'the soul is not immortal', that 'the soul dies with the body'. There is a host of difficult philosophical, religious, and historical issues here. It is all much more complex and uncertain than the questions about the status of Torah and the existence and nature of God. It seems fairly clear why the rejection of a providential God—a purposive God who issued the Law and who rewards those who obey it and punishes those who transgress it—and the denial of the continued validity of the Torah would warrant a serious sanction by a seventeenth-century Jewish community. Perhaps here it *is* obvious—even without concrete documentation but in the light of his mature opinions—why Spinoza was excommunicated. These principles go right to the heart of the Jewish religion, and their denial would, in the eyes of Spinoza's contemporaries, represent a threat not only to the faith but also to ordinary moral behavior.

What is *not* obvious, however, is why the immortality of the soul should have been a contributing factor—indeed, as I believe it was in Spinoza's case, an especially aggravating factor!—in the decision to ban him. Judaism's view(s) on the soul and its fate after death are much more ambiguous, more indeterminate, than its demand that one believe that God—a wise and just judge, the free creator of the world—revealed the Law to Moses, a Law binding on all Jews to the present day. Why should the denial of the immortality of the soul be counted as serious an offense as these other 'heresies'? How important a factor was it in the decision to punish Spinoza?[57] Moreover, *did* Spinoza, in fact, deny the doctrine of personal immortality? Was there a precedent in Jewish thought for his views on this question?

Now one might argue that the belief in the immortality of the soul is intimately linked to the other doctrines I have examined so far. For example, if God's providence plays itself out not only in this world but also in the distribution of eternal reward (for the righteous) and punishment (for the wicked) in some 'world to come', then the effective belief in such a providence would seem to require a robust conception of personal immortality.[58] Consequently, the denial of the immortality of the soul would *imply* the denial of an essential feature of God's providence. But it could just as well be argued, on a very good basis, that an individual Jew need not believe *anything* about the immortality of the soul.[59] Unlike questions of law, Judaism provides a good deal of latitude in matters metaphysical, and seems to require no particular beliefs or commitments on this issue. It all depends. And this is where Spinoza got into trouble.

Patriarchs, Prophets, and Rabbis 3

What must a Jew believe about the fate of the soul after death? Perhaps absolutely nothing. After all, this is a matter not of *halachah*, of law and prescribed ritual, but of *aggadah* (storytelling)—along with all the other spiritual, metaphysical, historical, political, and personal storytelling and mythologizing that make up so much of the richness of Jewish literature. To be sure, not all rabbinic authorities would agree with this response. Maimonides' thirteen principles of the Jewish faith demand not only a belief in the resurrection of the body after death for the righteous—a doctrine that would seem to require the postmortem persistence of the soul, which will be reunited with the body—but also a belief that the soul of a wicked person 'shall be cut off, so that it perishes and does not live eternally'. The soul of the righteous person, on the other hand, shall enjoy an eternal reward in the world to come. The person who rejects these doctrines 'has no real religion, certainly not Judaism'.[1]

But that is Maimonides' view. If the question is about whether there is *a* Jewish doctrine of the immortality of the soul, then the answer clearly must be no. What exists are numerous, sometimes reconcilable but more often contradictory viewpoints expressed by authoritative figures, indeed whole schools of thought, on the nature of the soul and what happens to it (or, in some cases, what does *not* happen to it) when a person dies. There is a good deal of divergence—and outright disputation—in the opinions of the prophets, rabbis, and sages over what the soul is and whether it perishes along with the body or enjoys a separate existence after the end of this life. And even among those who agree that the human soul persists after death, there is no unanimity over what that postmortem 'existence' amounts to. What apparently makes the question so difficult to resolve is the number of different kinds of issues at stake: not just metaphysical problems over the ontology or nature of the soul, its relationship to the body, and the 'topography' of the afterlife, but also moral and even political questions touching reward and punishment, ethical responsibility for one's actions, historical tendencies among schools of thought, and even the meaning and purpose of a human life.

It will be useful, in addressing the question, to examine a number of relevant Jewish texts of different kinds and of varying authoritative status. My goal in this chapter is certainly not to provide an exhaustive survey of Jewish views on immortality. Nor is it to discover what the 'Jewish tradition' is on this issue—on the contrary, I hope only to show, through a sampling of opinions, that there is no such thing; that, at best, there is a variety of Jewish traditions concerning the possibility and nature of immortality.[2]

Moreover, I shall not attempt to isolate exactly which of the many opinions or texts or traditions in the rabbinic literature were specifically of the greatest importance to and influence upon the Amsterdam Jewish religious leaders who were most concerned over Spinoza's claim that 'the soul dies with the body'. Undoubtedly, the rabbinic views on immortality that I do discuss (as well as others) were known to some of the authorities who were behind Spinoza's ban. The community's rabbis, if not its lay governors, were steeped in Jewish learning and scholarship. The most erudite Talmudist among them, Rabbi Mortera, was familiar with and did not hesitate to use standard rabbinic texts on the soul and the world to come as the occasion warranted; his homilies and treatises show this quite clearly. And as I shall discuss in Chapter 6, the Amsterdam rabbinate demonstrated a very strong concern for defending at least one of the general strains of rabbinic (and, in Aboab's case, kabbalistic) thought on this question.

However, the immediate concerns of Amsterdam's rabbis will have to wait. All that I want to accomplish in this chapter is to establish, through a broad but highly selective survey of some traditional Jewish statements on the postmortem fate of the person, a general context both for the views of Spinoza and his Jewish rationalist forebears on the immortality of the soul and for the *cherem* issued by the Amsterdam community against Spinoza, reportedly for his beliefs on this matter. I want, especially, simply to present enough material to show that there is no single Jewish doctrine of immortality, and to suggest that ordinarily there is nothing specific that a Jew needs to believe about the fate of the soul after death.

As in all *quaestiones Judaicae*, the first approach must be to the Torah, the first five books of the Hebrew Bible. Interestingly, for our purposes, the Pentateuch has very little to say on the immortality of the soul; and what it does say is either less than fully informative or entirely ambiguous.

The earliest biblical texts tell us that a person is (or, alternately, is endowed with) a *nefesh*, a 'spirit' or 'soul'. When God first created a human being (*ha'adam*), he 'breathed into his nostrils the breath of life [*nishmat chayim*], and the man became a living soul [*nefesh chayah*]' (Genesis 2: 7). While the *neshamah* appears to be something added to and contained within the body and that gives it life, the *nefesh* just *is* the person, and a *nefesh chayah* the animated or living being. When God commands Moses to return to Egypt to lead the children of Israel out of bondage, he tells Moses, who had killed one of Pharaoh's men, that it is safe for him to go back: 'for all the men who sought your life [*nefesh*] are dead' (Exodus 4: 19). Leviticus, on the other hand, notes that when a person dies, he or she is then a *nefesh met*, a 'dead soul' (21: 11).

Although it is frequently translated into English as 'soul', the meaning of the word *nefesh* should not be misconstrued. Neither a *neshamah* nor a *nefesh* is necessarily an immaterial principle or substance distinct from the body. The metaphysical dualism between mind and body that is so important in later Jewish thinking is conspicuously absent in the Torah. The *nefesh*, and thus the identity of the person, seems to be essentially bound up with the body. Thus, a priest may not go near a *nefesh met*, a dead *nefesh*, a corpse, lest he become defiled or unclean. A *nefesh*, alternately, could be a material principle of life or vitality internal to the body, an animating force belonging to it that may be active or extinct. It neither is separable from the body, nor is it capable of surviving the death of the body.

Most of the individuals named in the book of Genesis, when they come to the end of their days, simply die. There is no indication of an existence after one's life is over. To be sure, when Enoch passes away, we are told that 'God took him' (Genesis 5: 24), while Abraham was 'gathered to his people' (Genesis 25: 8). These seem, however, to be either metaphors (perhaps in the case of Enoch) or representations and remnants of heathen belief: the phrase 'gathered to his people' most likely derives from an earlier practice of ancestor worship (or, more generally, a cult of the dead) that later disappeared as the Israelites moved toward monotheism;[3] the expressions are not supported by any formal body of eschatological doctrine.[4] Later in the narrative Jacob warns his sons that he will not let them take Benjamin, his youngest son, back to Egypt, as the yet unrecognized Joseph has commanded them. 'For if any harm should happen to him by the way in which you go, you shall bring my gray hairs down to Sheol with sorrow' (Genesis 42: 36). This is the first mention of Sheol in the text of Scripture. However, far from being the realm of eternal punishment that appears in later literature, Sheol in the earliest biblical writings seems to be only an underground resting place for the dead. It is lacking all of the moral and picturesque features that are usually (and imaginatively) attributed to it in post-exilic Jewish eschatological writings, as well as in Christian descriptions of hell and purgatory. In fact, Sheol and its contents here appear to be beyond the scope of God's concern. A dead *nefesh* persists in Sheol, but that existence bears no moral relationship to the life that person led. The later Proverbs tells us that Sheol is populated with *rephaim*, literally 'sunken ones', usually translated as 'shades' or 'ghosts'. It is an attenuated form of existence, a material spirit—perhaps what remains of the body itself—emptied (or at least reduced) of all life force.

From the First Kingdom (established under Saul in the eleventh century) down through exile in the sixth century BCE, as the theological beliefs and historical circumstances of the Israelites changed, so did their conception of Sheol.[5] The other books of the Hebrew Scriptures —classified as the Nevi'im (Prophets) and the Ketuvim (Writings) —suggest a more nuanced and richer view of the abode of the dead. In the minds of some writers, descent to the underworld takes on moral and punitive overtones, and Sheol becomes a rather bleak, even repulsive domain. Ezekiel quotes God as saying to the inhabitants of Tyre that

> When I make you a desolate city, like a city where no man can live, when I bring up the primeval ocean against you and the great waters cover you, I will thrust you down with those that descend to the abyss, to the dead of all ages. I will make you dwell in the underworld as in places long desolate, with those that go down to the abyss. (26: 19–20)

According to Proverbs, the house of the harlot is 'the entrance to Sheol, which leads down to the halls of death' (7: 27). Sheol is the place of retribution, where sinners meet their end. But it is also something from which God can save one:

> Foolish men . . . are like sheep, they run headlong into Sheol, the land of Death; he is their shepherd and urges them on; their flesh must rot away and their bodies be wasted by Sheol, stripped of all honor. But God will ransom my life, he will take me from the power of Sheol. (Psalms 49: 13–15)

> The cords of death bound me, Sheol held me in its grip. Anguish and torment held me fast; so I invoked the Lord by name, 'Deliver me, O Lord, I beseech you; for I am your slave.' (Psalms 116: 3–4)

For Isaiah, the inhabitants of Sheol—to which sinners are 'brought down, to the depths of the abyss'—bear a faint resemblance to their living selves, although with a distinctive loss of vitality:

> Sheol below was all astir to meet you at your coming;
> She roused the ancient dead to meet you, all who had been leaders on earth;
> she made all who had been kings of the nations rise from their thrones.
> One and all they greet you with these words:
> 'So you too are weak as we are, and have become one of us.'
> Your pride and all the music of your lutes have been brought down to Sheol.
> (14: 9–11)

Once a person dies and has become one of the *rephaim* in Sheol, there is no hope of a return to life: 'The dead will not live again, those long in their graves [*rephaim*] will not rise; to this end you have punished them and destroyed them, and made all memory of them perish' (26: 14). Sinners descend into Sheol permanently. The righteous, on the other hand, escape it. However, it is not clear what lies in store for them. The reward for righteousness seems to be, in some cases, nothing eternal or extra-mundane, but rather simply continued life: the good get to live on, the wicked do not—they die and go to Sheol: 'For men of intelligence the path of life leads upwards and keeps them clear of Sheol below' (Proverbs 15: 24). The writer of Ecclesiastes, by contrast (perhaps in the first hint of a dualism between an immortal soul and the perishable body), insists that for the righteous 'the dust returns to the earth as it began and the spirit [*ruach*] returns to God who gave it' (12: 7).

Still, the earlier, more minimalist and barren picture of death persists in some of the Ketuvim. Soon after his travails begin, Job describes death as an eternal sleep. And all people eventually come to the same fate.

> Why was I not still-born,
> Why did I not die when I came out of the womb?
> Why was I ever laid on my mother's knees or put to suck on her breasts?
> Why was I not hidden like an untimely birth, like an infant that has not lived to see the light?
> For then I should be lying in the quiet grave, asleep in death, at rest, with kings and ministers who built themselves palaces, with princes rich in gold who filled their houses with silver.
> There the wicked man chafes no more, there the tired laborer rests; the captive too finds peace there and hears no taskmaster's voice; high and low are there, even the slave, free from his master. (3: 11–19)[6]

Job's complaint must, at the very least, express one way of thinking about death that was current among his people.[7] He insists that

> if a tree is cut down, there is hope that it will sprout again and fresh shoots will not fail. Though its roots grow old in the earth, and its stump is dying in the ground, if it scents water it may break into bud and make new growth

like a young plant. But a man dies, and he disappears; man comes to his end, and where is he? As the waters of a lake dwindle, or as a river shrinks and runs dry, so mortal man lies down, never to rise until the very sky splits open. If a man dies, can he live again? He shall never be roused from his sleep. (14: 7–12)

In the late biblical period, and with the writings attributed to Daniel in particular, an even fuller picture emerges of the extended moral dimensions of the fate awaiting one at death. Now when a person dies, he or she begins an extended period of waiting in Sheol. Sheol is the postmortem resting place of all individuals, although for some it is only an intermediate stage. At the 'end of days', with the coming of the Messiah, the righteous are recalled to life to join God, while the wicked simply remain in Sheol.[8] Thus, only virtue will be rewarded after this life in a kind of communal redemption. There is no unanimity on this, however, and some writers insist that *all* persons, righteous and wicked, are resurrected from Sheol at the end of time or the coming of the Messiah, and will then be judged accordingly. The good are permitted to move on to God's kingdom; the sinners will be punished and sent back to Sheol for ever. This appears, for example, to be Daniel's view: 'There will be a time of trouble, such as has never been since the nation came into being. But at that moment your people will be delivered, every one who is written in the book: many of those who sleep in the dust of the earth will wake, some to everlasting life and some to the reproach of eternal abhorrence' (12: 1–2). 'Everlasting life', *chayei olam*. Daniel's conception of the final judgment seems to involve a claim of personal immortality as the proper reward for the righteous. But he offers us no details on what the nature of that reward is, nor about the subject who receives it. Those who are awakened from 'the dust of the earth' may be merely bodily beings, and what passes for immortality may consist in the resurrection of one's 'shade'. It is certainly difficult to find here anything that can properly be called a 'doctrine'. Nor is there any clear commitment to a dualism of soul and body. If there is a distinction at all in these biblical writings, early and late, it is between *nefesh*, the whole individual being, and the *neshamah* or *ruach* which animates a person and that, according to Ecclesiastes, returns to God when a person dies.[9]

There is, then, no obvious and unambiguous reference to an immortal soul in the Torah itself; and the evidence from later biblical writings, given the variety both of their authors and of the historical and religious circumstances in which they were composed, suggests that the search is in vain.[10] As one scholar has noted, 'absolutely nowhere in the Bible do we find a unified view about life after death that reflects postmortem beliefs of the entire Biblical era, or even of any one period'.[11]

Judaism does have its heaven and hell—or, better, folklores surrounding paradise and its antipode. The embellishment of Sheol into a true domain of punishment, with all of the colorful retributive accoutrements that we have come to expect of the abode of eternal damnation, as well as the appearance of a divine realm of everlasting reward, is one of the philosophical products of the six centuries between the return from exile at the end of the sixth century BCE and the destruction of the second Temple in the first century CE. These developments in moral geography appear at times to be bolstered by the evolution—thanks, in some cases at least, to the influence of Greek philosophy—of an explicit metaphysical dualism between soul or mind and body. The soul now survives the demise of the body, from which it is separated at death. According to some religious figures (but certainly not all), it is the soul in a disembodied form that will either reap the benefits of righteousness or suffer the wages of sin. It will—on some accounts, temporarily—be reunited with the resurrected body at the end of time. But the soul's own fate is an eternal one, and morally dependent on the life one has led in this world. Or so some Jewish traditions would have it.

The collection of writings known as the Apocrypha and the Pseudepigrapha have no authoritative status in the Jewish canon. The 'events' these works relate, their stories and explanations of various phenomena, and—most of all—their pronouncements on matters of belief are without normative value. Indeed, it is not clear that they had much (or even any) influence at all within Jewish thought, since—given their noncanonical status and irregular availability and accessibility—Jews throughout the ages did not ordinarily read them.

Still, they do afford us insight into the Jewish mind at a certain extended historical moment. And what makes them striking for our purposes is the wealth of speculation they contain on the nature of the afterlife.

Among the apocalyptic works in Jewish literature perhaps none offers as rich and evocative a picture of the afterlife as the collection known as the Enoch texts, especially 1 Enoch. This pseudepigraphic work, probably composed around the third century BCE, tells the story of Enoch's spiritual wanderings in the worlds of Sheol or Gehinnom, on the one hand, and, on the other hand, heaven or paradise.[12] What Enoch sees in both domains is highly structured systems of punishment and reward, wherein the spirits of the dead receive their just dues. God will 'execute judgment upon all', he learns: for the righteous or elect, there will be salvation; for the wicked sinners, eternal destruction.

Guided on his tour by a number of archangels (including Raphael, Uriel, Gabriel, and Michael), Enoch first visits Sheol, where the spirits of the dead—now separated from the bodies they inhabited in life—assemble and wait until the day of their judgment, 'when the actions of men are weighed in the balance'. The terrain he sees is divided into four hollow places, 'deep and dark to look at'. The division is to separate the spirits of the righteous from the spirits of sinners.

> And this division [the angel answered] has been made for the spirits of the righteous, in which there is the bright spring of water. And this has been made for sinners when they die and are buried in the earth and judgment has not been executed on them in their lifetime. Here their spirits shall be set apart in great pain, till the great day of judgment, scourgings and torments of the accursed forever, so that there may be retribution for their spirits. There He shall bind them forever. (1 Enoch 22: 8–9)

When the day of judgment arrives, the bodies of all are resurrected and reunited with the souls: 'the earth shall give back that which has been entrusted to it, and Sheol also shall give back that which it has received. And hell shall give back that which it owes.' The souls of the righteous are, at the time of judgment, rewarded with passage to the 'dwelling places of the holy', where 'righteousness flows as water, and mercy like dew upon the earth. Thus it is among them for ever and ever' (1 Enoch 39: 5). It is, Enoch relates, a 'garden of life' (61: 12).

> Blessed are you, you righteous and elect, for glorious shall be your lot.
> And the righteous shall be in the light of the sun, and the elect in the light of eternal life:
> The days of their life shall be unending, and the days of the holy without number.
> And they shall seek the light and find righteousness with the Lord of Spirits:
> There shall be peace to the righteous in the name of the Eternal Lord. (58: 2–3)

Their glory and happiness will be eternal. 'They shall have been clothed with garments of glory, and they shall be the garments of life from the Lord of Spirits: And your garments shall not grow old, nor your glory pass away before the Lord of Spirits' (62: 15–16). The writer of 2 Enoch adds some material and imaginative detail. Paradise, he claims, is

> A garden—a place such as has never been known before for the goodliness of its appearance . . . tall trees of beautiful colors and their fruits ripe and fragrant and all kinds of fruits which they produced. And in the midst, the tree of life on which God rests when He comes into paradise . . . and on all sides in appearance it is like gold and crimson and transparent as fire . . . From its roots in the garden there go forth four streams which pour honey and milk, oil and wine . . . there are three hundred angels, very glorious, who keep the garden . . . this place, O Enoch, is prepared for the righteous who endure every kind of attack in their lives from those who afflict their soul; who turn away their eyes from unrighteousness . . . and also give bread to the hungry, and clothe the naked and raise the fallen, and assist the orphans who are oppressed, and who walk without blame before the face of the Lord and serve him only . . . For them this place is prepared as an eternal inheritance.

The souls of the wicked, on the other hand, are, 1 Enoch tells us, driven away to an eternal punishment for their sins. Those who did not experience judgment in their lifetime will experience the worst fate. On the day of judgment their temporary abode in the particular and painful 'hollow place' in Sheol will become an 'accursed valley' and they will be 'accursed forever', suffering in an 'abyss full of torment'. Those who were sinners in this life will be sent down and 'banished from off the face of the earth, and they shall perish for ever and ever'.

And I looked and turned to another part of the earth, and saw there a deep valley with burning fire. And they brought the kings and the mighty, and began to cast them into this deep valley. And there my eyes saw how they made these their instruments, iron chains of immeasurable weight. And I asked the angel of peace who went with me, saying, 'For whom are these chains being prepared?' And he said to me, 'These are being prepared for the hosts of Azazel, so that they may take them and cast them into the abyss of complete condemnation, and they shall cover their jaws with rough stones as the Lord of Spirits commanded.' (54: 1–6)

They will be 'cast into an abyss, full of fire and flaming, full of pillars of fire . . . And I saw at that time how a like fire of abyss was opened in the middle of the earth, full of fire, and they were judged and found guilty and cast into this fiery abyss, and they burned' (90: 24–6). 'Their souls will be made to descend into Sheol, and they shall be wretched in their great tribulation. And into darkness and chains and a burning flame where there is grievous judgment shall your spirits enter' (63: 10).

Among the spirits to be so punished are, appropriately enough, those who deny that the soul will, in the hereafter, enjoy the rewards of its righteousness or suffer the punishment for its wickedness—that is, those who deny the immortality of the soul and its moral dimensions.

And yet when you die the sinners speak over you:

'As we die, so die the righteous, and what benefit do they reap for their deeds? Behold, even as we, so do they die in grief and darkness, and what have they more than we? From henceforth we are equal. And what will they receive and what will they see forever? Behold, they too have died, and henceforth forever shall they see no light.' (102: 6–8)

We are, indeed, in this apocalyptic literature, a long way from the reserve of the biblical texts on the nature and fate of the soul. There is now a separation of body and soul at the moment of death. The body is buried, while the soul, conscious and endowed with thought and memory, descends to Sheol. The two are briefly reunited for the purposes of judgment—the doctrine of the resurrection of the body will become a standard, indeed a required feature of Jewish belief. The result of the judgment will be an eternal reward or punishment given to the soul itself.

This is all fairly visionary material. But the general idea behind it appears even in the more sober writings of the Apocrypha. The author of the Wisdom of Solomon, a Hellenistic writer of the first century, notes that 'God created man for immortality, and made him the image of his own eternal self.' Those who deny this are 'godless' in their words and deeds.

> They say to themselves in their deluded way: 'Our life is short and full of trouble, and when a man comes to his end there is no remedy; no man was ever known to return from the grave. By mere chance were we born, and afterwards we shall be as though we had never been, for the breath in our nostrils is but a wisp of smoke; our reason is a mere spark kept alive by the beating of our hearts, and when that goes out, our body will turn to ashes and the breath of our life disperse like empty air . . . A passing shadow—such is our life, and there is no postponement of our end; man's fate is sealed, and none returns.' (2: 1–5)

'Blinded by their own malevolence', the wicked fail to see God's hidden plan, never expecting that 'holiness of life would have its recompense; they thought that innocence had no reward'. On the contrary, the author insists, 'the souls of the just are in God's hand, and torment shall not touch them'. There is no mention here of the resurrection of the body. Rather, it is the soul that will enjoy the rewards of righteousness, 'in the moment of God's coming to them'. 'They are at peace, for though in the sight of men they may be punished, they have a sure hope of immortality; and after a little chastisement they will receive great blessings' (3: 1–5).

It is, of course, possible that all that the author of the Wisdom has in mind here is a figurative kind of immortality—namely, that which is acheived by a good name and reputation for virtue, what Homer and his Greek contemporaries called *kleos*. 'It is better to be childless, provided one is virtuous; for virtue held in remembrance is a kind of immortality, because it wins recognition from God, and from men too' (4: 1). The wicked, on the other hand, 'shall be full of anguish, and all memory of them shall perish' (4: 19). Their lives are compared to 'all those things that have passed by like a shadow, like a messenger galloping by; like a ship that runs through the surging sea, and when she has passed, not a trace is to be found, no track of her keel among the waves' (5: 9–10). What is eternal here is only metaphorically one's 'spirit'; living on in memory replaces true immortality in this weaker conception.

The author of 2 Esdras (Ezra), a near-contemporary of the writer of the Wisdom of Solomon, on the other hand, is clearly committed to the more robust and metaphysical apocalyptic picture.

> The entrances to this world were made narrow, painful, and arduous, few and evil, full of perils and grinding hardship. But the entrances to the greater world are broad and safe, and lead to immortality. All men must therefore enter this narrow and futile existence; otherwise they can never attain the blessings in store. Why then, Ezra, are you so deeply disturbed at the thought that you are mortal and must die? Why have you not turned your mind to the future instead of the present? (7: 12–16)

What that future holds in store is, first, a Messianic period of 400 years for those who are still alive at its inception (but not for those who have died). At the end of that 'kingdom', at the end of the world itself, the bodies of all the dead will be resurrected and reunited with their souls, which had been 'kept at rest' in 'storehouses'. 'The earth shall give up those who sleep in it, and the dust those who rest there in silence and the storehouses shall give back the souls entrusted to them' (7: 32–3). God will then appear in order to pass final judgment. The wicked will be sent to eternal punishment, while the righteous and just will receive an eternal reward. 'Then the place of torment shall appear, and over against it the place of rest; the furnace of hell shall be displayed, and on the opposite side the paradise of delight . . . Look on this side, then on that: here are rest and delight, there fire and torments' (7: 36–8). Only a few will be fortunate enough to enjoy happiness in 'the eternal world to come'; most will suffer misery in the 'place of torment'. But everyone deserves their fate: 'It was with conscious knowledge that the people of this world sinned, and that is why torment awaits them.'

Ezra, revealing a metaphysical curiosity, actually asks his guide about what happens at death, 'when every one of us gives back his soul'. 'The spirit', he is told, 'leaves the body to return to the One who gave it, and first of all to adore the glory of the Most High' (7: 78). The soul of the just person, freed from the confines of the mortal body, will, before the final judgment, be present before God and will contemplate his being. Until they receive 'the glory waiting for them in the next age', they will enjoy 'the rest which they are now to share in the storehouses, guarded by angels in deep silence'. There they will remain until they are 'set free [for] the spacious life which will soon be theirs to enjoy for ever and ever' (7: 96). The souls of the wicked, on the other hand, are condemned to wander aimlessly, anticipating with dread the final sentence they will receive in the future world. 'Those who have rejected the ways of the Most High and despised his law, and who hate all that fear God, their spirits enter no settled abode, but roam thenceforward in torment, grief and sorrow.'

What remains of a person after death, for many Hellenistic Jewish authors, is no longer a mere 'shade', a depleted physical existent, but a true soul or spirit ontologically distinct from the body and modeled, almost certainly, on the Greek *psyche* or Platonic *nous*. This soul, or *nefesh* (or, in some cases, *ruach*), survives as an individual, conscious being, one that remembers its past life and contemplates (with joy or sorrow) its eternal condition. It is a metaphysical remnant of a moral being. As such, it—apparently along with the body, with which it is eventually reunited—is the subject of divine punishment or reward.

The apocalyptic writings of the last three centuries BCE and the first century CE did, to be sure, elaborate on some themes that are thinly present in the Hebrew Bible (such as Sheol and divine judgment). The authors of these works seem to take themselves to be saying things that are not only consistent with Scripture, but perhaps also implied therein. But—and this is the important point—there is nothing in these later texts that is to be regarded as *dogma*; they are noncanonical works, mostly visionary storytelling, and do not possess any halachic value. They must also have had little actual influence on later, more mainstream Jewish writings. But at least some of the elements of the doctrines of immortality and the afterlife that they contain also appear, in one form or another, in the classic rabbinic works that were of normative authority.

One of the most important developments in the post-Exile era for the later development of Judaism as a relatively unified religion, with a generally (but not completely) consistent set of doctrines and beliefs, was the division—both political and religious—between the Sadducees and the Pharisees. And according to the historian Josephus, writing late in the first century, the question of the immortality of the soul stands as one of the defining aspects of this division. The more urbane and upper-class Sadducees, representing the conservative viewpoint of the priesthood, basically argued that when you are dead, you are dead; there is no immortality of the soul. The Pharisees, on the other hand, 'believe that souls have an immortal vigor, and that under the earth there will be rewards and punishments, according as they have lived virtuously or viciously in this life; and the latter are to be detained in an everlasting prison, but the former will have the power to revive and live again'.[13]

The Pharisees eventually won the day, and their views constitute the core of later rabbinic doctrine. This does not mean, however, that there is universal agreement among the sages of the Talmud and the *midrashim* (or rabbinic commentaries) over what exactly the 'afterlife'—for those who agree that there is one—holds in store for the soul. There is no consensus or uniformity in rabbinic views on the nature and immortality of the soul, nor on the moral and theological importance of such doctrines. There still is no dogma here, and rabbis and other authorities had a good deal of latitude for speculation, exposition, interpretation, and interpolation on this question of metaphysical *aggadah*. To be sure, the resurrection of the body (*techiyyat hametim*, literally the 'animation of the dead') is—from the Mishnah to Maimonides—nearly unanimously regarded as a nonnegotiable belief. (So much so that it appears repeatedly in the Amidah, still the central set of prayers in Jewish worship.) Maimonides includes it among the thirteen required articles of the Jewish faith, while both the Tannaim (the authorities of the Mishnah) and the Amoraim (the talmudic commentators on the Mishnah) claim that those who deny that the resurrection of the body is pronounced by the Torah will have no share in the world to come.[14] But there is a great deal of diversity in opinions about where or when this resurrection will take place, who will be included, and how it relates to any particular theories of personal immortality[15] or national redemption. It would be very difficult to argue that there is anything universal and normative included in this doctrine aside from the general and ambiguous claim that the dead will be brought to life again by God. Still, there are some things about which there is at least broad authoritative agreement and that can be recognized as 'Jewish belief', although—and this bears repeating—they fall not under *halachah* but only *aggadah*.

The rabbinic period witnessed the development of a full-bodied metaphysical dualism of mind and body. With some exceptions, the rabbis seem to have been in agreement that while the body is material, divisible, and corruptible, the soul is a simple, immaterial, and incorruptible being.[16] On this view, the soul is clearly ontologically distinct from the body, and thus survives the demise of the body. 'Until three days [after death] the soul keeps on returning to the grave, thinking that it will go back [into the body]; but when it sees that the facial features have become disfigured, it departs and abandons [the body].'[17]

On some accounts, the soul is tripartite, constituted by *nefesh*, *ruach*, and *neshamah*. The *nefesh*, or vegetative and nutritive soul, is responsible for appetite and basic bodily and sensory functioning. *Ruach* is animal soul, and is bound up with animal emotion and human passion. It is essentially what the Greeks called *thumos*, or 'high spirit'. It is distinct from, yet intimately related to, *neshamah*, the intellect, the subject of our higher cognitive functions. It appears that for some rabbinic authorities, *nefesh* is inseparable from the body, perhaps even a part of the body; it remains with the corporeal parts upon a person's death, and is thus necessarily mortal. A more prevalent view, however, is that all three parts of the soul, while functionally distinct, form an indissoluble unity: the soul is one. Rabbi Samuel, for example, is reported to have claimed that *neshamah*, the soul, is identical with both *nefesh* and *ruach*.[18] What survives the body after death is often interchangeably called *nefesh*, *ruach*, and *neshamah*.

What awaits the soul is 'the world to come', *olam haba*. According to one body of opinion, a soul departs for the world to come immediately upon a person's death (or perhaps a few days afterwards); the world to come is thus, on this view, a separate realm contemporaneous with this world. According to another set of views, however, the world to come is a posthistorical domain, arriving only at the end of time, after all of the souls that have been created by God have participated in life in this world.[19] One of the great sources of divergence among the rabbis (as among later Jewish philosophers) is what relationship the world to come bears to the Messianic era—the period ushered in by the coming of the Messiah and the establishment of his kingdom on earth—and to the time of the resurrection of the body. The dominant view among those who adopt a posthistorical understanding of the world to come is that it will arrive after the end of the Messianic era, and after the resurrection of the body and its reunion with the soul.

The world to come is, practically all the rabbis agree, a place or time of moral reckoning. 'In the hereafter, there will be judgment and reckoning,' declares one midrash text.[20] The world, Rabbi Jacob declares, 'is like an antechamber before the world to come. Get ready in the antechamber, so you can go into the great hall.'[21] What awaits one in that 'great hall' is God the judge, 'who, if he puts me to death puts me to death forever'.[22] It is not clear, however, whether what is judged is simply the soul alone or the soul and body together. For one midrashic authority, the soul, that which 'fills the body . . . [and] carries the body', will also 'outlast the body', and it alone shall stand before God.[23] But another rabbi believes that this is both to mistake the locus of moral responsibility and to forget the doctrine of the resurrection of the body.

God will say to the soul: 'Why have you sinned before me?' And the soul will answer: 'O master of the universe, it is not I that sinned, but the body that has sinned. Why, since leaving it, I am like a clean bird flying through the air. As for me, how have I sinned?' God will also say to the body: 'Why have you sinned before me?' And the body will reply: 'O master of the universe, it is not I who have sinned, but the soul that has sinned. Why, since it left me, I am cast about like a stone thrown upon the ground. Have I then sinned before you?'

What will the Holy One, blessed be He, do to them? He will bring the soul and force it into the body, and judge both as one.[24]

According to this view—and it is by no means an isolated or even a minority opinion—when the soul is reunited with the resurrected body, it is forever. What this represents is not so much an account of the immortality of the soul alone, but rather a robust conception of resurrection. The subject of God's judgment is a reanimated human being, body and soul together. There is, in fact, a general tendency in rabbinic thinking either towards a conflation of the two doctrines of the resurrection of the body and the immortality of the soul, or at least towards an ambiguity between them in statements on the afterlife. On either account, there is a strong conception of personal immortality.

The result of God's judgment—either for the soul alone or for the soul in union with the resurrected body—will be either reward with entry into the world to come, considered as a kind of everlasting life; or punishment, consisting either in eternal death or (according to most texts) descent into Sheol or Gehinnom. 'Is it only the living who are in God's hand, and not the dead? No, but the righteous even after their death may be called living, whereas the wicked, both in life and in death, may be called dead.'[25] Rabban Jochanan ben Zakkai was reportedly filled with anxiety over his eternal fate.

When Rabban Jochanan ben Zakkai fell ill, his disciples went in to visit him. When he saw them he began to weep. His disciples said to him, 'Lamp of Israel, pillar of the right hand, mighty hammer! Why do you weep?' He replied, 'If I were being taken today before a human king who is here today and tomorrow in the grave, whose anger if he is angry with me does not last forever, who if he imprisons me does not imprison me to everlasting death, and whom I can persuade with words and bribe with money, even so I would weep. Now that I am being taken before the supreme King of Kings, the Holy One, blessed be He, who lives and endures for ever and ever, whose anger, if He is angry with me, is an everlasting anger, who if He imprisons me imprisons me forever, who if He puts me to death puts me to death forever, and whom I cannot persuade with words or bribe with money—nay, more, when there are two ways before me, one leading to Paradise [Gan Eden] and the other to Gehinnom, and I do not know by which I shall be taken, shall I not weep?[26]

It is the righteous alone who will have a place in the world to come. This constitutes their ultimate reward. 'The future world', Rav was reportedly fond of saying, 'is not like this world. In the future world there is no eating nor drinking nor propagation nor business nor jealousy nor hatred nor competition, but the righteous sit with their crowns on their heads feasting on the brightness of the divine presence, as it says, *And they beheld God, and did eat and drink*.'[27] What awaits the righteous in the world to come is their perfection and pure fulfillment. It is, in other words, heaven, paradise, Gan Eden:

> In the hereafter, the Holy One, blessed be He, will prepare a feast for the righteous in the Garden of Eden, and there will be no need either of balsam or of choice spices, for the north wind and the south wind will sweep through and sprinkle about all the perfumes of *Gan Eden*, and they will exhale their fragrance . . . In the hereafter, the Holy One will give them [those who occupied themselves with Torah] to drink of the wine that is preserved in its grapes since the days of creation, and will let them bathe in rivers of milk.[28]

The rewards of virtue in the world to come are, of course, eternal: 'Although all experience death, every righteous person has an eternity of his own.'[29]

According to at least one strain of talmudic tradition, there are in paradise only the *souls* of the righteous. Twelve months after the death of the body (during which time the *nefesh* 'ascends and descends'), the soul of the righteous individual is freed. It is gathered to the 'divine treasury' (*otzar*), on at least one account, where it will 'hide under the Throne of Glory'.[30] Who is to be included among 'the righteous'? Will all virtuous persons, of whatever ancestry or creed, Gentiles as well as Jews, 'the righteous of all nations', be admitted to the world to come? Or will only righteous members of the nation of Israel be awarded entry? Or will, in fact, *all* Jews, as members of God's chosen nation, ultimately find an eternal reward there, accompanied perhaps by righteous Gentiles? There seems to be no agreement whatsoever on this issue. The Mishnah appears to answer the question when it states that 'all Israelites have a share in the world to come'.[31] But this claim, rather than resolving the problem, represents only the starting point for later debate. Some rabbis insist that by 'all Israelites' the Tannaim were referring to all righteous persons,[32] while others claim that the assertion must be read more restrictively. Even if all Jews are guaranteed, by virtue of belonging to the nation of Israel, a place in *olam haba*, there are certain sins for which one could lose that birthright. Those who deny the doctrine of the resurrection of the body, or claim that it is not taught by the Torah; those who deny that the Torah is not of divine origin; those who read heretical books; someone who 'pronounces the divine name as it is spelled out'; 'the generation of the flood' and 'the generation of the dispersion'; the men of Sodom; those who put their neighbors to shame, and many other classes of people (including those who speculate on the world to come!): 'these are the ones who have no portion in the world to come'.[33] It is interesting to note that the list of offenses for which one could be excluded from *olam haba* includes not only actions, but doctrines and beliefs as well.

If the righteous—or, more accurately, the souls of the righteous—will enter paradise, the wicked, on the other hand, have a different, much more miserable fate in store: 'The wicked are condemned to death like a beast, and do not enter the world to come.'[34] It may be that the punishment of the wicked consists only in death itself, in a loss of access to life in the world to come. When we are told that the wicked will be 'cut off' (*hikaret*), this may be all that is meant. Thus, Maimonides, in his commentary on some of these texts, notes that 'utterly evil punishment consists in the cutting off of the soul so that it perishes and does not live eternally'.[35] Or, more ominously, if there is—as many rabbis insist—life after death for the souls of the wicked as well as of the righteous, it lies in the 'valley of destruction', the 'horrible pit': Gehinnom. This is the realm of punishment, and it involves a period of painful retribution leading (for some, at least) to restoration. It is the temporary or permanent destination not just for sinners among the Gentiles, but also for a large number of classes within Israel (including 'he who follows his wife's counsel', at least according to Rav[36]). It is a realm of darkness, snow, hail, itching, brimstone, smoke, and, of course, fire: 'Ordinary fire is a sixtieth of the fire of Gehinnom.'[37] This fire of heretofore unexperienced intensity will 'burst upon the heads of the wicked'.[38] When they feel its heat, 'they will cry out "Oh!, oh!", and it will be followed by snow, at which they cry out "Woe! Woe!" '

The sojourn of a soul (or a soul and a resurrected body together) in this hell may be for only a limited term (twelve months seems to be a common period, although it varies according to the seriousness of one's sins and the degree of one's repentance). In this case, it has a purifying function, and at the end of the period the soul is able to move on to Gan Eden. Sometimes, however, a person's sins are so heinous that Gehinnom is the eternal abode of their soul. 'All who descend into *gehinnom* [subsequently] reascend', Rabbi Chanina says, 'excepting three, who descend but do not reascend, viz. He who commits adultery with a married woman, publicly shames his neighbor, or fastens an evil epithet upon his neighbor.'[39] Eternal punishment also awaits 'those who abandon the ways of the community, and those who spread terror in the land of the living'; they will be punished in Gehinnom 'for all generations . . . *Gehinnom* will be consumed but they will not be consumed.' These are the 'thoroughly wicked'—distinguished from both the thoroughly righteous and the intermediate—and they will 'forthwith be inscribed definitively as doomed to *gehinnom*, as it says *And many of them that sleep in the dust of the earth shall awake, some to everlasting life and some to reproaches and everlasting abhorrence.*'[40]

What can be concluded from this cursory examination of the most central and important writings of the Jewish canon, along with a number of noncanonical but fascinating texts? Is there a Jewish doctrine of the immortality of the soul? Perhaps it is better to say that, among Jewish rabbinic traditions, there is a dominant tendency toward belief in personal immortality, with a fair amount of disagreement on the detailed nature of what happens to the soul after death. There is a general dualism of soul and body in rabbinic and early medieval Judaism. The human soul is a substance that is distinct from the body, separable from it at death. It involves both animating and intellectual functions. This metaphysics is accompanied by an eschatology, a moral structuring of time and the cosmos. The soul survives the death of the body, but it will be reunited with a resurrected body at a determinate moment in the future, generally before a final judgment is pronounced. For some rabbis, the soul will (at least for the righteous) find its ultimate reward and eternal home in a disembodied state; according to others, it is the whole *person*, understood as a reensouled resurrected body, who is granted eternal life in the world to come. On either account, there is a kind of personal immortality. But again it is important to stress that all of this speculating and theorizing and philosophizing is a matter of *aggadah*, of extracurricular storytelling and mythologizing. It is not the laying down of any legal rulings or principles, and none of the rabbis suggests that those who disagree with their specific views on the metaphysics of the soul or the contents and topography of the afterlife have violated Jewish *law* or denied some necessary proposition of the faith.[41] Nor are they called heretics.[42]

Not everyone was satisfied to leave it at that. Maimonides, for one, tries to take things further and transform the principle of immortality into a quasi-dogma. In his grand attempts to summarize, systematize, and interpret the teachings of the Talmud and rabbinic tradition, he does not include a belief in personal immortality explicitly in any of his listings of the thirteen essential articles of the Jewish faith. He does, however, note that among those articles is not just the doctrine of the resurrection of the dead, but also the claim that 'God rewards those who perform the commandments of the Torah and punishes those who transgress its admonitions. The greatest reward is the world to come; the worst punishment is extinction.'[43] It is a theme that runs throughout his halachic works:

> The good reserved for the righteous is life in the world to come, a life that is immortal . . . The reward of the righteous is that they will attain this bliss and abide in this state of happiness; the punishment of the wicked is that they will not attain this life but will be cut off and die . . . [for the wicked] the soul, after its separation from the body (at the close of its existence) on earth, will not attain life in the world to come but will be cut off from that life also.[44]

There can be no question that Maimonides sought to make certain previously nonobligatory beliefs essential to and required for

Judaism.[45] And for him, the immortality of the soul (and the concomitant doctrine of eternal reward and punishment) has the status of a 'grand principle' (*ikkar gadol*), a 'pillar of the law' (*amod ha-torah*). It is, along with the belief in God's unity, 'the beginning and the end' of Torah. In his mind, at least—and his was an influential mind indeed—there *is* a doctrine of immortality, one which is more than just a 'true opinion': despite its metaphysical content, it is, if not a halachic principle in its own right, then at least a necessary condition for proper halachic observance.[46]

Now it is a commonplace to claim that Judaism is not, in fact, a religion of dogmas. 'The whole project of creed formulation is alien to biblical–rabbinic Judaism,' writes one scholar.[47] To be sure, the question of the *general* relationship between Judaism and dogmatic belief is a notoriously complex one, and I have no intention of entering into it here. However, what *is* historically clear is that whenever an attempt is made to establish for Judaism an explicit code of necessary beliefs—such as we find in Maimonides—the result is tension in the ranks and resistance from substantial intellectual quarters. Isaac Abravanel, for example, a fifteenth-century Jewish thinker, denies that Judaism has *any* beliefs that qualify as fundamental principles of the faith: there are no dogmas for Jews. He claims, in fact, that Maimonides knows this, and that he was offering his 'principles' only as pedagogical devices to guide the masses, not as definitive statements of dogma. Everything in the Torah, Abravanel insists, is simply to be accepted as true, 'even the smallest thing'. To go further and engage in philosophical speculation on the 'fundamental beliefs' of Judaism is unnecessary and even dangerous.[48]

More relevant to the issues at hand in this study is the response of Joseph Albo, a philosophical contemporary of Abravanel. Albo stresses the open-ended nature of discussion on the question of immortality and the world to come. Taking Maimonides head-on, he denies that the doctrine of resurrection—and, presumably, the immortality of the soul as well—is either a fundamental or even a derivative principle of Jewish law. Rather, he insists, what is essential is simply a belief in divine reward and punishment; differences of opinion on the details, on the nature of that reward and punishment, should be tolerated. It may be that it all takes place in the hereafter, but perhaps it takes place only in *this* world.

> As long as one believes in reward and punishment generally, whether corporeal, in this world, or spiritual, in the world to come, he does not deny a principle of the Law of Moses if he disbelieves in resurrection . . . Belief in the Messiah and in the resurrection of the dead are principles peculiar to Christianity which cannot be conceived without them. But resurrection and the Messiah are [in Judaism] like branches issuing from the principles of Reward and Punishment and are not root principles in themselves.[49]

Abravanel and Albo were far from alone in their antireductive, anti-dogmatizing efforts, on this and other issues.[50]

While the views on the imortality of the soul (or of the person) and the world to come found in the Talmud and other rabbinic writings may constitute a 'doctrine'—or, better, an ambiguous body of doctrines—they certainly do not constitute a single set of dogmas. In fact, what we find in all of the writings surveyed in this chapter is not even so much an elaboration of doctrine as the gradual unfolding in the mainstream of Jewish religious thought of the development of some views on the nature of the soul and its life after death. And given the generally aggadic (that is, nonhalachic) nature of the issues, a tolerance and latitude on the question of personal immortality and the afterlife seems to have survived later attempts to systematize and reduce it to a single, unequivocal, and required dogma. Thus, Moses ben Joshua of Narbonne (in Provence; he was also called Moses Narboni), a learned and respected fourteenth-century philosopher in the Maimonidean tradition, clearly denies that there is anything personal or individual about immortality. Adopting a variation of Averroes' conception of the numerical unity of intellect in all human beings, Narboni argued that when a person dies his soul, unified with the universal Agent Intellect through the pursuit of knowledge in this life, loses all particularity and identity and merges entirely with that higher Intelligence.[51] Now Averroism was strongly attacked in the world of Christian faith and learning, most prominently by Albert the Great and St Thomas Aquinas; and it was officially condemned by the Bishop of Paris in 1277, just because it threatened the orthodoxy on immortality. The response from within Judaism, however, was entirely different. Moses Narboni had his critics—most notably, Chasdai Crescas—but no one accused him of heresy for his views. He was certainly not punished for his opinions on such a philosophical matter. As we shall see in the next chapter, it is not even clear that Maimonides himself believed that, in the end and in philosophical truth, immortality was a truly personal affair.

The Philosophers 4

Jewish tradition is, by and large, rabbinic tradition. The Talmud and the midrash compilations set the agenda—and, in a sense, the content—for all later Jewish writing. To be sure, despite the efforts of Maimonides and others, Judaism remained a relatively undogmatic religion; when it comes to belief and theory (as opposed to law and action), there was—as we have seen in the case of the afterlife—a good deal of latitude. Still, any theological or philosophical discussion, even that involving speculation on metaphysical matters, had at least to address and take account of the basic teachings of some of the more prominent rabbis whose views are portrayed in those central works. Even as great and renowned a figure as Maimonides had to explain himself very carefully if it appeared as though, in his views on the nature of the soul and its postmortem fate, he was departing too much from what his authoritative forebears are reported generally to have asserted.[1] While philosophy found within medieval Judaism quite a bit more free rein than it was granted within Christianity, it still had to answer to a higher authority.

A discussion of Jewish philosophical views on the immortality of the soul before Spinoza could be a vast enterprise, a book in its own right. It would begin where most surveys of Jewish philosophy begin, with Philo of Alexandria, and proceed up through Saadya ben Joseph (Saadya Gaon), the tenth-century rationalist of Babylon who devoted several 'treatises' within his *Kitab al-Amanat wal-I'tiḳdat* ('Book of Beliefs and Opinions') to the nature of the soul and the afterlife, and then on to the 'Golden Age' of Jewish philosophy in the high and late Middle Ages. But my interest here is not with such a general survey. My discussion of Jewish philosophers before Spinoza is highly selective, but not arbitrarily so. It is geared toward making sense of Spinoza's own views on the question of immortality. And there are two Jewish philosophers in particular whose thought is of special importance for understanding both Spinoza's early intellectual development and his mature metaphysical, epistemological, and moral doctrines. The first is Maimonides—Rabbi Moses ben Maimon (1135?–1204), also known by the acronym RaMBaM. The other is Gersonides—Rabbi Levi ben Gershom (1288–1344), or RaLBaG—the Rambam's fourteenth-century intellectual descendant, and arguably the greatest medieval Jewish philosopher after Maimonides. Both Maimonides and Gersonides adopted a general conception of *olam haba* that, in its fundamentals, owed much to the standard rabbinic accounts. But their views on the nature and immortality of the soul and on its place in the world to come were profoundly influenced by the Aristotelian philosophy to which they, unlike their rabbinic predecessors, were deeply committed. In the eyes of their many critics, in fact, it was a question of too much philosophy and not enough concession to tradition, on these matters and others. Spinoza, on the other hand, found in their works exactly what he was looking for.[2]

Maimonides wrote in a great array of literary forms (and in both Arabic and Hebrew) and for a variety of audiences. There are responsa that he composed in his capacity as community rabbi; textual commentaries (including the monumental *Commentary on the Mishnah*); his great legal code, the *Mishneh Torah*, a grand summation of Jewish law; letters to various individuals and communities; works on particular issues (such as the *Ma'amar Techiyat Hametim*, 'Treatise on Resurrection'); ethical writings, medical treatises, and halachic rulings. And then there is his masterpiece of philosophical thinking, the grand synthesis of Judaism and (Aristotle's) philosophy, *The Guide of the Perplexed*. The *Guide* represents Maimonides' attempt to present in a systematic manner his views—as informed not just by the categories but also by the substance of Aristotelian thought—on some classic problems of philosophy and religion: the existence and nature of God, the proper method of reading the Bible, the workings of prophecy and providence, cosmology, and the nature of knowledge. But the final chapters of the work are devoted to what, since Socrates, has been considered *the* most important question of philosophy: What is the good life for a human being? It is here that Maimonides sets forth an account of human happiness and the perfection and fate of the soul. With their stark intellectualism, there seems to be some tension between these chapters and his writings on immortality and the world to come in his halachic works. But they also inspired both Gersonides and Spinoza to rethink what exactly human immortality consists in.

Maimonides is a philosopher who is extraordinarily sensitive to the variety of meanings, both concrete and abstract, that words can have. This is particularly true for terms or phrases that are often used in the Bible equally to describe God, humans, and other creatures, and where a failure to grasp their ambiguity can lead to gross misunderstandings (such as the belief that God is a corporeal being). One such problematic term is 'soul'.

> *Soul* [*nefesh*] is an equivocal term. It is a term denoting the animal soul common to every sentient being. Thus: *Wherein there is a living soul.* And it is also a term denoting blood. Thus: *Thou shalt not eat the soul with the flesh.* It is also a term denoting the rational soul, I mean the form of man. Thus: *As the Lord liveth that made us this soul.* And it is a term denoting the thing that remains of man after death. Thus: *Yet the soul of my lord shall be bound in the bundle of life.* It is also a term denoting the will. Thus: *To bind his princes according to his soul*, which means: through his will.[3]

A true understanding both of the nature of the human soul and of its highest perfection is an issue not just of metaphysical interest, but also of great import for our happiness and moral well-being. The challenge, as Maimonides sees it, is to offer a philosophically sophisticated explanation of what the soul is that, at the same time, can help us make sense of the rabbinic tradition on the world to come.

Taking as his starting point the basic categories of Aristotle's metaphysics, Maimonides, in the *Mishneh Torah*, argues that every 'substance', every individual existing thing, is composed of two ingredients: matter and form. This is the traditional (for Aristotelians) 'hylomorphic' conception of the nature of things. Matter (in ancient Greek, *hyle*) is the physical 'stuff' that gives the substance its numerical identity, that individuates it spatially and temporally from other things (particularly things that belong to the same species or kind: the particular matter belonging to one horse distinguishes it from any other horse; the lump of bronze that goes into one statue distinguishes that statue numerically from any other bronze statue; and the body of one human being numerically individuates him from any other human being). Form (*morphe*), on the other hand, is what gives the individual its identity and character—it is what makes a horse a horse and a human being a human being.[4] Just as the form given by a sculptor to one bronze statue (say, of a person) differentiates it not numerically but qualitatively from another bronze statue of a different kind of being (of a horse), so things in the world are distinguished qualitatively into kinds and individuals through their respective forms. In the latter-day Aristotelian philosophy that Maimonides inherited, form, although it inheres in matter, is itself immaterial, and thus a fundamentally different kind of reality than matter.[5] Still, form and matter always coexist in bodily substances; in the physical world there can be no form without matter, and no matter without form.[6] As Maimonides himself puts it, 'you will never see matter [*golem*] without form [*tzurah*] . . . the bodies that are found are all a combination of matter and form'.[7]

The form of the human being, the immaterial component that, while distinct from the body, nevertheless commingles with it to produce a person, is the soul (*nefesh*). 'The soul of all flesh is the form which it was given by God.'[8] Maimonides stresses that this form should not be confused with the visible shape of the body. Nor is it the same as the more simple forms (or actualizations of bodily capacities) that explain the vegetative and animal functions in nonhuman creatures. Although it is single and simple, the human soul is certainly capable of a variety of kinds of actions, some of them very much like those more basic functions in plants and animals. 'I say that there are five [activities] of the soul: nutritive, sentient, imaginative, appetitive and rational.'[9] The human *form*, the soul, nourishes and animates the human being by causing all the internal motions of the body that give it life, such as digestion, excretion, and procreation; it is responsible for the body's sentience (sight, hearing, taste, smell, and touch); it is the source of our imaginative powers, our ability to recall and recombine various sensory impressions of objects in the world; and it is the seat of desire, emotion, and passion: 'From this power originate such actions as seeking something or fleeing from it, as well as being attracted to something or avoiding it; rage and agreeableness, fear and boldness, cruelty and compassion, love and hatred, and many such disturbances of the soul.'[10] Thus the human soul, although generically different from other kinds of forms, performs many functions that are similar to the functions performed in other living creatures by their proper forms. But unlike the forms belonging to other living beings, the soul of the human being has an 'extra dimension': knowledge, intellectual capacity, rational thought. All of the other powers of the soul—nutrition, sensation, imagination, and appetite—require the soul to use the body as an instrument. But the highest activity of the soul, rational thought, does not; it is a purely intellectual affair. Moral reasoning, mathematical apprehension, and other forms of abstract thinking and knowing are all activities of the soul alone. They can be engaged in by disembodied souls (such as angels).

> The rational part is the power found in man by which he perceives intelligibles, deliberates, acquires the sciences, and distinguishes between base and noble actions. Some of these activities are practical and some are theoretical. Of the practical, some are productive and some are reflective. By means of the theoretical, man knows the essence of the unchanging beings. These [theoretical activities] are called sciences without qualification. The productive is the power by means of which we acquire occupations, such as carpentry, agriculture, medicine, and navigation. The reflective is that by which one deliberates about a thing he wishes to do at the time he wishes to do it—whether it is possible to do it or not and, if it is possible, how it ought to be done.[11]

Within the soul, then, *nefesh* or *ruach* is distinguished from *neshamah*.[12] The latter is essentially and functionally related to the body, since it animates the body and governs physical functions. The activities of the *neshamah* will thus cease with the body's decomposition. 'When the matter [of the body] . . . decomposes, the *neshamah* ceases to exist—for the *neshamah* exists only together with the body.' The *nefesh*, the rational part of the soul, on the other hand, is, Maimonides insists, independent of the body; when the body decomposes, 'the *nefesh* will not be cut off . . . it does not require [the body] for its activities [*ma'asim*]. Rather, it knows and comprehends knowledge which is above matter.'

This intellect, the highest part of the soul, is like the soul's own form. 'Know that this single soul, whose powers or parts are as described, is like matter, and the intellect is its form.' Its actualization and fulfillment represent the greatest achievement for a human being, his supreme perfection as the kind of being he is. We are naturally fitted for knowledge, and to the extent that we realize this capacity we perfect ourselves. It represents, in fact, the way in which the human being has been created in God's image.

> The extra dimension which is found in the soul of man is the form of man who is perfect in his knowledge. Concerning this form, the Torah states: 'Let us make man in our image and in our likeness'—that is, granting man a form which knows and comprehends ideas that are not material, like the angels, who are form without body, until he can resemble them.[13]

The intellect is what, for Maimonides, is immortal in a human being. In the *Guide* he notes that '[soul, or *nefesh*] also denotes the rational soul, I mean the form of man . . . and it is a term denoting the thing that remains of man after death'.[14] The intellect comes directly 'from God, from heaven', it 'exists forever', and will, upon the death and disintegration of the body, 'return to God who granted it'.[15] In fact, Maimonides believes that the immortality of the soul or intellect is not a miraculous event, as it is for many thinkers, but rather a part of the ordinary course of nature. Forms, being immaterial, are not subject to the corruption that affects matter. 'All bodies subject to generation and corruption are attained by corruption only because of their matter; with regard to form and with respect to the latter's essence, they are not attained by corruption but are permanent. Do you not see that all the specific forms are perpetual and permanent?'[16] The soul will—all things being equal—naturally persist after the body's demise.

Of course, all things are not always equal. Given the moral dimensions of human immortality, it is not the case that all souls will enjoy their natural fate and remain eternally. Many will be refused this postmortem survival, the ultimate reward. Maimonides turns to this question numerous times in his halachic writings.

> The Torah's intent in regard to reward is to the ultimate goal, which is life in the world to come, and in regard to punishment is to the ultimate end, which is extinction from the world to come.[17]

The punishment of the wicked will consist in their souls being 'cut off' from the world to come, from the eternal blessedness that awaits the righteous.

> The reward of the righteous is that they will attain this bliss and abide in this state of happiness; the punishment of the wicked is that they will not attain this life but will be cut off and die. He who does not attain this life will be dead, in the sense that he will never live again but will be cut off in his wickedness and perish like the brute beast. This is the penalty of *excision*, referred to in the Torah, as it is written, 'That soul shall utterly be cut off, his iniquity shall be upon him' (Numbers 15: 31): which has been traditionally interpreted as follows: ' "cut off" (*karet*), in this world; "utterly cut off" (*hikkaret*), in the world to come.' This means that that soul, after its separation from the body (at the close of its existence) on earth, will not attain life in the world to come but will be cut off from that life also.[18]

The same view is reiterated in his commentary on Mishnah, *Sanhedrin*, chapter 10:

> Utterly evil punishment consists in the cutting off of the soul so that it perishes and does not live eternally. This is the penalty of *karet* to which the Torah refers, as in the phrase: 'That soul shall be utterly cut off' (Numbers 15: 31). Interpreting this phrase, our sages said: 'The word *hikkaret* refers to the world to come' . . . It follows that if a person has deliberately and regularly chosen physical delights, has despised the truth and loved falsehood, he will be cut off from that high level of being and remain disconnected matter.[19]

For Maimonides, *olam haba* is a purely spiritual realm, where disembodied souls enjoy a state of perfect happiness, unencumbered by the restrictions and interferences of the body. The occasional rabbinic conflation of (or ambiguity between) the doctrines of the resurrection of the body and the immortality of the soul is absent from Maimonides' conception of the world to come. And it is not the entire soul that achieves this supreme condition, he reminds us, but only the intellect. 'The soul, whenever mentioned in connection [to the world to come], is not the vital element requisite for bodily existence, but that form of the soul which is identical with the intelligence [*hada'ah*] which apprehends the creator, as far as it is able, and apprehends other abstract concepts and other things.'[20] The human intellect, he explains, 'is created separate . . . and exists longer than any body . . . People in the world to come have separate souls, that is to say, intellects.'[21] Because this part of the soul is now freed from the body, it will achieve a state of perfect rationality, acting through nonsensory intellectual cognition, something previously granted only to spiritual beings without bodies: 'In the world to come souls without bodies will exist like angels.'[22]

The world to come is a world of incomparable *spiritual* delight, a condition of pure intellectual 'bliss beyond which there is nothing more blissful'. The immortal soul will enjoy eternal happiness through the eternal exercise of its intellectual functions alone. Maimonides stresses this aspect of the world to come because he is trying to counteract a good deal of speculation on what *olam haba* is like, and particularly to discourage those who picture it as a garden of earthly delights, full of *physical* pleasures, a 'Garden of Eden, a place in which one eats and drinks without any physical work or effort'. There are people who insist that in the world to come 'there are houses made of precious stones, beds of silk, rivers flow with wine and fragrant oils, and many other things of that sort. This same group believes that the evil is Gehinnom, a place of raging fire, in which bodies are burned and agonies of all sorts are inflicted upon men.'[23] On the contrary, Maimonides insists, 'in the world to come there is nothing corporeal, and no material substances; there are only the souls of the righteous without bodies'.[24] Because there are no bodies in the world to come, Maimonides argues, there are—and can be—no physical pleasures there. 'In the world to come there is no corporeal existence, as the sages, of blessed memory, said: "There is no eating and no drinking and no sexual intercourse." '[25] What the soul will find is its own proper kind of happiness: understanding, knowledge, an intellectual communion with God. 'In the world to come, our souls will become wise with the knowledge of God the creator . . . Souls enjoy blissful delight in this attainment of knowledge of the truly essential nature of God the creator, a delight which is like that experienced by the holy angels who know his existence first-hand.'[26] In the world to come the soul will be able to contemplate the divine essence, undistracted by the temptations and demands of the senses.

(Maimonides' contemporary Jewish critics—most notably, Samuel ben Ali, the Gaon of Baghdad—believed that he went too far in his spiritualistic depiction of the world to come.[27] They charged that by eliminating all traces of the physical from *olam haba*, and by making it a purely spiritual realm of disembodied souls, he was, in effect, *denying* the doctrine of the resurrection of the body. This occasioned Maimonides to compose his *Treatise on Resurrection*, where he re-emphasizes the importance of the doctrine of resurrection for the Jewish faith, but argues that the reunion of the soul with the body (from which it was separated at death) will occur during the Messianic era, and for the righteous will be only temporary; a final separation of the soul from the body will occur for those who are to enter the world to come.[28])

The upshot of Maimonides' discussion of immortality and the world to come in his halachic writings is that the ultimate goal of human life is moral and, more importantly, intellectual perfection, leading to a postmortem, everlasting state of pure spiritual existence. It looks as though what the afterlife holds in store for a righteous person—someone who has faithfully studied and kept to the commandments of the Torah—is an individual and personal immortality whereby the soul of a human being reaps the benefits in the world to come for virtue in this life. This immortality seems to involve the disembodied intellect experiencing both a conscious enjoyment of its present activity (an intellectual love of God) and a blissful memory of the good it achieved in this life.[29]

There is a problem here, however, in understanding just *how* the disembodied intellect is supposed to retain its individuality and personal dimension. For Maimonides, as for many Aristotelians, the work of individuation (or numerical identity) is performed by matter alone.

In whatever is not a body, multiplicity cannot be cognized by the intellect, unless the thing in question is a force in a body, for then the multiplicity of the individual forces would subsist in virtue of the multiplicity of the matters or substances in which these forces are to be found. Hence, no multiplicity at all can be cognized by the intellect in the separate things, which are neither a body nor a force in a body, except when they are causes and effects.[30]

Now if the soul, or at least that part of it that is immortal, is, as we are told in the *Mishneh Torah*, nothing but a form, then what remains of a person after death—the intellect, or the form of the soul itself—would seem not to be able to retain the individuality that it had during its embodied existence and that was explained by the matter that it informed.[31] Maimonides, however, appears (at least in this context) to be unconcerned by this problem facing his account.

Maimonides' legalistic works were composed for a broad and not necessarily philosophically sophisticated audience. The message they were intended to convey was, by and large, an orthodox and fairly uncomplicated one. But sometimes Maimonides did not write for the common people. He believed that there are some truths to which they should not be exposed. These deepest principles of the Torah are so difficult to comprehend that the philosophically uninitiated individual, in his unprepared attempt to understand them and the resulting confusion, could suffer a loss of faith. They are truths that should be concealed and never communicated openly and in a public forum. Maimonides is quite insistent on this point, and it does not demand any kind of commitment to the latter-day exegetical theory of 'esoteric' writing to see it.[32] Maimonides explicitly asserts that it is not right that the 'ignorant multitude', the 'vulgar', or mere 'beginners in speculation' should try to understand everything.[33]

This may explain why a somewhat different picture of the immortal soul—slightly more problematic, from a rabbinic point of view—emerges from a careful reading of Maimonides' philosophical masterpiece, the *Guide of the Perplexed*. In this work there is still the emphasis on intellectual perfection of the human being and its importance for our supreme happiness and blessedness. But when one looks closely at what the perfected soul or intellect consists in, and what is said to remain of a person after his death, it becomes harder to see Maimonides' doctrine of immortality as a classical one of the *personal* survival of the individual soul. And his critics did not hesitate to point this out.[34]

In the *Guide* Maimonides distinguishes between four varieties of human perfection. At the bottom of the ranking there is the perfection of possessions, where an individual has acquired a great deal of material and social wealth: money, clothing, land, slaves, and even power. Then there is physical perfection, 'the perfection of the bodily constitution and shape'. Both of these 'lower' types of perfection are fleeting and mutable. Wealth and health are easily subject to change and usually due to circumstances beyond our control. More significantly, they do not represent the improvement of a human being *as* a human being. More desirable is the perfection of the moral virtues. These are the character traits that, on Maimonides' view, dispose us to be useful to other human beings: generosity, courage, temperance, and so on. While also useful to its possessor, this 'excellence in moral habits' is not really an intrinsic perfection of the person himself. It is more a matter of relative perfection and a kind of social good. 'For if you suppose a human individual is alone, acting on no one, you will find that all his moral virtues are in vain and without employment and unneeded, and that they do not perfect the individual in anything; for he only needs them and they again become useful to him in regard to someone else.'[35] Practical virtue is thus not an end in itself and not our ultimate goal. Rather, it is of merely instrumental value, 'good as a means toward' something higher.

'True human perfection', on the other hand, consists—as in the halachic writings—in intellectual perfection, or what Maimonides now calls 'the acquisition of rational virtues'. 'I refer to the conception of intelligibles, which teach true opinions concerning the divine things. This is in true reality the ultimate end; this is what gives the individual true perfection, a perfection belonging to him alone; and it gives him permanent perdurance; through it man is man.'[36] Through knowledge and wisdom, the soul can achieve a non-relational perfection within itself; it may perfect itself intrinsically as an intellect. Important to this perfection, of course, is a rational understanding of the natures of things in the world, of the laws and order of Nature itself, and of the nature and ordering of the celestial realm. All of this belongs to natural science. But this is only a preliminary stage on the way to the greater and more important divine science, that is, to an understanding of the highest possible object of apprehension: God. Through an intellectual grasp of the essence of God—'the apprehension of His being [*metziyut*] as He, may He be exalted, is in truth'—and of his actions, we enter into a state of worshipful union with God.[37] And this, according to Maimonides, is what we should all strive for. The practical virtues are useful and good, especially in our relations with others. But the perfection of the intellect is the true and highest good, the *summum bonum* of human existence.[38]

Now when the intellect ordinarily comes to know a thing, what happens is that the form of the object—but not its matter—enters the soul of the knower. When a person knows a horse, the human intellect assumes the form of 'horse'. The intellect does not literally become a horse, of course, since the appropriate matter is lacking. It does, however, become 'informed' by the essence of horse, and so in a very literal sense becomes one with its object: the same form that, in the matter, makes a horse a horse now exists cognitively in the knower's soul and makes him a horse-knower.[39] In knowledge, the mind thus becomes identical in character with its object (the mind of the horse-knower is, in an important sense, truly horselike). To know a thing is to move from a state of potentiality (that is, from being merely 'receptive' to the forms of things) to a state of actualization (that is, actually assuming the form of one known object or another). Here is how Maimonides puts it:

> Know that before a man intellectually cognizes a thing, he is potentially the intellectually cognizing subject. Now if he has intellectually cognized a thing (it is as if you said that if a man has intellectually cognized this piece of wood to which one can point, has stripped its form from its matter, and has represented to himself the pure form—this being the action of the intellect), at that time the man would become one who has intellectual cognition in

actualization. Intellect realized in actualization is the pure abstract form, which is in his mind, of the piece of wood. For intellect is nothing but the thing that is intellectually cognized.

The intellect so actualized, Maimonides concludes, just *is* its content or object, the form of the thing. Before knowing, the intellect is mere potential or capacity, that is, nothing actual. In a state of knowing, on the other hand, what is actual is the form that now constitutes the mind.

Accordingly, it has become clear to you that the thing that is intellectually cognized is the abstract form of the piece of wood, that this form is identical with the intellect realized in actualization, and that these are not two things —intellect and the intellectually cognized form of the piece of wood. For the intellect in actualization is nothing but that which has been intellectually cognized.[40]

The actualized intellect, the intellect that is in a state of knowing, is not distinct from *what* it knows. On the contrary, the former is reduced to the latter; they are 'always one and the same thing'. 'That which has been assumed to be an intellect in actualization has nothing belonging to it except the form of the piece of wood. Accordingly, it is evident that whenever intellect exists in actualization, it is identical with the intellectually cognized thing.'

It now becomes clear what it is that is immortal for Maimonides. In the halachic writings he spoke of the intellect—*nefesh*, as distinct from the *neshamah*—as the 'form' of the soul, and as that which, when perfected, remains after a person's death. When we thus strive for our specific perfection—the perfection of the intellect—and seek to acquire knowledge of the highest kind, what we are really striving for is the greatest actualization of our intellects. In his philosophical writings he explains that the intellect is, when actualized, nothing but the forms of the things known. Or, in other words, the actualized intellect—also called the 'acquired intellect'—is nothing but the contents of the knowing mind, or the objects known *as* they are known. Thus, it is this knowledge alone that will remain after the death of the body. If a person is righteous, it is this that will be granted entry into the world to come.

The souls that remain after death are not the soul [*neshamah*] that comes into being in man at the time he is generated. For that which comes into being at the time a man is generated is merely a faculty consisting in preparedness, whereas the thing that after death is separate from matter is the thing that has become actual and not the soul that also comes into being; the latter is identical with the spirit that comes into being.[41]

And if a person has followed the path of true intellectual perfection, the actualized intellect that will remain after death just is the knowledge of God. The halachic writings themselves say as much: 'There is nothing which remains eternally except the knowledge of the creator of the world.'[42] As God is the highest of all possible objects of knowledge, the knowledge of God is the supreme good of the rational intellect; and it is a knowledge that partakes of the character of its object. The pursuit of intellectual perfection—the pursuit of the knowledge of God—thus leads to immortality, but only because the knowledge thus acquired is itself (like its object) eternal. 'The soul . . . refers to the form of the soul, the knowledge of the Creator which it has comprehended according to its potential . . . This is the form that we described in chapter four of *Hilchot Yesodei haTorah* [of the *Mishneh Torah*]. This life, because it will not be accompanied by death . . . is called "the bond of life".'[43] Now it seems very difficult to find much here that could, in any interesting sense, be viewed as an individual and *personal* kind of immortality. To what extent can a body of knowledge—which is all that the perfected intellect consists in—be seen as my *self*? Can memory and consciousness belong to it once it is separated from the body and the other, mortal faculties of the soul? How, in fact, can one perfected intellect, outside of the body and the space-time parameters that define existence in this life, be distinguished from another? What, in other words, is personal and individual about the perfected intellect?

It is this question—one that is raised by the accounts of immortality in both the halachic works and the *Guide*—that puzzled Maimonides' contemporary critics, as well as later scholars.[44] It also gave at least one of his intellectual disciples the opportunity he was looking for to move carefully but (I believe) deliberately even closer to depersonalizing the immortal soul.

Unlike Maimonides, whose views on the immortality of the soul need to be gleaned from a variety of his halachic and philosophical writings, Gersonides devoted an entire book of his philosophical *magnum opus* explicitly to this issue. The opening fourteen chapters of his *Sefer Milchamot haShem* ('The Wars of the Lord') are entitled *behasha'arut hanefesh* ('On the Immortality of the Soul'). His, too, is a thoroughly Aristotelian conception of the human soul and of its capacity for immortality. But it also stands in stark contrast to the views of earlier Aristotelians, such as Alexander of Aphrodisias (a second-century Greek commentator on Aristotle's works) and Averroes, or ibn Rushd, the great but highly controversial twelfth-century Arabic philosopher and the author of several important commentaries on Aristotle.[45] The topic of the immortality of the soul is of supreme importance for Gersonides, for upon it depends not just the metaphysical fate of the soul, but also our happiness and well-being—and not only in the afterlife, but in this life as well.

Gersonides begins his discussion by singling out that part of the soul that is the prime candidate for immortality.

> Since the intellect [*hasekhel*] is the most fitting of all the parts of the soul [*nefesh*] for immortality—the other parts are obviously perishable together with the corruption of the body because they use a bodily organ in the exercise of their functions—it is necessary that we inquire into the essence of the human intellect before we investigate whether it is immortal or not, and whether if it is immortal, in what way it is immortal.[46]

Although Gersonides uses *nefesh* to refer to the soul as a whole, the echoes of Maimonides' distinction between *neshamah*, or the part of the soul that governs and depends upon the body and thus perishes with it, and *nefesh* or *ruach*, the rational part of the soul, are unmistakable here. The soul, for Gersonides, is likewise composed both of parts that use the body in their functioning (such as sensibility and imagination) and of pure intellect, *hasekhel*.

That part of the soul that does depend on the body—and, in particular, on the senses and the imaginative faculty—for its operations is called the 'material intellect' (*hasekhel ha-hayulani*). The material intellect is pure potentiality, the bare capacity for thought. Like all potentialities, it must reside in a subject; it cannot be a substance in its own right. Gersonides argues at length against the view that the subject of this disposition is a soul understood as an incorporeal substance distinct from the body.[47] If such were the case, the disposition would belong to an actual intellect—a form—and (as forms are pure actualities) would not have any potentialities.[48] In fact, Gersonides argues, the material intellect is a disposition of the body (with 'body' understood in Aristotelian terms as a substance composed of both matter and form).[49] It is a capacity or potentiality that the animated human body has, because it is 'informed', to contribute to the acquisition of knowledge through the mediation of sensation and imagination. It is basically the living human organism's capacity to transform sensory input into knowledge.[50] The material intellect is also, therefore, along with the body, corruptible and mortal—it comes to an end with a person's physical death.

Left to its own devices, however, the material intellect will not generate knowledge. True knowledge is the intellectual grasp of abstract, universal truths—it is, in other words, conceptual in nature, not sensory—and the unaided material intellect can receive only the images of particular things. The senses and the imagination give us only limited access to individual objects in the world around us. What supplements the material intellect and makes it possible for a knower to transcend this acquaintance with particulars and apprehend more general things—such as essences, mathematical truths, and the laws of nature[51]—is what Gersonides calls the Agent Intellect. Understanding just how this higher intellect functions requires a brief excursion into the cosmos itself.

In medieval Aristotelian cosmology the universe as a whole is finite and globelike, with an absolute center and an outermost limit. It is, in fact, a series of concentric material (crystalline) spheres. On some accounts, there is, first, an outermost sphere encompassing the universe as a whole; its turning initiates the motions of the inner spheres. Gersonides himself, however, rejects such a 'starless sphere' undergoing diurnal motion.[52] For him, the outermost sphere of the universe is the sphere holding the fixed stars. In the space enclosed by this sphere lie the other spheres that, in their perpetual circular motion, each carry around either one of the five known planets, the sun, or the moon.[53] At the center of the universe, within the innermost sphere of the moon, stands the earth itself. The spheres themselves are animate beings. Like all substances, they are constituted of matter and form. They are also, therefore, intelligent, 'ensouled' beings, and their motion is explained in part by their desire and volition.

Now associated with each sphere, but distinct from it, is what is called a 'separate intellect' (*hasekhel hanifrad*). This is the immaterial spirit or incorporeal intelligence that governs that sphere. It needs to be distinguished from the indwelling soul that animates each sphere. In fact, the separate intellect is that whose perfection a sphere's indwelling soul desires to emulate. Each separate intellect explains (again, only in part) the motion of its corresponding sphere (as that sphere's desire to emulate a perfect being gives rise to its own circular—that is, pefect—motion) and the arrangement of its contents. All of the separate intellects[54] 'flow'or 'emanate' from God, and serve, in a sense, as God's intermediaries for the spheres they govern. Maimonides, whose account differs from that of Gersonides in some significant respects, believes that the separate intellects are, in fact, the angelic natures, and describes them in this way: 'In existence, there are separate intellects that are in no way a body. All of them overflow from God, may He be exalted, and they are the intermediaries between God and all these bodies.'[55] Gersonides does not identify them as angels, but like Maimonides he does insist that, while the separate intellects emanate from God, they do not derive eternally from God but God caused them to come into being by an act of will.[56]

The separate intellect governing the sublunary realm—that is, the earth and the phenomena that lie between the earth and the moon—is called the Agent (or Active) Intellect (*hasekhel hapo'el*). This incorporeal soul, which emanates from the higher separate intellects, plays two roles in the world. The first role is causal. The Agent Intellect is causally responsible for all of the physical phenomena in nature: their natures, their arrangements and sequences, and their lawlike interactions. It is also causally responsible for almost all events in the realm of human action and thought.[57] While God is the remote and ultimate cause of everything in the sublunary realm, the more proximate agent (and working on God's behalf) is the Agent Intellect.[58]

The generation and decay of things in the sublunary realm is, at the most fundamental physical level, the result of the combination and separation of the four elements: air, fire, earth, and water. And the motion of these basic terrestrial elements—their 'mixture', their balance, and especially their coming together in a manner appropriate for the production and reception of sublunary natural forms—is caused by the motions of the celestial spheres and the 'rays' of influence from the planets and stars. '[The heavenly bodies] do preserve [the cycle] of generated phenomena in the terrestrial world as one contrary [element] prevails at one time and another contrary [element] prevails at another time. This can occur either by virtue of the difference in the positions of the heavenly bodies . . . or the differences among the heavenly bodies themselves.'[59] But it is the Agent Intellect itself that, for Gersonides, is primarily 'the agent that generates things in the sublunary world'.[60] This is because, first of all, these celestial influences take place according to a plan emanating from God through the superior separate intellects to the Agent Intellect.[61] But, more importantly, the Agent Intellect is the proximate cause of the generation of the forms in the prepared matter.[62] And by being the generative source of all the forms constituting natural things, the Agent Intellect is the cause of substances and of the order and hierarchy among them, as well as of the general course of nature. The Agent Intellect thus actively governs the dynamics of the natural world.[63]

Because the Agent Intellect is an intelligent cause, it possesses full knowledge—the 'maker's knowledge'—of the order it imposes on the world.

> Since the agent responsible for the [existence] of all beings in the sublunary world must possess the knowledge of the order [obtaining in this world]—just as the craftsman must have an idea of the order obtaining among the things he is to create—and since . . . this agent is the Agent Intellect . . . it follows that the Agent Intellect possesses the knowledge of the order obtaining in the sublunary world.[64]

By generating the natural sublunary forms, it is the cause of substances; and because it emanates from the higher intellects, it knows fully the plan it is thereby carrying out.

> The separate agent responsible for all these things [substances] should know the law, order and rightness inherent in these sublunary phenomena, since these things acquire their very existence from the intelligible order of them in the soul of this separate agent.[65]

The Agent Intellect contains the concepts of all beings, organized comprehensively and systematically, such that the totality of what the Agent Intellect knows constitutes an exhaustive body of science. While each of the higher separate intellects contains a partial knowledge, derived from God, of the plan of the sublunary world—namely corresponding to the partial, contributing influence that its own sphere has upon the motions of matter in that world[66]—the Agent Intellect emanating from them conceives the whole plan, just as it is in God.[67] Its knowledge is thus a kind of complete and archetypal blueprint for the world it governs.[68] 'The Agent Intellect . . . possesses [the knowledge] of the plan and order [of the terrestial domain].' Gersonides, in fact, refers to it as 'the rational order of the terrestrial world', although its science also includes knowledge of all celestial phenomena as well.[69] It is an eternal and incorruptible order—indeed, he calls it 'the law' of the sublunary world[70]—in contrast to the changing, corruptible, and temporal procession of things and events in the world that instantiates and dynamically exemplifies it. This knowledge in the Agent Intellect exists in 'a perfect and unified manner'.[71]

The second role played by the Agent Intellect is epistemological, related to human knowledge. It is a role made possible, in fact, by its first role as intelligent cause, as the agent (or executor) of the astral determinism that operates in the sublunary realm. The Agent Intellect is responsible for 'illuminating' human minds and generating human cognition of the general concepts of things and of universal truths, that is, 'true science'. Because of the intellectual union between the human intellect and this higher, separate intellect, the potential of the material intellect can be actualized and the human being can acquire a knowledge of things that goes beyond mere sensory acquaintance through particular images.[72] The world, in effect, becomes 'intelligible' to the human intellect via the Agent Intellect. If knowledge is the apprehension of the forms of things, the grasp of their essential and general features, then what the Agent Intellect does is, through its own knowledge of the forms, cause the human intellect's understanding of them. 'The material intellect cannot apprehend any form except those of the sublunary world and can apprehend them only after the Agent Intellect makes them intelligible.'[73]

The forms of things are just their general natures.[74] 'It is necessary that the general nature exist actually in every one of the individuals of which it is the common nature.' The general nature of horse is in every horse. Through repeated sensory perception, that is, through the reception of particular images in the imaginative faculty of the material intellect, the human mind (moved by the Agent Intellect) can abstract from the particularities that distinguish one specific sensible encounter with an object of a certain kind from another of the same kind and reach an understanding of that common nature.[75] After seeing a number of horses, for example, one comes to understand what a 'horse' is essentially. The Agent Intellect makes this process possible by illuminating the human intellect with that eternal order it contains; it 'informs' the human intellect with the general knowledge required for it to make intelligible sense of sensible particulars.

> The Agent Intellect works upon the material intellect and enables it to become cognitive in actuality after having been cognitive only potentially. Accordingly, the Agent Intellect renders the image intelligible in actuality after having been intelligible potentially merely in an accidental sense.[76]

What we are ultimately after is, in fact, not just the essence of this or that particular kind of being. Part of what is contained in a 'nature' is a set of functions that will allow one to see a (kind of) thing in all of its intrinsic and relational characters. What we truly seek is a complete and unified system of such truths. The real object of knowledge for a human being is the intelligible 'order of things' as contained within the Agent Intellect, what one commentator calls 'the formal structure of nature'.[77] It is, in essence, the laws of the astral providence that governs this world.[78] Because this order is eternal, universal, and immutable, it exclusively possesses the characteristic features of true knowledge.

The intelligible [order] of the image possessed by the Agent Intellect is more appropriately an object of knowledge for us than the image itself. For, since the image becomes intelligible to the material intellect because of the conceived order pertaining to it in the Agent Intellect, that conceived order ought to be the object of knowledge of the material intellect rather than the image . . . For the image in no way becomes intelligible, since the particular is, as particular, not knowable; rather, what is known is the order corresponding to the image as present in the Agent Intellect.[79]

This, then, is how the human mind—initially limited by its union with a material body—moves past sensible cognition via images to the apprehension of the intelligibles, of the forms of things without their matter, and ultimately of the plan of nature itself. Through this process, aided by the intelligent cause of the sublunary world's order, the human mind comes to an understanding of the true order of the world. Its knowledge grows, in fact, to mirror (as much as possible for human beings) the knowledge that is in the Agent Intellect itself. We become 'enlightened'.

The result of all of this in the knower—'the cognition of the very order inherent in the Agent Intellect'—is what Gersonides calls the 'acquired intellect' (*hasekhel hanikneh*).[80] It is, essentially, the same thing that Maimonides referred to as the 'actualized' or 'perfected' intellect. Gersonides notes that 'it is clear that the acquired intellect is the perfection of the material intellect brought about by the Agent Intellect'.[81] The acquired intellect is a body of conceptual knowledge. It is an intellectual attainment on the part of the knower; it just *is* that person's knowledge of eternal truths. Because it is only a partial grasp of a larger whole, and a not entirely systematic one at that, the acquired intellect is not identical with the knowledge in the Agent Intellect itself. 'The knowledge acquired by us is [really] not identical with the knowledge in the Agent Intellect; for knowledge in the Agent Intellect exists in a unified manner.'[82] But the content of the acquired intellect reflects to some degree the knowledge in that higher spirit. As one scholar has described it, the acquired intellect is 'the sum total of intellectual cognitions attained by an individual throughout his lifetime'.[83]

And this brings us, finally, to immortality. What is immortal in a human being is, for Gersonides, nothing beyond the acquired intellect. Despite the fact that the acquired intellect is generated *in us*, it does not follow that it is corruptible; Gersonides rejects Aristotle's claim that 'everything generated is corruptible'.[84] Because the rational order of the world in the Agent Intellect is eternal and incorruptible, our knowledge of that order (once it is acquired) must likewise be eternal and incorruptible, since knowledge (being identical with what is known) takes its character from the object known. Moreover, he argues, the acquired intellect (unlike the material intellect) is both immaterial and separable from the body, and thus not subject to the forces that destroy the body. 'The acquired intellect is immaterial, and an immaterial substance does not have the conditions requisite for corruption.'[85] Hence, he concludes, 'the acquired intellect is immortal'. When a person dies, the soul understood as the material intellect ceases along with the body. As a result, all further acquisition of knowledge necessarily comes to an end as well. But the acquired intellect remains. The immortality available to any human being consists only in this persistence, after the death of the body, of the knowledge that he or she has acquired in this lifetime.

To his contemporaries, Gersonides must have seemed to be treading perilously close to—if not right into the eye of—the Averroist storm. Averroes' writings, especially his commentaries on Aristotle, were the subject of several virulent condemnations in the thirteenth century. His views were regarded as inconsistent with a number of Christian dogmas, indeed, with the whole notion of there being a single, Christian truth. In fact, Averroes saw himself as simply laying out the proper understanding of Aristotle's views, and philosophers and theologians in the Latin West who were committed to the Aristotelian system had to drive a wedge between the master and his important but heretical commentator.

Among the Arabic Aristotelian's greatest sins, at least in the eyes of his Christian critics, was the denial of an individual, personal immortality. Averroes had argued that the material intellect in a human being is not a particular product of the union of a body (matter) and an individual soul (form), but rather simply the manifestation in that person of the single, all-embracing Agent Intellect. Thus, a person's 'soul'—the form animating his body—is nothing but the Agent Intellect itself; and his cognitive powers and achievements are simply the direct activity in him of that higher intellect, which actualizes certain potentialities in his body. All human beings, that is, literally share the same form—the Agent Intellect is common to them all. And a person 'thinks' only because of his union or 'conjunction' with the Agent Intellect and the intelligibles it contains.

Although in itself general, the Agent Intellect undergoes a temporary process of 'individuation' when it is attached to and embodied in an individual human being in a lifetime. But since the Agent Intellect is, in truth, *one*, and thus the same in and for all individuals, when a person dies all such individuation acquired through the body disappears and his 'soul' reverts back to its transcendent, separate, impersonal existence as the pure Agent Intellect. There is no *personal* immortality for Averroes.[86]

Gersonides is aware of the philosophical problems here. For example, if all human beings literally share the same intellect, he argues, then how can we account for the different intellectual attainments of different people? But of even greater importance, it seems, are the religious and theological objections he has in mind. As Gersonides goes to great lengths to distinguish his own view of the soul from that of Averroes, he concentrates especially on the issue of personal immortality. If the human intellect is really nothing but the Agent Intellect, then immortality is of no practical value or moral consequence. For, he suggests, it would follow that *all* human beings, whatever their character or virtue—'be he fool or sage', good or evil—will, because they literally share the same eternal soul, obtain this alleged immortality. Moreover, if immortality is indeed a totally impersonal affair, as Averroes claims, then it can have no relevance for our very personal and particular lives. If it is not *I* who survive postmortem, then that eternal existence can be of no interest to me and have no connection to (and play no motivating role in) what I do in *this* lifetime. 'It has no utility at all', Gersonides says of Averroes' view; in it 'theoretical knowledge plays no role in the attainment of human perfection'.[87]

But does Gersonides himself have a doctrine of *personal* immortality? After a person's death, can the body of knowledge that constitutes his acquired intellect be distinguished from that of another person? More importantly, since it is presumably one's *self* that is rewarded with immortality, can that person's acquired intellect, postmortem, be linked up with his life and identified as his self? Gersonides apparently thinks so. Each person's acquired intellect is, he argues, a 'unity' (*echad*), 'numerically one', and thus can be distinguished—without any reference to the body at all—from other acquired intellects, even if those intellects have some knowledge in common. 'One piece of knowledge can be common to Reuben and Simon yet differ in them insofar as the kind of unity differs in them; so that, for example, the unity in the acquired intellect of Reuben differs from the unity in the acquired intellect of Simon.' What gives each acquired intellect its unity and identity is both the amount of knowledge it involves and the content or character of that knowledge—not just its items, but also the way they are connected or synthesized.

> These differences [between the acquired intellects of Reuben and Simon] are attributable to the differences in the acquisition of this knowledge with respect to quantity and quality. For when someone acquires more knowledge within a particular science, the unity of his knowledge in [his acquired intellect] differs from the unity of knowledge who has acquired less knowledge in that science. Similarly, he who has acquired knowledge in a science different from the science in which another has acquired knowledge, his acquired intellect differs from the acquired intellect of the other. In this way, the levels of intellectual perfection are considerably differentiated.[88]

Different people acquire different, and different amounts of, intellectual knowledge. This will presumably allow one disembodied acquired intellect to be distinguished from another. And Gersonides seems to think that a sense of selfhood will accompany this unity. He speaks of the happiness and pleasure that the immortal soul will feel when, having been released from the body, it will contemplate the knowledge it acquired during its temporal, embodied existence.[89]

But what Gersonides offers seems like both a rather thin kind of unity and an accidental kind of individuality for the acquired intellect to possess. It is not a unity that accrues to a collection of bits of knowledge because of the substantial unity of the knower or consciousness (or 'soul') to which they belong, much in the way a bunch of grapes has a unity because of the stem to which the grapes are connected. There is nothing to the acquired intellect beyond the knowledge itself; the content does not literally *belong to* something. Nor is there anything here similar to the 'internal' phenomenological unity—the unity that we *perceive* and are conscious of—that memory provides for our states of consciousness. Gersonides' acquired intellect is not a consciousness, nor even a true substance; it is a body of knowledge. And it would seem to be theoretically possible for two persons, in their lifetimes, to acquire exactly the same amount and kind of knowledge about exactly the same things. To use Gersonides' own words, two minds might 'approximate the unity of knowledge in the Agent Intellect' in precisely the same way and to the same degree, in which case each possessor of that knowledge has attained the same 'level of perfection'.[90] Would not the acquired intellects of two such people be indiscernible from each other, particularly after the death of their bodies? If the quantity and content of their intellectual attainments are the same, then how could the acquired intellect of the one be distinguished from the acquired intellect of the other? And if the acquired intellects cannot be at least qualitatively distinguished, how can they be personalized, that is, identified with one human life rather than another?[91] Moreover, whence does this alleged sense of self derive? What explains the consciousness and memory that Gersonides seems to attribute to the immortal acquired intellect?[92]

Gersonides does not appear to be worried by such questions. In his mind, the philosophical and theological advantages of his own account of immortality over the Averroist doctrine are obvious. And the consequences for our happiness and well-being—certainly in this life, and more importantly in the world to come—are immense. True human happiness consists in the intellectual achievement represented by the perfecting of the mind, by the attainments of the acquired intellect.

The true reward and punishment [for righteousness and sin] do not consist of these [material] benefits and evils that we observe [in this life]. For the reward and punishment that accrue to man insofar as he is a man have to be good and evil that are truly human, not good and evil that are not human. Now human good consists of the acquisition of spiritual happiness, for this good concerns man as man, and not of the pursuit of good food and of other sensual objects.[93]

In this lifetime we can enjoy some measure of this perfection. The knowledge it affords us will grant us a degree of protection from the vicissitudes of this world.[94] It is good and useful for navigating life in this world to possess a knowledge of nature that approximates that of nature's maker. But the demands of the body and the force of worldly circumstances often stand in the way of the enjoyment of true perfection. Thus, even virtuous people—those who have devoted their lives to the search for true knowledge—are subject to the elements, to the disturbances and imperfections of the world. It is only when they die that they are capable of enjoying their highest happiness to the highest degree.

It is important to realize that each man who has attained this perfection enjoys the happiness resulting from his knowledge after death. We have some idea of this pleasure from the pleasure we derive from the little knowledge we now possess which subdues the animal part of our soul [so that] the intellect is isolated in its activity. This pleasure is not comparable to the other pleasures and has no relation to them at all. All the more so will this pleasure be greater after death; for then all the knowledge that we have acquired in this life will be continuously contemplated and all the things in our minds will be apprehended simultaneously, since after death the obstacle that prevents this kind of cognition, i.e., matter, will have disappeared . . . After death, [the intellect] will apprehend all the knowledge it has acquired during life simultaneously.[95]

The true reward for virtue, for pursuing the life of knowledge and intellectual achievement, will, Gersonides believes, be in the world to come.

The view of our rabbis (of blessed memory) is that true reward and punishment occur in the world to come and that there is no necessity for reward and punishment in this world to be such that the righteous and the sinner receive material benefits and evils, respectively.[96]

The immortality of the soul understood as the eternity of a body of knowledge—this is surely a far cry from what the rabbis of the Talmud and the *midrashim* had in mind. Both Maimonides and, perhaps to a greater extent, Gersonides offer a highly intellectualized conception of immortality, one that seems to threaten the personal character of this, the ultimate reward. This may even have been their intention. To Maimonides, reducing immortality to the persistence of abstract knowledge may have appeared to be the most effective means of discouraging metaphysical speculation about the world to come, and especially the overly simplistic and materialistic pictures of that realm being offered by his contemporaries. But neither philosopher, however rationalistic his commitments, was willing to dispense altogether—at least openly and explicitly—with the broad Jewish conception of immortality and the world to come, especially its moral dimension as the domain of ultimate reward for virtue. It would take a bold thinker indeed to do so.

Eternity and Immortality 5

When Spinoza died in 1677, at the age of 44, he had published only two works: the 'geometrical exposition' of Descartes's *Principles of Philosophy*, along with an appendix entitled 'Metaphysical Thoughts', in 1663; and the astonishingly bold—and, to orthodox religious sensibilities, blasphemous—*Theological–Political Treatise*, which appeared anonymously in 1670. Although by the time he died he had been working on his philosophical masterpiece the *Ethics* for almost fifteen years, and was even close to publishing it at one point, it did not appear in print until just after his death, when his friends issued two posthumous editions (Latin and Dutch) of his writings. The work had been circulating in manuscript among his friends for some time, but he was always cautious about revealing too much of it, especially to strangers. Leibniz, for one, was anxious to see or at least learn about Spinoza's much anticipated work when he was in Paris in the early 1670s and in contact there with Walter Ehrenfried von Tschirnhaus, one of Spinoza's acquaintances. Tschirnhaus apparently had a copy of a draft of the *Ethics*, but Spinoza made it clear that he did not want it shown to Leibniz, whom he did not know very well.[1]

Spinoza was under no illusions about the reception his metaphysical, theological, and moral views would receive, particularly after the uproar and scandal caused by the *Treatise*. He knew that his views on God, nature, and the human being would not receive a fair hearing, and, given the intellectual and political climate, would most likely only exacerbate his reputation for atheism and materialism. I suspect that he was also quite concerned about how people would react to his denial of personal immortality—indeed, of any life after death. This was an especially important issue in theological circles in the seventeenth century. Ecclesiastic and university authorities came down hard on those who denied the immortality of the soul, or even those whose principles were deemed inconsistent with the doctrine—the reviled Socinians are only one of the more prominent cases—and were ever on the lookout for this particular brand of heresy.

Given at least part of his philosophical pedigree, it would have been very easy for Spinoza to proclaim the soul to be immortal. His historically most proximate philosophical mentor, Descartes, in fact, devoted an entire work ostensibly to proving the immortality of the soul.[2] And yet Spinoza's thinking on the human being and his *eudaimonia*, his happiness and well-being, is as much the result of his education in Jewish philosophy as of his reading in the 'moderns'. The categories of Spinoza's metaphysics and his theory of knowledge may owe the greatest debt to his Cartesian heritage, but his moral philosophy (including his views on eschatology) has its roots in more ancient terrain.[3] In fact, what I take to be Spinoza's denial of personal immortality is, in many respects, simply the logical culmination of what Maimonides and Gersonides had claimed about the soul and immortality. It also follows, of course, quite naturally from his more general metaphysical views, which constitute the subject matter of the first part of the *Ethics*.

Spinoza's fundamental insight in the early, metaphysical portions of the *Ethics* is that Nature is a unity, a self-sufficient system, an indivisible and uncaused substantial whole—in fact, it is the *only* substantial whole. Outside of Nature, there is nothing. Everything that exists is a part or effect of Nature and is brought into being by Nature with a deterministic necessity. This, in itself, would be troubling to Spinoza's contemporaries, especially those who believed that there are (or, at least, have been) miracles—that is, divinely caused exceptions to the laws of nature—and that there is some kind of freedom available for human beings. But the truly astounding thesis of the book, what would so scandalize his critics, is the additional claim that this unified, unique, productive, necessary being just *is* God.[4]

Part One of the *Ethics*, 'On God', begins with some deceptively simple definitions of terms that would be familiar to any seventeenth-century philosopher. 'By substance I understand what is in itself and is conceived through itself'; 'By attribute I understand what the intellect perceives of a substance, as constituting its essence'; 'By God I understand a being absolutely infinite, i.e., a substance consisting of an infinity of attributes, of which each one expresses an eternal and infinite essence.' The definitions of Part One are technically Spinoza's absolute starting points, although some of his critics complained that they already assumed too much. To a query by his friend Simon de Vries, however, he replied that a definition need not be true or provable, but only 'explain a thing as we conceive it or can conceive it'.[5] The definitions are, in effect, simply clear concepts that ground the rest of his system. They are followed by a number of axioms that, he assumes, will be regarded as obvious and unproblematic by the philosophically informed ('Whatever is, is either in itself or in another'; 'From a given determinate cause the effect follows necessarily'). From these starting points, the first proposition necessarily follows, and every subsequent proposition in the work can be demonstrated using only what precedes it.

In propositions 1 through 15 Spinoza presents the basic elements of his picture of God. God is the infinite, necessarily existing (that is, uncaused), unique substance of the universe. There is only one substance in the universe; it is God; and everything else that is, is in God.

He begins his argument by showing that substance is, by its nature, uncaused, and thus necessarily exists. If two substances have different attributes—that is, if they differ in essential nature—then they have nothing in common with each other. But one thing can be the cause of another only if there is some common nature between them. Thus, if two things have nothing in common with each other, one of them cannot be the cause of the other. After showing that in nature there cannot be two or more substances of the same nature or attribute (that is, that each substance is unique in its kind), and hence that no substance has anything in common with any other substance, Spinoza concludes that one substance cannot be produced by another substance. It follows, then, that it pertains to the nature of substance to exist.

Spinoza then proceeds to demonstrate that substance is necessarily infinite, and that therefore it has (also by its nature) infinite attributes or essences, each of which must be conceived through itself and not through anything else (such as some other attribute). Proposition 11 represents the culmination of this first stage of Spinoza's argument: God, or a substance consisting of infinite attributes, each of which expresses eternal and infinite essence, necessarily exists. (The proof of this proposition consists simply in the classic ontological proof for God's existence. Spinoza writes that 'if you deny this, conceive, if you can, that God does not exist. Therefore, by axiom 7 ["If a thing can be conceived as not existing, its essence does not involve existence"], his essence does not involve existence. But this, by proposition 7, is absurd. Therefore, God necessarily exists, q.e.d.'.)

Once the existence of God has been established, Spinoza finds it easy to conclude, further, that, except for God, no substance can be or be conceived. That is, God—an infinite, necessary and uncaused, indivisible being—is the only substance of the universe. For if no two substances can share an attribute or essence (proposition 5); and if there is a substance with all possible attributes (i.e., God) (proposition 11), then it follows that the existence of that infinite substance precludes the existence of any other substance. For if there *were* to be a second substance, it would have to have *some* attribute or essence. But since God has *all* possible attributes, then the attribute to be possessed by this second substance would be one of the attributes already possessed by God. But it has already been established that no two substances can have the same attribute. Therefore, there can be, besides God, no such second substance.

If God is the only substance, and (by axiom 1) whatever is, is either a substance or *in* a substance, then everything else must be in God. 'Whatever is, is in God, and nothing can be or be conceived without God' (proposition 15).

Much of the technical language of Part One is, to all appearances, right out of Descartes. But even the most devoted Cartesian would have had a hard time understanding the full import of the first fifteen propositions. What does it mean to say that God is substance and that everything else is 'in' God? Is Spinoza saying that rocks, tables, chairs, birds, mountains, rivers, and human beings are all *properties* of God, and hence can be predicated of God (just as one would say that the table 'is brown')? It seems very odd to think that objects and individuals—what we ordinarily think of as independent 'things' to which properties belong—are, in fact, merely properties of a thing. Spinoza was sensitive to the strangeness of this kind of talk, not to mention the philosophical problems to which it gives rise. When a person feels pain, does it follow that the pain is ultimately just a *property* of God, and thus that God feels pain? What Spinoza has in mind, however, is not so much a picture of God as the subject or substratum underlying all things, but rather the double dependency —conceptual and causal—that all things have on God. First, the adequate conception of any finite being will necessarily involve God. And this is because, second, God is the ultimate, universal cause of everything real (and, as axiom 4 tells us, 'the knowledge of an effect depends on and involves the knowledge of its cause'). Thus, by proposition 16, God is described not so much as the underlying substance of all things, but as the universal, immanent, and sustaining cause of all that exists: 'From the necessity of the divine nature there must follow infinitely many things in infinitely many modes (i.e., everything that can fall under an infinite intellect)'.

According to the traditional Judeo-Christian conception of divinity, God is a transcendent creator, a being who causes a world distinct from himself to come into being by creating it out of nothing. God produces that world by a spontaneous act of free will, and could just as easily have not created anything outside himself. By contrast, Spinoza's God is the cause of all things because all things follow causally and necessarily from the divine nature. Or, as he puts it, from God's infinite power or nature 'all things have necessarily flowed, or always followed, by the same necessity and in the same way as from the nature of a triangle it follows, from eternity and to eternity, that its three angles are equal to two right angles'.[6] The existence of the world is, thus, mathematically necessary. It is impossible that God should exist but not the world. This does not mean that God does not cause the world to come into being freely, since nothing *outside* of God constrains him to bring it into existence. But Spinoza does deny that God creates the world by some arbitrary and undetermined act of free will. God does not act by will at all.[7] Nor is it the case that God could have done otherwise. There are no possible alternatives to the actual world, and there is no contingency or spontaneity within that world. Everything is absolutely and necessarily determined.[8]

[Ip29] In nature there is nothing contingent, but all things have been determined from the necessity of the divine nature to exist and produce an effect in a certain way.

[Ip33] Things could have been produced by God in no other way, and in no other order than they have been produced.

There are, however, differences in the way things depend on God. Some features of the universe follow necessarily from God—or, more precisely, from the absolute nature of one of God's attributes—in a direct and unmediated manner. These are the universal and eternal aspects of the world, and they do not come into or go out of being. They include the most general laws of the universe, together governing all things in all ways. From the attribute of extension there immediately follow the laws governing all extended objects (the truths of geometry) and laws governing the motion and rest of bodies (the laws of physics); from the attribute of thought there follow laws of thought (the principles of logic).

Particular and individual things, on the other hand, are causally more remote from God. They exist at a more determinate level, being nothing but 'affections of God's attributes, or modes by which God's attributes are expressed in a certain and determinate way'.[9] An individual body, for example, is simply a particular manifestation of the general nature of extension.

There is, of course, an intersection between the universal and eternal aspects of the world, on the one hand, and, on the other hand, the series of transitory finite individuals. There are two causal orders or dimensions governing the production and actions of particular things. First, they are determined by the general laws of the universe that follow immediately from God's natures. All bodies, for example, instantiate the nature of extension and must obey the laws of matter and motion. But in addition, each particular thing is determined to act and to be acted upon by other particular things. Thus, the actual state or behavior of a body in motion is a function not just of the essence of extension and the universal laws of motion, but also of the other bodies in motion and rest surrounding it and with which it comes into contact.[10] Finite things, in this way, follow not directly and immediately from God's nature alone—as the laws of nature themselves do—but only indirectly, in conjunction with other factors, some of which are themselves finite and determined.

Spinoza's metaphysics of God is neatly summed up in the famous phrase that occurs in the Latin edition of the *Ethics*: 'God or Nature', *Deus sive Natura*: 'That eternal and infinite being we call God, or Nature, acts from the same necessity from which he exists.'[11] Despite appearances, the idea behind the phrase is not a simplistic identification of God with the whole of Nature. He claims that there are, in fact, two sides of Nature. First, there is the active, productive aspect of the universe—Substance and its attributes, from which all else follows. This is what Spinoza calls *Natura naturans*, 'naturing Nature'. Strictly speaking, this is what is identical with God. The other aspect of the universe is that which is produced and sustained by the active aspect, *Natura naturata*, 'natured Nature'.

> By *Natura naturata* I understand whatever follows from the necessity of God's nature, or from any of God's attributes, i.e., all the modes of God's attributes insofar as they are considered as things that are in God, and can neither be nor be conceived without God.[12]

There is nothing that does not, in both its essence and its existence, depend—both causally and in terms of our understanding of it—in a very intimate way on God/*Natura naturans*.

> [Ip25] God is the efficient cause, not only of the existence of things, but also of their essence.
>
> Demonstration: If you deny this, then God is not the cause of the essence of things; and so the essence of things can be conceived without God. But (by

[Ip15], which states that 'whatever is, is in God and nothing can be or be conceived without God') this is absurd.

Therefore, God is also the cause of the essence of things.

This causal and epistemic dependence of all things upon God will play an important role in Spinoza's conception of human well-being and, consequently, his doctrine of the eternity (but *not* the immortality) of the mind.

In Part Two of the *Ethics* Spinoza turns to the nature of the human being. The two attributes of God of which we have cognizance are extension and thought. This, in itself, involves what would have been an astonishing thesis in the eyes of his contemporaries, one that was usually misunderstood and always vilified. When Spinoza claimed in proposition 2 that 'Extension is an attribute of God, or God is an extended thing', he was almost universally—but erroneously—interpreted as saying that God is literally corporeal. For just this reason, 'Spinozism' became, for his critics, synonymous with atheistic materialism.

What is in God is not matter itself, however, but extension as an essence, as a *kind* of reality.[13] And extension and thought are two distinct essences that have absolutely nothing in common. Extension is complex three-dimensionality. Thought is simple, indivisible, and dimensionless (although, while not composed of parts, it nonetheless has an internal complexity). The modes or particular expressions of extension are physical bodies; the modes of thought he calls 'ideas'. Because extension and thought have nothing in common, the two realms of matter and mind are causally closed systems. Everything that is extended follows from within the attribute of extension alone, both from its general nature as extension and from other extended things. Every bodily event is part of an infinite causal series of bodily events and is determined only by the nature of extension and its laws, in conjunction with its relations to other extended bodies. Similarly, every idea follows only from within the attribute of thought. Any idea is an integral part of an infinite series of ideas and is determined by the nature of thought and its laws, along with its relations to other ideas. There is, in other words, no causal interaction between bodies and ideas, between the physical and the mental. There is, however, a thoroughgoing correlation and parallelism between the two series. For every mode in extension that is a relatively stable parcel or collection of matter, there is a corresponding mode in thought. In fact, he insists, 'a mode of extension and the idea of that mode are one and the same thing, but expressed in two ways'.[14] Because of the fundamental and underlying unity of Nature, or of Substance, Thought and Extension are just two different ways of 'comprehending' one and the same Nature. Every material thing thus has its own particular idea—a kind of mentalistic correlate—that expresses or represents it. Since that idea is just a mode of one of God's attributes—Thought—it is in God, and the infinite series of ideas constitutes God's mind. As he explains,

> A circle existing in nature and the idea of the existing circle, which is also in God, are one and the same thing, which is explained through different attributes. Therefore, whether we conceive nature under the attribute of Extension, or under the attribute of Thought, or under any other attribute, we shall find one and the same order, or one and the same connection of causes, i.e., that the same things follow one another.

It follows from this, he argues, that the causal relations between bodies is mirrored in the logical relations between God's ideas. Or, as Spinoza notes in proposition 7, 'the order and connection of ideas is the same as the order and connection of things'.

One kind of extended body, however, is significantly more complex than any other in its composition and in its dispositions to act and be acted upon. That complexity is reflected in its corresponding idea. The body in question is the human body; and its corresponding idea is the human mind or soul.

> [Ip11] The first thing that constitutes the actual being of a human mind is the idea of a singular thing which actually exists.

> [Ip13] The object of the idea constituting the human mind is the body, or a certain mode of extension which actually exists, and nothing else.

The human body, like any other body, is a particular parcel of extension (or mode of Extension). It is a specific ratio of motion and rest among material parts that constitute a relatively stable collection, related in space and time to other relatively stable collections of material parts.[15] And for the human body, as for any body in nature, there is a corresponding mode of (or expression within) Thought (that is, an idea). This is the human mind.

Spinoza rejects some of the most basic elements of Descartes's conception of the mind. For Descartes, the mind (or soul) is a substance in its own right. It is thinking substance, *res cogitans* (as opposed to the extended substance, body, *res extensa*). 'The substance in which thought immediately resides is called mind.'[16] Like any finite substance, the mind is ontologically distinct and independent, and requires no other thing (except God[17]) for its existence. It certainly does not depend on the body for its being; and it depends on the body for only *some* of its modifications or activities (for example, sensations). Spinoza's mind, on the other hand, is most definitely not a substance. It is, like any other idea, simply one particular mode of God's attribute Thought. It is the expression in Thought of the body, which is a particular mode of the other attribute, Extension.

Thus, every aspect of the body has a corresponding aspect in the mind. Whatever is true of or happens in the body is necessarily reflected or expressed in the mind. More particularly, every event or effect in the body is represented by an 'idea' in the mind. In this way, the mind perceives, more or less obscurely, what is taking place in its body. This is true for *all* affections—both passive and active—of the body. Not all of these perceptions are at a conscious level, of course, but they are nonetheless a part of the makeup of the human mind.

> [Ip12] Whatever happens in the object of the idea constituting the human mind must be perceived by the human mind, or, there will necessarily be an idea of that thing in the mind; i.e., if the object of the idea constituting a human mind is a body, nothing can happen in that body which is not perceived by the mind.

Through its body's interactions with other bodies, and particularly the effects those bodies have in the human body, the mind is also aware of (or represents) what is happening in the physical world around it. But the human mind no more interacts with its body than any mode of Thought interacts with a mode of Extension.

One of the pressing questions in seventeenth-century philosophy, and perhaps the most celebrated legacy of Descartes's mind–body dualism, is the problem of how two radically different substances such as mind and body enter into a union in a human being and generate effects in each other. How can the extended body causally engage the unextended mind, which is incapable of contact or motion, and 'move' it, that is, cause mental effects such as pains, sensations, and perceptions? How can the mind 'push' or 'move' the body in voluntary action if it cannot literally *touch* it? By moving away from Descartes's conception of the mind, Spinoza, in effect, makes the problem disappear. He denies that the human being is a union of two *substances*. The human mind and the human body are two different expressions—under Thought and under Extension—of one and the same thing, perhaps best called 'the person'. And because there is no alleged causal interaction between the mind and the body, the so-called mind–body problem does not, technically speaking, arise.

Spinoza's account of the nature of the human mind grounds it deeply in the nature of the human body.[18] The richness of activity and capacity of the human mind is a function of the greatness of structure and aptitude of the human body.

[IIp13s] In proportion as a body is more capable than others of doing many things at once, or being acted on in many ways at once, so its mind is more capable than others of perceiving many things at once. And in proportion as the actions of a body depend more on itself alone, and as other bodies concur with it less in acting, so its mind is more capable of understanding distinctly. And from these [truths] we can know the excellence of one mind over the others.

[Ip14] The human mind is capable of perceiving a great many things, and is the more capable, the more its body can be disposed in a great many ways.

Indeed, as propositions 11 and 13 above indicate, the *existence* of the human mind depends on the existence of the human body. There is a fundamental unity in these two aspects of a human being. This unity is *so* fundamental, in fact, that the mind—like the material intellect of Spinoza's Jewish philosophical forebears—may turn out to be as corruptible as the body, and immortality nothing but a convenient but pernicious ecclesiastic fiction.

Descartes prided himself on the felicitous consequences of his philosophy for religion. In particular, he believed that by so separating the mind from the corruptible body, his radical dualism offered the best possible defense of and explanation for the immortality of the soul. 'Our natural knowledge tells us that the mind is distinct from the body, and that it is a substance . . . And this entitles us to conclude that the mind, insofar as it can be known by natural philosophy, is immortal.'[19] Though he cannot with certainty rule out the possibility that God has miraculously endowed the soul with 'such a nature that its duration will come to an end simultaneously with the end of the body', nonetheless, because the soul (unlike the human body, which is merely a collection of material parts) is a substance in its own right, and is not subject to the kind of decomposition to which the body is subject, it is by its nature immortal. When the body dies, the soul —which was only temporarily united with it—is to enjoy a separate existence.

By contrast, Spinoza's views on the immortality of the soul—like his views on many issues—are, at least in the eyes of most readers, notoriously difficult to fathom. One prominent scholar, in what seems to be a cry of frustration after wrestling with the relevant propositions in Part Five of the *Ethics*, claims that this part of the work is 'an unmitigated and seemingly unmotivated disaster . . . rubbish that causes others to write rubbish'.[20] Another, more equanimous scholar insists that 'in spite of many years of study, I still do not feel that I understand this part of the *Ethics* at all'. He adds, 'I feel the freedom to confess that, of course, because I also believe that no one else understands it adequately either.'[21] Because of the complexity and opacity of his account of the eternity of the mind, which involves some of the most difficult and puzzling propositions of the *Ethics*, there has been, since the posthumous publication of his writings, a great deal of debate over whether Spinoza believes in personal immortality or rejects it; even today no consensus has emerged.

A number of scholars have thought that what Spinoza is up to, at least in the *Ethics*, is a denial of personal immortality, although there is very little agreement on just how he accomplishes this. Thus, Stuart Hampshire notes that, for Spinoza, while there is an eternal aspect of the mind, what survives the death of a person cannot possess any individuality. 'The possible eternity of the human mind cannot . . . be intended to mean that I literally survive, as a distinguishable individual, in so far as I attain genuine knowledge; for in so far as I do attain genuine knowledge, my individuality as a particular thing disappears and my mind becomes so far united with God or Nature conceived under the attribute of thought.'[22] While he does not necessarily find such an Averroist-type doctrine in the *Ethics*, Curley agrees with Hampshire's general point. Despite the difficulty he claims to have in understanding Part Five, he says that 'Spinoza does not have a doctrine of personal immortality. What "remains" after the destruction of the body is not a person . . . whatever the doctrine of the eternity of the mind does mean, it does not mean that *I* can entertain any hope of immortality.'[23] James Morrison, too, is of this opinion, although he insists that this is not because, as Hampshire claims, the mind is absorbed into the infinite attribute of thought, but because the essential condition of individuation for Spinoza—that is, the existence of the body—no longer obtains.[24] Although Yovel sees yet other reasons for denying that Spinoza held a robust doctrine of postmortem survival, he sums up this general line of interpretation nicely: 'The transcendent-religious idea of an afterlife, in which our existence will be modified in proportion to what we have done in this life, is foreign to [Spinoza].'[25] There is, in other words, no personal immortality for Spinoza.

Now this is indeed a very tempting reading of Spinoza. It is, in fact, the one I shall argue for (although I shall offer different reasons as to why there is and can be no personal immortality in Spinoza's system). However, the more popular interpretation of Spinoza seems to be that which somehow finds in his philosophy an account of personal immortality, in one or another of that doctrine's classical senses. Generally speaking, one can hold that the soul is immortal either because as a 'substance' (or, so as not to conflict with Spinoza's own terminology, 'thing') in its own right that is ontologically distinct from the mortal body, the entire soul persists after death (the so-called 'Platonic' view); or because there is at least a *part* of the soul—which is in fact not a self-subsisting substance but the inseparable 'form' of the body, most of which dies with the body—that remains after death (for example, such as Gersonides' acquired intellect; this is the 'Aristotelian' view).[26] On either account, there is a spiritual element of the person—either the whole soul itself or some part of it—that persists, disembodied, after that person's death; an element that is identifiable with that person's self and that bears some relationship to the life he led. Spinoza is usually alleged to have held some version or another of one of these two positions.

Alan Donagan, for example, in much of his work on Spinoza, has adopted this reading. He insists that Spinoza's 'affirmation of personal immortality' is not irreconcilable with the rest of his system, and that what remains of a person after his death is a particular, individuated, and personal essence—one, moreover, that bears a strong sense of self. Immortality for Spinoza, he claims, is a 'personal and individual affair'; what persists postmortem is 'a part of the individuating primary constituent of each mind . . . a part which retains its individuality'.[27] I shall return to his arguments for this position below. More recently, Tamar Rudavsky has claimed that 'Spinoza's theory of human immortality can in fact be rescued in a way that preserves individuality.' Without saying why his views on the mind need such rescuing,[28] she insists that 'what we call immortality of soul, characterized as eternity of mind, for Spinoza must be personal. Within this unity of mind with God/Substance, there is still something of "me" that remains.'[29]

Perhaps the most extreme version of this reading of Spinoza, however, is also the most prominent one. Harry Wolfson, in his magisterial and justly celebrated study of Spinoza's philosophy, sees in the *Ethics* as strong a doctrine of personal immortality as one could hope for. In fact, according to Wolfson Spinoza is 'merely reaffirming an old traditional belief', namely, that 'the bliss and happiness of the immortal souls consist in the delight they take in the knowledge of the essence of God'.[30] Immortality for Spinoza is, on his account, entirely personal: 'the eternal preservation of something that was peculiar to a particular human being during his lifetime . . . the thought element of the mind that survives death bears the particular characteristics of the individual during his lifetime . . . the immortality of the soul, according to Spinoza, is personal and individual'.[31] Indeed, Wolfson insists, Spinoza's goal is the entirely conservative project of defending the traditional rabbinic view of immortality against its latter-day critics: '[Spinoza's] main object was to affirm the immortality of the soul against those of his own time who denied it.'[32] Spinoza is also concerned to show that there is nothing supernatural about immortality, that it is simply a part of the ordinary course of nature. (In what is the most astounding feature of his interpretation, Wolfson goes so far as to say that Spinoza 'retains the traditional vocabulary and speaks of the immortality of the soul'.[33] In fact, nothing could be further from the truth: Spinoza obviously goes to great lengths to avoid the traditional vocabulary. The phrase 'immortality of the soul' (*immortalitas animae*) does not once appear in Spinoza's own account in the *Ethics*. He consistently—and, I am sure, self-consciously—uses instead the phrase 'eternity of the mind' (*mentis aeternitas*)'.[34] Wolfson's continuous use of the words 'immortality of the soul' to describe Spinoza's view is thus very puzzling indeed.[35])

Despite the vigorous debate around this question, all hands would agree on at least one thing: the question of immortality was of concern to Spinoza from the beginning to the end of his relatively brief philosophical career. It is an issue that is central not only to his metaphysics of the person, but also to his views on religion, morality, and the state. However, it is equally important to see—as a result of both a close reading of his writings and a broader understanding of his philosophy as a whole—that Spinoza *did*, without question, deny the personal immortality of the soul. Given everything he believed about the nature of the soul, and more importantly about true virtue and the happiness of a human being, he *had* to deny that the soul is immortal. And he did so with absolute satisfaction.

The evidence for this from an early work—the incomplete and never published *Korte verhandeling van God, de Mensch en der zelfs welstand* ('Short Treatise on God, Man and his Well-Being')—is sketchy and inconclusive, and warrants only a brief discussion. Chapter 23 of the second part of the treatise bears the title 'Van des Ziels Onsterfelijkheid', 'On the Immortality of the Soul'. Spinoza seems perfectly comfortable with using the term 'immortal' (*onsterfelijk*) to describe the soul in this work.[36] But it is not clear what such an 'immortality' is supposed to amount to, and especially whether it is of a personal variety.

The chapter is very brief, and in its entirety reads as follows:

> If we once consider attentively what the Soul is, and where its change and duration arise from, we shall easily see whether it is mortal or immortal.
>
> We have said, then, that the Soul is an Idea which is in the thinking thing, arising from the existence of a thing which is in Nature. From this it follows that as the duration and change of the thing are, so also are the duration and change of the Soul must be. Moreover, we have noted that the soul can be united either with the body of which it is the idea or with God, without whom it can neither exist nor be understood.
>
> From this, then one can easily see that:
>
> 1. If it is united with the body only, and the body perishes, then it must also perish; for if it lacks the body, which is the foundation of its love, it must perish with it; but that
> 2. If it is united with another thing, which is, and remains, immutable, then, on the contrary, it will have to remain immutable also. For through what would it then be possible that it should be able to perish? Not through itself, for as little as it was able, when it did not exist, through itself to begin to exist, so little is it able, now that it exists, [through itself] to change or perish. So what alone is the cause of the soul's existence [i.e., God], would also, when the soul came to perish, have to be the cause of its nonexistence, because it [i.e., God] changed or perished.[37]

There is obviously nothing definitive being said here about the immortality or permanence of the soul. In itself, the chapter presents only a disjunction, a set of possibilities: if the soul is united only to the body, then it is as mortal as the body; if it is united to something immutable, then it too (apparently by a kind of parasitic association) is immutable. But in an appendix at the very end of the extant manuscripts of the treatise Spinoza concludes the work with these words: 'And from all of this (as also because our soul is united with God, and is a part of the infinite Idea arising immediately from God), we can see clearly the origin of clear knowledge, and the immortality of the soul.' So, Spinoza is, in this early work, willing at least to *say* of the soul that it is immortal; or, better, that it can 'make itself eternal [*eeuwig*]' by uniting itself to something that is intrinsically eternal.[38]

The *Short Treatise*, composed around 1660–1, is a first but abandoned approach to the philosophy presented more substantially and systematically in the *Ethics*, and it contains, often in a rather cryptic form, many of the theses of the later, more mature work. This should put the reader on guard against placing too much weight on the language that Spinoza uses in it; he is still struggling for a clear and definitive expression of his ideas. What the *Short Treatise* calls the soul's 'union' with God appears to be both a state of being—an ontological union with God, with the soul as a mode of one of God's attributes, Thought—and a state of knowing, an intellectual union with God, with God's nature as the object of our apprehension. But what is the nature of the 'immortality' that he here appears to grant to the soul? Is it a robust, personal type of immortality, something we can take comfort in (or fear) as a postmortem survival? Or is it simply the kind of nonpersonal persistence of an idea or a body of knowledge such as we find in Gersonides and, later—now called the 'eternity of the mind'—in the *Ethics* itself? Spinoza does not say, and his language, which includes both 'immortal' and 'eternal' to describe the soul after death, is ambiguous.[39] As we shall see, there are good reasons for believing that, even at this early stage in his thinking, Spinoza was denying personal immortality, even if he did not yet have in place his technical philosophical vocabulary for doing so, and especially the later conceptual resources for explaining in what exactly the eternity of the mind consists.

In the *Ethics* the word 'immortality' (*immortalitas*) occurs once and only once. It appears in a context in which Spinoza is describing the foolish beliefs of the multitude, who are often motivated to act virtuously only by their hope of an eternal reward and their fear of an eternal punishment. If they were not convinced that the soul lived on after the body, then morality—difficult as it is—would, in their eyes, not be a burden worth bearing. Such an opinion, he notes, 'seems no less absurd to me than if someone, because he does not believe he can nourish his body with good food to eternity, should prefer to fill himself with poisons and other deadly things, or because he sees that the Mind is not eternal, *or* immortal, should prefer to be mindless, and to live without reason.'[40] The main point of his discussion here is the importance and value of virtue in *this* life; that virtue is, in essence, its own reward. But the passage might also seem important with respect to the question of Spinoza's views on immortality. Spinoza does, as we shall see, argue for the *eternity* of the mind, and this text makes it look as though he is willing to equate the thesis of the eternity of the mind with the thesis of the immortality of the soul. However, he is here only describing, in a rather derisive way, the naive and potentially self-destructive opinions of the vulgar who feel that a life of virtue is worth living only if it leads to the alleged eternal rewards in the fictitious afterlife described by manipulative preachers. It is clearly a view that he holds in great contempt.[41]

When the *Ethics* does get around to discussing the fate of the mind or soul after a person's death, Spinoza is obviously very careful to avoid any talk of *immortalitas*, lest his reader—on the lookout for individual immortality—mistake the whole moral of his story. There are parts of the mind that will persist after the demise of the body, Spinoza allows, but the eternity belonging to them is nothing personal.

Spinoza defines 'eternity' simply as that which stands outside of all duration or time. 'Eternity can neither be defined by time nor have any relation to time.'[42] Something is not eternal merely if its duration is without beginning or end; this is nothing but sempiternity, or everlastingness in time. True eternity, which Spinoza explicitly contrasts with sempiternity,[43] stands outside of all temporal categories whatsoever. 'Before', 'after', 'now', 'later', and all such ascriptions are completely inapplicable to what is eternal.[44] God, or substance, is eternal; so are the attributes Thought and Extension. In a certain respect, particular finite things are also eternal—when they are considered not in their temporally and (in the case of bodies) spatially bound relationships to other finite things, that is, when what is in question is their actual, durational existence, but rather when they are considered from a more abstract perspective as atemporal essences—what Spinoza calls *sub specie aeternitatis*. This way of looking at things will play a twofold role in Spinoza's account of the eternity of the mind.

The human mind partakes of eternity in two distinct ways.[45] First, there is the eternity that belongs to it because it is the idea—or the expression in the attribute of Thought—of the material essence—in the attribute of Extension—of the human body.

[Vp22] In God there is necessarily an idea that expresses the essence of this or that human body, under a species of eternity [*sub specie aeternitatis*].

Demonstration: God is the cause, not only of the existence of this or that human body, but also of its essence, which therefore must be conceived through the very essence of God, by a certain eternal necessity, and this concept must be in God.

Any actually existing human body persists durationally, in time and within the causal nexus of other finite things that affect it and determine it. Toes stub against tables; arms throw balls; snow forts come crashing down on us. This sequence of affairs begins in time, pursues its course in time, and comes to an end in time. The duration of the body as actually existing is limited; so are all the numerous modifications of the body that come about through its interactions with other finite modes. But every human body—in fact, every existing body of any type—also has an aspect *sub specie aeternitatis*, 'under a form of eternity'. There is an essence of that body in its extensional being, an extended nature abstracted from its temporal duration. Whether it is a case of a table, a baseball, a snow fort, or a human body, its essence would be a type of formulaic mathematical or dimensional mapping of that body that identifies it as the particular parcel of extension that it is, as the particular possible way of being extended that that body represents. Any body is nothing but a specific ratio of motion and rest among a collection of material parts. Its unity consists only in a relative and structured stability of minute bodies.[46] And this is what is reflected in its essence, its eternal being. At this level, no question whatsoever is raised about whether the body actually exists in nature or not. Because it is outside all duration, making no reference to time, this essence of the body is eternal.

Now the essence of a body as an extended mode is in God (or Substance) under the attribute of Extension. It is 'eminently' contained within Extension as one of its infinite potentialities or possible generations. It is, in other words, just one out of an infinitely many ways of being extended. Given Spinoza's general parallelism between the attributes of Extension and Thought, and given the resulting and more particular parallelism in a human being between what is true of the body and what is true of the mind, there are, then, likewise—and necessarily—two aspects of the human mind, which is nothing other than the idea *of* the body. First, there is the aspect of the mind that corresponds to the durational existence of the body. This is the part of the mind that reflects the body's determinate relationships in time with the other bodies surrounding it. Sensations and feelings—pain, pleasure, desire, revulsion, sadness, fear, and a host of other mental states—are all the expression in the mind of what is concurrently taking place in the body in its temporal interactions with the world. I feel pain when I stub my toe. These passions belong to the mind to the extent that the human being is a part of 'the order of nature' and, through his body, subject to being affected by the world around him.[47]

The parallelism also requires, however, that this part of the mind comes to an end when the duration of the body comes to an end, that is, at a person's death. When the body goes, there are no more pleasures and pains, no more sensory states. All of the affections of the body of which these sensations, images, and qualia are mental expressions cease at death—the body is no longer 'in the world' responding to its determinations. Thus, their correlative expressions in the mind cease as well. But there is another part of the mind—namely, that aspect of it that corresponds to the eternal aspect of the body. This is the expression in the attribute of Thought of the body's extended essence. Like its correlate in extension, this aspect of the mind is eternal.[48] It is a part of the mind that remains after a person's death.

[Vp23] The human mind cannot be absolutely destroyed with the body, but something of it remains which is eternal.

Demonstration: In God there is necessarily a concept, or idea, which expresses the essence of the human body (by [Vp22]), an idea, therefore, which is necessarily something that pertains to the essence of the human mind. But we do not attribute to the human mind any duration that can be defined by time, except insofar as it expresses the actual existence of the body, which is explained by duration and can be defined by time, i.e., we do not attribute duration to it except while the body endures. However, since what is conceived, with a certain eternal necessity, through God's essence itself is

> nevertheless something, this something that pertains to the essence of the mind will necessarily be eternal. There is, then, this idea which expresses the essence of the body under a species of eternity, a certain mode of thinking, which pertains to the essence of the mind, and which is necessarily eternal.

The mind thus includes, as an essential and eternal component, an idea-correlate in Thought of the essence of the body in Extension. This idea-correlate is eternal because it, like the essence of the body it represents, is situated nondurationally within one of God's/Nature's eternal attributes. The mind as the idea of (the eternal essence of) the body is itself eternal.

Notice, however, that this is a very minimal kind of eternity. It is not something in which human beings can take any pride or comfort, for it is an eternity that belongs to *all* things, human and otherwise. Given Spinoza's metaphysics, and especially the universal scope of the parallelism between Extension and Thought, or bodies and ideas, there is nothing about this eternity of the mind that distinguishes the human being from any other finite being—or, more properly, there is nothing that distinguishes this eternity belonging to the human mind from the eternity belonging to the idea of any other finite body. What Spinoza claims with respect to the general parallelism between modes of extension and modes of thought applies necessarily in this particular case as well: 'The things we have shown . . . are completely general and do not pertain more to man than to other individuals . . . and so whatever we have said of the idea of the human body must also be said of the idea of anything.'[49] Human minds are, naturally, significantly different from the Thought-modes or ideas corresponding to other, non-human bodies—they have more functions and greater capacities (including memory and consciousness), because the actually existing bodies of which they are the ideas are themselves more complex and better endowed than other bodies (such as trees).

> In proportion as a body is more capable than others of doing many things at once, or being acted on in many ways at once, so its mind is more capable than others of perceiving many things at once. And in proportion as the actions of a body depend more on itself alone, and as other bodies concur with it less in acting, so its mind is more capable of understanding distinctly.[50]

But this means only that what remains in Thought after a person's death is, like the essence of the body it expresses, more internally complex, so to speak, than the ideas that remain after the dissolution of some other kind of body.[51] It is not, however, more eternal.

Nor is it more 'personal'. It is only the correlate in Thought of a specific ratio of motion and rest in Extension. It expresses a particularly complex ratio, to be sure, but it is generically no different from the idea of the essence of any other body.[52] And there is nothing distinctly personal about this eternal idea of the body—nothing that would lead me to regard it as my 'self', identical to the self I currently am in this life. I shall return to this below.

There is, however, another variety of eternity for the mind in Spinoza's system. It, too, involves the kind of atemporal being characteristic of ideas of essences. But it is, in fact, an eternity that is available *only* to human minds, since it is acquired by rational agents alone.[53]

According to Spinoza, all creatures are essentially (and necessarily) moved by the pursuit of self-interest; they naturally strive for what will aid their self-preservation.

[IIIp6] Each thing, as far as it can by its own power, strives to persevere in its being.

[IIIp7] The striving by which each thing strives to persevere in its being is nothing but the actual essence of the thing.

This, in fact, constitutes (for moral agents, at least) virtue. To act virtuously is to do what will most effectively serve to preserve one's being.

[IVp20] The more each one strives, and is able, to seek his own advantage, i.e. to preserve his own being, the more he is endowed with virtue; conversely, insofar as each one neglects his own advantage, i.e. neglects to preserve his being, he lacks power.

Human beings, when they are acting rationally, strive naturally for knowledge. Since we are, among all creatures, uniquely endowed with reason and the capacity for understanding—that is, with intelligent minds—we recognize that our own proper good, our ultimate perfection and well-being, consists in the pursuit of what benefits this our highest part. But what else could benefit our highest intellectual faculties except knowledge? Thus, if virtue is the pursuit of what is in one's own self-interest, as Spinoza insists; and if the acquisition of knowledge is what is in our own self-interest, then human virtue consists in the pursuit of knowledge.[54]

But Spinoza is concerned here not just with the pursuit of any ordinary kind of knowledge. Rather, what is most beneficial to a rational being is a particular sort of deep understanding that he calls 'intuitive knowledge', *scientia intuitiva*, or 'the third kind of knowledge'. This is an intuitive understanding of individual things in their relations to higher causes, to the infinite and eternal aspects of Nature, and it represents the highest form of knowledge available to us.

The human mind, like God's attribute of Thought, contains ideas. Some of these ideas—sensory images, 'feels' (like pains and pleasures), perceptual data—are imprecise qualitative phenomena. They are, as we have seen, nothing but the expression in thought of states of the body as it is affected by the bodies surrounding it. Such ideas do not convey adequate and true knowledge of the world, but only a relative, partial, and subjective picture of how things presently seem to be to the perceiver given the perspectival limitations of his physical place. There is no systematic order to these perceptions, nor any critical oversight by reason. 'As long as the human Mind perceives things from the common order of nature, it does not have an adequate, but only a confused and mutilated knowledge of itself, of its own Body, and of external bodies.'[55] Under such circumstances, we are simply determined in our ideas by our fortuitous and haphazard encounter with things in the external world. This superficial acquaintance will never provide us with knowledge of the essences of those things. In fact, it is an invariable source of falsehood and error. This 'knowledge from random experience' is, for Spinoza, the 'first kind of knowledge', and results in the accumulation of what he calls 'inadequate ideas'.

'Adequate ideas', on the other hand, are formed in a rational and orderly manner. They are necessarily true and reveal certain essential natures. The second kind of knowledge, 'Reason', is the apprehension of an essential truth through a discursive, inferential procedure. It is somewhat unclear, however, whether for Spinoza what we apprehend through reason, in knowledge of the second kind, is only *general* truths and principles—'common notions' or 'universal notions'—or also truths about *individuals*.

On the one hand, he insists that we can know adequately features that are common to a number of particulars (for example, certain truths about bodies generally, such as the laws governing their motions and the properties that characterize them universally). One way in which we can arrive at such knowledge is through deductive reasoning from other adequate general or common notions, since 'whatever ideas follow in the mind from ideas that are adequate in the mind are also adequate' (IIp40). It also seems that we can arrive at common notions inductively, through abstraction from sensory acquaintance with particulars.[56]

On the other hand, it sometimes seems to be the case that in the second kind of knowledge what is apprehended includes truths about individuals. In particular, knowledge of the second kind involves grasping a thing's causal connections not just to other objects but, more importantly, to the attributes of God and the infinite modes (the laws of nature) that follow immediately from them. That is, what one sees in the second kind of knowledge but not in knowledge of the first kind is how the thing is ultimately determined by the nature or essence that it instantiates. In the adequate idea of a particular body, for example, the body will be embedded not only in its mechanistic relations to other bodies, but also within the laws of motion and rest and the nature of matter (extension) itself. (In fact, it is these that render those mechanistic relations lawlike and necessary.) The adequate idea of a thing thus clearly and distinctly situates its object in all of its causal nexuses and shows not just *that* it is, but *how* and *why* it necessarily is. As Yovel puts it, in knowledge of the second kind we 'explicate the object externally, by the intersection of mechanistic causal laws', until we achieve 'a point of saturation . . . when a network of lawlike explanations has, so to speak, closed in on the object from all relevant angles'.[57] The person who truly knows a thing sees the reasons why the thing was determined to be and could not have been otherwise.

'It is of the nature of Reason to regard things as necessary, not as contingent.'[58] The belief that something is accidental or spontaneous —that is, causally undetermined—can be based only on an inadequate grasp of the thing's causal explanation, on a partial and 'mutilated' familiarity with it. To perceive by way of adequate ideas is to perceive the necessity inherent in Nature. Sense experience alone could never provide the information conveyed by an adequate idea. (At one point Spinoza suggests that the difference between an adequate idea of a thing and an inadequate one is not unlike the contrast between simply knowing a conclusion versus seeing how the conclusion follows from specific premises.[59]) The senses present things only as they happen to appear from a given perspective at a given moment in time. An adequate idea, on the other hand, by showing how a thing follows necessarily from one or another of God's attributes, ultimately presents it in its 'eternal' aspects—*sub specie aeternitatis*—and leads to a conception of the thing without any relation to time or finite and partial perspective. 'It is of the nature of Reason to regard things as necessary and not as contingent. And Reason perceives this necessity of things truly, i.e., as it is in itself. But this necessity of things is the very necessity of God's eternal nature. Therefore, it is of the nature of Reason to regard things under this species of eternity.'

If knowledge of the second kind does indeed provide this ratiocinative understanding of individuals, then the third kind of knowledge, intuition, takes what is known by Reason and grasps it in a single and comprehensive act of the mind. Where the second kind of knowledge moves discursively through various stages, from the initial starting point (causes) through intermediate steps to its final conclusion (effect), in the third kind of knowledge there is an immediate perception of the necessity of a thing and the way it depends on its ultimate, first causes.

> This kind of knowing proceeds from an adequate idea of the formal essence of certain attributes of God to the adequate knowledge of the formal essences of things.[60]

> The third kind of knowledge proceeds from an adequate idea of certain attributes of God to an adequate knowledge of the essences of things.[61]

Intuition synthesizes into a metaphysical truth—an essence—what Reason knows only discursively. It thereby generates a deep causal understanding of a thing, that is, an 'internal' knowledge of its essence (in contrast with what Yovel calls 'explicating the object externally'). Such an internal essential knowledge situates the thing immediately and timelessly in relation to the eternal principles of Nature that generated and govern it. This conception of ultimate knowledge is already present early in Spinoza's *œuvre*, in the *De Intellectus Emendatione Tractatus* ('Treatise on the Emendation of the Intellect') from the late 1650s.

> The essences of singular, changeable things are not to be drawn from their series, or order of existing, since it offers us nothing but extrinsic denominations, relations, or at most, circumstances, all of which are far from the inmost essence of things. That essence is to be sought only from the fixed and eternal things, and at the same time from the laws inscribed in these things, as in their true codes, according to which all singular things come to be, and are ordered. Indeed these singular changeable things depend so intimately, and (so to speak) essentially, on the fixed things that they can neither be nor be conceived without them.[62]

Spinoza's conception of adequate knowledge reveals an unrivaled optimism in the cognitive powers of the human being. Not even Descartes believed that we could know all of nature and its innermost secrets with the degree of depth and certainty that Spinoza thought possible. Spinoza's friend Lodewijk Meyer, in his preface to Spinoza's *Descartes's Principles of Philosophy*, alerts the reader to this difference between the two philosophers.

> We must not fail to note that what is found in some places [of this work]—viz. *that this or that surpasses the human understanding*—must be taken . . . as said only on behalf of Descartes. For it must not be thought that our Author offers this as his own opinion. He judges that all those things, and even many others more sublime and subtle, can not only be conceived clearly and distinctly, but also explained very satisfactorily—provided only that the human Intellect is guided in the search for truth and knowledge of things along a different path from that which Descartes opened up and made smooth.[63]

Most remarkably, because Spinoza thought that the adequate knowledge of any object, and of Nature as a whole, involves a thorough knowledge of God—its cause—and of how things relate to God and its attributes, he also had no scruples about claiming that we can, at least in principle, know God.

[IIp45] Each idea of each body, or of each singular thing which actually exists, necessarily involves an eternal and infinite essence of God.

Demonstration: The idea of a singular thing which actually exists necessarily involves both the essence of the thing and its existence. But singular things cannot be conceived without God—on the contrary, because they have God for a cause insofar as he is considered under the attribute of which the things are modes, their ideas must involve the concept of their attribute, that is, must involve an eternal and infinite essence of God.

As we come to a greater understanding of nature, we necessarily come to a greater understanding of God. 'The more we understand singular things, the more we understand God.'[64] There is a particularly fine expression of this idea in the *Theological-Political Treatise*:

Since all our knowledge, and the certainty that banishes every possible doubt, depend solely on the knowledge of God—because, firstly, without God nothing can be or be conceived, and secondly, everything can be called into doubt as long as we have no clear and distinct idea of God—it follows that our supreme good and perfection depends solely on the knowledge of God. Again, since nothing can be or be conceived without God, it is clear that everything in Nature involves and expresses the conception of God in proportion to its essence and perfection; and therefore we acquire a greater and more perfect knowledge of God as we gain more knowledge of natural phenomena. To put it another way, since the knowledge of an effect through its cause is nothing other than the knowledge of a property of that cause, the greater our knowledge of natural phenomena, the more perfect is our knowledge of God's essence, which is the cause of all things.[65]

Moreover, it is thoroughly possible—albeit difficult—for us to know God perfectly and adequately. 'The knowledge of God's eternal and infinite essence that each idea involves is adequate and perfect.'[66] 'The human Mind has an adequate knowledge of God's eternal and infinite essence.'[67] No other philosopher in history has been willing to make this claim. But, then again, no other philosopher identified God with Nature.

We strive, then, to acquire the third kind of knowledge: an intuitive understanding of the natures of things not merely in their finite, particular, and fluctuating causal relations to other finite things, not in their mutable, durational existence, but through their unchanging essences. And to truly understand things essentially in this way is to relate them to their infinite causes: substance (God) and its attributes. What we are after is a knowledge of bodies not through other bodies but through Extension and its laws, and a knowledge of ideas through the nature of Thought and its laws. It is the pursuit of this kind of knowledge that constitutes human virtue and the project that represents our greatest self-interest as rational beings.

[Vp25] The greatest striving of the mind, and its greatest virtue, is understanding things by the third kind of knowledge.

Demonstration: The third kind of knowledge proceeds from an adequate idea of certain attributes of God to an adequate knowledge of the essence of things, and the more we understand things in this way, the more we understand God. Therefore, the greatest virtue of the mind, i.e., the mind's power or nature or its greatest striving, is to understand things by the third kind of knowledge.

[Vp29s] We conceive things as actual in two ways: either insofar as we conceive them to exist in relation to a certain time and place, or insofar as we conceive them to be contained in God and to follow from the necessity of the divine nature. But the things we conceive in this second way as true, or real, we conceive under a species of eternity [*sub specie aeternitatis*], and to that extent they involve the eternal and infinite essence of God.

Sub specie aeternitatis: when we understand things in this way, we see them from the infinite and eternal perspective of God, without any relation to or indication of time and place. When we perceive things in time, they appear in a continuous state of change and becoming; when we perceive them 'under a form of eternity', what we apprehend abides permanently. This kind of knowledge, because it is atemporal and because it is basically God's knowledge, is eternal. It is, above all, not connected to the actual existence of any finite, particular thing, least of all the existence in time of the human body.

Now Spinoza suggests, first of all, that the acquisition of true and adequate ideas is beneficial to a person in this lifetime, as the source of an abiding happiness and peace of mind that is immune to the slings and arrows of outrageous fortune. When a person sees the necessity of all things, and especially the fact that the objects that he or she values are, in their comings and goings, not under one's control, that person is less likely to be overwhelmed with emotions at their arrival and passing away. The resulting life will be tranquil, and not given to sudden disturbances of the passions. I shall return to this in the next chapter. But there is an additional reason why we should strive to acquire and maintain our store of adequate ideas: they represent for us the closest thing available to what is usually called 'immortality'.

Because adequate ideas are nothing but an eternal knowledge of things, a body of eternal truths that we can possess or tap into in this lifetime, it follows that the more adequate ideas we acquire as a part of our mental makeup in this life—the more we 'participate' in eternity now—the more of us remains after the death of the body and the end of the durational aspect of ourselves. Since the adequate ideas that one comes to possess are eternal, they are not affected by the demise of the body and the end of our (or any) temporal and durational existence. In other words, the more adequate knowledge we have, the greater is the degree of the eternity of the mind.

[Vp38] The more the mind understands things by the second and third kind of knowledge, the less it is acted on by affects which are evil, and the less it fears death.

Demonstration: The mind's essence consists in knowledge; therefore, the more the mind knows things by the second and third kind of knowledge, the greater the part of it that remains, and consequently the greater the part of it that is not touched by affects which are contrary to our nature, i.e., which are evil.

Now, as we shall see, it is a bit misleading to say, as I have above, that this eternal knowledge is a part of *me* that remains after death. Rather, what remains is something that, while I lived and used my reason, belonged to me and made up a part—the eternal part—of the contents of my mind. The striving to increase my store of adequate ideas is, in this way, a striving to increase my share of eternity. Thus, Spinoza claims, the greater the mind's intellectual achievement in terms of the acquisition of adequate ideas, 'the less is death harmful to us'. Indeed, he insists, 'the human mind can be of such a nature that the part of the mind which we have shown perishes with the body is of no moment in relation to what remains'.[68]

The echoes here of Gersonides' view are remarkable.[69] Spinoza's third kind of knowledge, the body of adequate ideas that persist after one's death, is, for all intents and purposes, the acquired intellect of Gersonides' theory. It represents the sum of a person's intellectual achievements in this life. And because the pursuit of such knowledge is, for both philosophers, the life of virtue, the eternity that ensues after death is, in a sense, the reward for virtue.

However, if what one is looking for after this temporal existence is a personal immortality in the world to come—a conscious, full-blooded (but body-less) life after death in Gan Eden or *olam haba*—then the eternity of the mind held out by Spinoza will seem a very thin and disappointing recompense for having lived a life of good. Since the pursuit of knowledge just *is* virtue, for Spinoza, it can indeed be said that, in a sense, the increased share in eternity that accrues to a person from the acquisition of adequate ideas is the 'reward' for virtue in this life. The degree of one's participation in eternity is thus affected by a person's virtue in his or her lifetime. Nonetheless, it is hard to see Spinoza's account of the eternity of the mind as a doctrine of personal immortality of the soul. Indeed, I believe that he set out to deny, in his own terms, that there is any such thing.

The question of 'personal immortality' involves two issues. The first concerns the survival of the soul, in whole or in part, as a discrete, individual entity. Any robust theory of personal immortality should hold the soul (or whatever aspect of it persists after death) to be, at the very minimum, quantitatively distinguishable from any other soul-like entity after the demise of the body. Numerical individuality is surely a necessary condition for individuality *tout court*. Without quantitative identity, a person's disembodied, postmortem soul would then have no individuality at all (this was Averroes' problem). The second issue concerns the recognizable continuity of specific (and not just generic) identity between the soul in this life and in the afterlife. It must be possible to distinguish *qualitatively* one postmortem soul from another and identify it as the soul that belonged to *this* once-living person and not that one. It must be possible, that is, to take the soul after death and link it up somehow to the life that was a person's durational existence. Only in this way can it be said that it is the soul of *this* person (as opposed to *that* person) that is immortal.

The second question is, in the context of Spinoza's thought, easier to address. One thing is, first of all, perfectly clear. Spinoza will absolutely *not* allow it to be said that a *person* is immortal. For Spinoza, my person or self is an actually existing body together with the mind that is its expression. Or, more precisely, a person is the mode that expresses itself in time as an actually existing body in Extension and as a corresponding mind (or idea) in Thought. A person is not a soul or mind that just happens to be embodied, as many philosophers from Plato onwards have pictured it; nor is it the body alone—it is, instead, the unity of the two. 'A man consists of a Mind and a Body.'[70] Because, as Spinoza makes clear, the bodily component of a person must be an actually existing human body,[71] there can be no persistence of a *person* after his death. The end of durational existence is the end of the person.

But what about saying that the mind that does persist after one's death, while not the person, can nonetheless be identified as the mind of this or that person? Spinoza makes it very difficult to sustain this claim as well. One solution to this question must be ruled out from the start. It cannot be the case that the eternal mind carries *within itself* any direct reference to what was the person's durational existence—to the existing constituent parts and events that make up a person's lifetime. As we have seen, what is eternal bears no reference to time whatsoever. There will be, in the eternal mind, no traces of durational existence.

Still, might it not be possible to find some way of distinguishing one eternal mind from any other and drawing a connection from it to one particular durational lifetime? The problem with this approach, on Spinoza's terms, is that it is hard to see *how* one eternal mind—or, rather, the body of eternal adequate ideas that once belonged to a person's mind—could be qualitatively differentiated or individuated from another. Or, to put it more precisely, there is no reason why two eternal minds should *necessarily* be distinguishable from one another. Wolfson, for one, believes that Spinoza's approach to this issue is similar to that of Gersonides. Recall that for Gersonides one acquired intellect is supposed to be distinguished, disembodied and post-mortem, from another acquired intellect through its contents, that is, through the quantity and character of the knowledge belonging to each. As different people reach in their lifetimes different levels of intellectual achievement, this will be reflected in their acquired intellects. In this way, Wolfson argues, for Spinoza as well it is the case that 'though all souls are immortal and all of them are united with God, there exist certain differences between the individual souls which remain after death . . . Immortality is in a sense personal and individual.'[72] But these eternal minds—like Gersonides' acquired intellects—are composed only of abstract ideas or knowledge, and there is nothing in principle to keep them from having identical contents. The limiting case of such a scenario would be perfect knowledge, whereby a mind, having achieved comprehensive understanding of the entirety of Nature, would mirror God's total and eternal understanding of things—that is, the totality of ideas under the attribute of Thought. Two minds having attained this state would, because their contents are the same, be qualitatively indistinguishable. Of course, no finite mind can achieve such a perfect state of knowledge. But even with lesser degrees of understanding, what is to keep two minds from having acquired in this life exactly the same collection of adequate ideas? Since adequate ideas reflect reality *sub specie aeternitatis*, there would not even be any difference of perspective on the objects so cognized. It may not be a likely event, but it is at least possible. (Spinoza suggests that it may even be a desirable state of affairs. He makes it fairly clear that the more adequate ideas two minds have, the more they 'agree with each other'.[73] This is the road to social peace and political well-being.) And this means that there is nothing in the nature of an eternal mind that guarantees that it will be qualitatively distinguishable from another.

Individuating a postmortem eternal mind and distinguishing it from others not by its contents, by the knowledge it contains, but by connecting it with a particular durational consciousness in this lifetime, and thus conferring upon it a truly *personal* dimension, is equally problematic. As long as a person lives, the eternal part of his mind—being simply his knowledge of adequate ideas—is a part of that person's consciousness. But it would seem that at the moment of death, the link between that body of knowledge and the consciousness to which it belonged is necessarily broken. For Spinoza, consciousness and memory (the latter, in essence, is nothing but that which gives unity to consciousness) seem to be intimately tied to the (full) person. At one point in the *Ethics* Spinoza suggests that someone who has undergone a radical change in consciousness has, *ipso facto*, undergone a radical change in personhood. 'Sometimes a man undergoes such changes that I should hardly have said he was the same man. I have heard stories, for example, of a Spanish Poet who suffered an illness; though he recovered, he was left so oblivious to his past life that he did not believe the tales and tragedies he had written were his own.'[74] It would seem to be the case, as well, that a radical change in personhood through extreme alteration or destruction of the body would, through the parallelism of mind and body, entail a radical change in, or even loss of, consciousness.

Now Spinoza explicitly links self-consciousness to the actual existence of the body, and particularly to the way it interacts with other existing bodies. 'The mind does not know itself, except insofar as it perceives the ideas of the affections of the body.'[75] This alone is enough to suggest that after death a person's particular and personal consciousness comes to an end.[76] But if, in addition, consciousness and personhood are so closely connected, then it would seem that as personhood goes (which, as we have seen, ends with the body's demise) so goes consciousness. A postmortem mind, then, would no longer be endowed with its living consciousness. Even if it had *a* consciousness—and I see no reason for thinking that it could—it would certainly have no memory of the conscious life it led in its durational term, for memory itself also depends upon the actually existing body: 'The mind can neither imagine anything, nor recollect past things, except while the body endures.'[77] Spinoza suggests, in fact, that the belief in a conscious immortal soul that is linked via memory to its durational (lived) consciousness is simply to fall prey to a popular misconception of what persists after a person's death, a misconception that involves projecting onto the eternal mind features that properly characterize only a living, embodied consciousness. 'If we attend to the common opinion of men, we shall see that they are indeed conscious of the eternity of their mind, but that they confuse it with duration, and attribute it to the imagination, or memory, which they believe remains after death.'[78] An eternal mind looks like nothing but a body of knowledge permanently cut off from any kind of consciousness (including access to an earlier consciousness). There will thus be no connection, at least *within* consciousness, between the mind in duration and the mind *sub specie aeternitatis*.

So how can an eternal mind be qualitatively individuated and given a personal dimension, a connection to the life led by a particular person? One final possibility suggests itself, namely, through the body. This is precisely how a mind is individuated in this lifetime—by being the expression in Thought of a particular, actually existing body. So why might not a similar approach work for the mind postmortem? Since the eternal mind is eternal, it cannot bear any direct reference either to an actually existing body or (more relevantly) to the historical (temporal) existence that its own body once enjoyed. However, it is important to remember that there are two eternal aspects to the human mind: in addition to the store of adequate ideas that constitute one kind of eternity for the (rational) mind, there is that eternity (common to *all* modes of Thought) that it acquires by being the idea of the eternal essence of the body (defined as a particular ratio of motion and rest between material particles). So, belonging to an eternal mind there is, in addition to its adequate ideas, that ideal component corresponding to the eternal remnant (in Extension) of the particular body that once made up a person. In this way each eternal mind would seem, through its makeup, to pick out a particular body that at one time belonged (durationally) to a person. To put it another way, if a *person* is an actually existing body (as a modal expression within Extension) with its correlative durational mind (as a modal expression within Thought), then, since the eternal mind bears, as one of its constituents, an idea of the eternal essence of that body, is not that mind simply the eternal, ideal expression of the *person*? Will not this suffice to distinguish one eternal mind from another and give it a connection to a human life? If it cannot be done by the adequate ideas the mind contains, surely it can be done by the essence of the once-existing body to which the mind ideally and eternally refers?

This is exactly the approach to Spinoza's account taken by Donagan. In duration, he insists, human minds 'are complex ideas individuated by their primary constituents: ideas of existing human bodies'.[79] This is no less true of eternal minds, with the difference being that the body whose idea does the individuating is no longer existing.

> Spinoza's proof that something of the mind remains, which is eternal, confirms Wolfson's emphatic statement that he conceived immortality as 'personal and individual'. For in it, he set out to show, not that ideas which are common to different minds remain after death, but that a part of the individuating primary constituent of each mind does so, a part that retains its individuality.

That constituent of the eternal mind that accounts for its individuating is 'an idea of the formal essence of its body'.[80]

However, there is a problem with this approach as well. It is potentially very troublesome, given Spinoza's conception of a body, to individuate bodies outside of duration, that is, outside of their mutual spatial, temporal, and causal relations as actually existing bodies. 'What constitutes the form [*forma*] of the human body consists in this, that its parts communicate their motions to one another in a certain fixed proportion.'[81] If a body *sub specie aeternitatis* is nothing but a generic, eternal mathematical formula specifying a parcel of extension—through a relatively stable ratio of motion and rest between material parts—and bearing no reference to time and duration, then, like the collection of adequate ideas that persists after one's death, it too need not *in principle* be distinguishable from the mathematical, atemporal formula constituting the essence of another, qualitatively similar body. Two bodies may be precisely alike in all of their 'intrinsic' qualities, and distinguishable only through the different relations in which they stand to other bodies (relative place and time, causal interactions, etc.) and, thus, only as long as they actually exist.

This is a problem that infects the Cartesian account of bodily individuality generally. If, as Descartes claims, a body just *is* extension, then it is nothing but geometrical figure; and, outside of time and physical place, two similar geometrical figures are indistinguishable—one circle looks just like another of the same size; only context allows one to differentiate them. Thus, the abstractness of the eternal essence of a human body might preclude one from being able to distinguish it from the eternal essence of another human body—this could be the case, for example, with ball bearings or (if we concentrate, for the sake of argument, only on external appearance) with perfectly identical twins—and thus from being able to use that component of an eternal mind to distinguish *it* from another.

So much for the question of the *qualitative* individuality of the eternal mind. The first issue raised above, regarding the *quantitative* distinction among eternal minds—or what might be called the mind's ontological *integrity* after death—is more difficult to resolve. Is the postmortem mind even an identifiable *thing*, one that is at least numerically different from other eternal minds? Or, to put the question another way, is there in fact a plurality of eternal minds for Spinoza? The answer to this question is not very clear. Nevertheless, here is a tentative suggestion. The adequate ideas that remain after one's death are not bound together in any way and thus separated from any other 'collection' of adequate ideas (say, those that belonged to someone else). Bear in mind that there is no consciousness or memory to unite them, as there was during that person's lifetime; these features of the mind ended with the death of the person. Moreover, all of the evidence points to the mind's integrity as a thing being solely a function of, and thus dependent upon, the actual existence of the body. Proposition 13 of Part Two states that 'the object of the idea constituting the human mind is the body, or a certain mode of Extension that actually exists, and nothing else'.

My suggestion—and it is, I admit, only a suggestion—is that for Spinoza, after a person's death, what remains of the mind eternally—the adequate ideas, along with the idea of the essence of the body—all disperses and reverts back to the infinite intellect of God (the attribute of Thought), since they just are God's knowledge of things.

[Vp40s] Our mind, in so far as it understands, is an eternal mode of thinking, which is determined by another eternal mode of thinking, and this again by another, and so on, to infinity; so that together, they all constitute God's eternal and infinite intellect.[82]

This passage seems to imply that the eternal mind is a discrete and identifiable mode of Thought, distinguishable from any other eternal mind or mode of Thought. And yet, the adequate ideas themselves all are, always have been, and always will be nothing more than ideas in God's infinite intellect, modes of the attribute Thought. For an all too brief span of time they stand in a certain determinate relationship with one another as they enter into the composition of an existing human mind—a mind that, in truth, is nothing but an idea that is a collection of ideas. And for that duration of a person's lifetime, God's knowledge of the objects of those ideas 'passes through' the human mind in so far as the ideas form a part of that specific collection. 'When we say that the human mind perceives this or that, we are saying nothing but that God, not insofar as he is infinite, but insofar as he is explained through the nature of the human mind, or insofar as he constitutes the essence of the human mind, has this or that idea.'[83]

This is, of course, all very vague, and I am genuinely puzzled about how to answer the question of the postmortem integrity of the 'collection' of adequate ideas constituting an eternal mind. But if my proposed account is right, then there is just one set of eternal, adequate ideas, a body of knowledge that each of us, in this lifetime, is able to tap into. To this extent, we as knowers can 'participate' in eternity. In knowing, in the pursuit of a rational understanding of nature and of ourselves, we can transcend our own individuality and temporality. This is, in fact, something that we can be consciously aware of in this life, and it is a source of joy. As he says at one point, 'we feel and know by experience that we are eternal'.[84]

The fascinating thing about all of this is that Spinoza's account of the eternity of the mind—and especially his blatant rejection of personal immortality—appears to be the culmination of a certain trend in Jewish rationalism. When read in the light of the theories of Maimonides and Gersonides, Spinoza's views seem to be simply a case of pushing a particular intellectualist account of the mind to its ultimate logical conclusion.[85] What Spinoza is saying, in essence, is that if Maimonides and Gersonides are right, if virtue is nothing but the pursuit of an intellectual understanding of certain eternal truths and if that (call it either the 'acquired intellect' or the adequate ideas of the 'third kind of knowledge') is all that remains after we are dead, then the traditional claims about the personal immortality of the soul are nothing but fictions.

Things do not look good for those who want to find a doctrine of personal immortality in Spinoza's philosophy. But, in fact, anyone who even tries to do so fails to grasp one of the essential, large-scale aspects of Spinoza's philosophical project. Regardless of what one thinks of my reading of Spinoza's doctrine of the eternity of the mind, and irrespective of the strength or weakness of the arguments that I offer for that reading, there is one very good reason—indeed, to my mind the strongest possible reason—for thinking that Spinoza intended to deny the personal immortality of the soul: such a religiously charged doctrine goes against every grain of his philosophical persuasions. To believe that Spinoza's philosophy allows for personal immortality is deeply to misunderstand Spinoza.

The Life of Reason 6

Philosophers are, as a breed, rationalistic. The life of reason is generally deemed to be of greater value, more 'worth living', than a life of passion. In his dialogue *Phaedrus*, Plato has Socrates express his pride in being a person of self-control, one who does not allow his emotions to get the better of him. 'I am the master of myself', he claims, 'rather than the victim of love.'[1] Socrates compares the soul to a chariot, with a driver in charge of two horses, one white and one black. The charioteer, the 'soul's pilot', is reason. The white steed is noble and good, and willingly does his master's bidding. He is a lover of glory, and pursues the course the charioteer dictates. The other horse is unruly, 'hot-blooded, consorting with wantonness and vainglory; shaggy of ear, deaf, and hard to manage with whip and goad'.[2] This horse, representing base desire, needs to be controlled by the charioteer with his obedient helper. The healthy soul is a well-ordered soul, with reason governing the other parts.[3]

Plato's literary talents are undeniable. But few philosophers have argued as rigorously—and with such historical immediacy—as Spinoza for the importance of being governed by reason, for leading a life by the guidance of our intellect and not our emotions. Like the Stoics before him, he believed that true happiness came to those who were able to control their passions. We cannot eliminate them entirely, he insists, but there is much we can do to moderate their effects and diminish their ability to overwhelm us. This is the path of virtue and the route to personal, social, and political well-being.

The title of Part Four of the *Ethics* sums up very well Spinoza's view of the ordinary human life: 'On Human Bondage, or the Powers of the Affects'. We are, he claims, slaves to the passions. 'Man's lack of power to moderate and restrain the affects I call Bondage. For the man who is subject to affects is under the control, not of himself, but of fortune, in whose power he so greatly is that often, though he sees the better for himself, he is still forced to follow the worse.'[4]

The passions, or 'passive affects', are in effect those things that happen in us the causes of which lie outside of our own nature; we feel passions when we are being acted upon by the world around us. The spectrum of human emotions are all functions of the ways in which external things affect our powers or capacities. Love, for example, is simply our awareness of a thing that brings about some improvement in our constitution. We love the external object that benefits us and causes us joy. Hate, on the other hand, is nothing but 'sadness with the accompanying idea of an external cause'. We hate the object that harms us and makes us unhappy.[5] Thus all of the human emotions, in so far as they are passions, are constantly directed outward, toward things and their tendencies to affect us one way or another. Aroused by our passions and desires, we seek or flee those things that we believe cause joy or sadness. 'We strive to further the occurrence of whatever we imagine will lead to Joy, and to avert or destroy what we imagine is contrary to it, or will lead to Sadness.'[6] Our hopes and fears fluctuate depending on whether we regard the objects of our desires or aversions as remote, near, necessary, possible, or unlikely.

What we so often fail to keep in mind, however, is the fact that the things that stir our emotions, being external to us, do not answer to our wills. I have no real power over whether what I hate is near me or distant, whether the person I love lives or dies. The objects of our passions are completely beyond our control. (This is, of course, all the more so in the absolutely deterministic universe that Spinoza describes.) Thus, the more we allow ourselves to be controlled by these objects—by their comings and goings—the more we are subject to fluctuating passions and the less active and free (that is, self-controlled) we are. The upshot is a fairly pathetic picture of a life mired in the passions and pursuing and fleeing the changeable and fleeting objects that occasion them:

'We are driven about in many ways by external causes, and . . . like waves on the sea, driven by contrary winds, we toss about, not knowing our outcome and fate.'[7] It is, he says, a kind of disease to suffer too much love for a thing that is mutable and never fully under our power, even when we do, for a time, have it within our possession.

Sickness of the mind and misfortunes take their origin especially from too much love toward a thing which is liable to many variations and which we can never fully possess. For no one is disturbed or anxious concerning anything unless he loves it, nor do wrongs, suspicions and enmities arise except from love for a thing which no one can really fully possess.[8]

The solution to this predicament is an ancient one. Since we cannot control the objects that we tend to value and that we allow to influence our well-being, we ought instead to try to control our evaluations themselves and thereby minimize the sway that external objects and the passions have over us. We can never eliminate the passive affects entirely. We are essentially a part of nature, and can never fully remove ourselves from the causal series that link us to the world of external things.

It is impossible that a man should not be a part of Nature, and that he should be able to undergo no changes except those which can be understood through his own nature alone, and of which he is the adequate cause . . . From this it follows that man is necessarily always subject to passions, that he follows and obeys the common order of Nature, and accommodates himself to it as much as the nature of things requires.[9]

But we can, ultimately, counteract the passions, control them, and achieve a certain degree of relief from their turmoil.

The path to restraining and moderating the passions is through virtue. As we have seen, virtue for Spinoza consists in the pursuit of knowledge and understanding: the acquisition of adequate ideas and the intellectual intuition of the essences of things. When we perceive things *sub specie aeternitatis*, through the second and third kinds of knowledge and in relation to God, what we apprehend is the deterministic necessity of all that happens.

[IIp44c2] It is of the nature of reason to perceive things under a certain species of eternity.

Demonstration: It is of the nature of reason to regard things as necessary and not as contingent. And it perceives this necessity of things truly, that is, as it is in itself. But this necessity of things is the very necessity of God's eternal nature. Therefore, it is of the nature of reason to regard things under this species of eternity.

We see that all bodies and their states and relationships—including the condition of our own body—follow necessarily from the essence of matter and the universal laws of physics; and we see that all ideas, including all the properties of minds, follow necessarily from the essence of thought and its universal laws. Such insight can only weaken the power that the passions have over us. When we come to this level of understanding and realize that we cannot control what nature brings our way or takes from us, we are no longer anxious over what may come to pass, and no longer obsessed with or despondent over the loss of our possessions. We regard all things with equanimity, and we are not inordinately and irrationally affected in different ways by past, present, or future events. The result is self-control and a calmness of mind.

The more this knowledge that things are necessary is concerned with singular things, which we imagine more distinctly and vividly, the greater is this power of the Mind over the affects, as experience itself also testifies. For we see that Sadness over some good which has perished is lessened as soon as the man who has lost it realizes that this good could not, in any way, have been kept. Similarly, we see that [because we regard infancy as a natural and necessary thing], no one pities infants because of their inability to speak, to walk, or to reason, or because they live so many years, as it were, unconscious of themselves.[10]

Spinoza's ethical theory is, to a certain degree, Stoic,[11] and recalls the doctrines of thinkers such as Cicero and Seneca:

We do not have an absolute power to adapt things outside us to our use. Nevertheless, we shall bear calmly those things that happen to us contrary to what the principle of our advantage demands, if we are conscious that we have done our duty, that the power we have could not have extended itself to the point where we could have avoided those things, and that we are a part of the whole of nature, whose order we follow. If we understand this clearly and distinctly, that part of us which is defined by understanding, i.e., the better part of us, will be entirely satisfied with this, and will strive to persevere in that satisfaction. For insofar as we understand, we can want nothing except what is necessary, nor absolutely be satisfied with anything except what is true.[12]

The third kind of knowledge, by revealing how all things ultimately depend on God (or Nature) and its attributes, puts one in an intellectual union with the highest possible object of human knowledge. As this state of knowing represents our *summum bonum*, we strive to maintain it; and because its object is eternal and unchanging, we can do so. What, in the end, replaces the passionate, unstable love for ephemeral 'goods' is an abiding intellectual love for an eternal, immutable good that we can fully and stably possess, God.

[Vp32] Whatever we understand by the third kind of knowledge we take pleasure in, and our pleasure is accompanied by the idea of God as a cause . . .

Corollary: From the third kind of knowledge, there necessarily arises an intellectual love of God. For from this kind of knowledge there arises Joy, accompanied by the idea of God as its cause, i.e., Love of God, not insofar as we imagine him as present, but insofar as we understand God to be eternal. And this is what I call intellectual love of God.

It follows from this, Spinoza argues, that

[Vp33] The intellectual love of God, which arises from the third kind of knowledge, is eternal.

For since the third kind of knowledge is eternal, the joy it involves (because such knowledge represents an increase in our active powers) is likewise eternal. But then so must be the resulting love for the object which is that joy's (eternal) cause. The third kind of knowledge generates an eternal love for its eternal object, and this love consists in not a passion, but blessedness itself.[13]

Taking his cue from Maimonides' view of human *eudaimonia*, Spinoza argues that the mind's intellectual love of God *is* our understanding of the universe, our virtue, our happiness, our well-being, and our 'salvation'.[14] It is also our freedom and autonomy, as we approach the condition wherein what happens to us (especially in our states of mind) follows from our own, intrinsic nature as thinking beings and not as a result of the ways external things affect us. Spinoza's 'free person'—'one who lives according to the dictate of reason alone'[15]—bears the gifts and losses of fortune with equanimity, does only those things that he believes to be 'the most important in life', takes care for the well-being of others (doing what he can to insure that they, too, achieve some relief from the disturbances of the passions through understanding), and is not anxious about death. His understanding of his place in the natural scheme of things brings to the free individual happiness and true peace of mind.

The two passions or emotions that clearly concern Spinoza the most are hope and fear. Both relate to an uncertainty over what the future may bring. Hope, he claims, is simply 'an inconstant Joy which has arisen from the image of a future or past thing whose final outcome we doubt'. We hope for a thing whose presence, as yet uncertain, will bring about joy. We fear, however, a thing whose presence, equally uncertain, will bring about sadness.[16] When that the outcome of which was doubtful becomes certain, hope is changed into confidence, while fear is changed into despair. To live a life according to hope and fear is to be governed by an anxious state of expectation or dread that is essentially incurable. Spinoza, no doubt, is in basic agreement with Seneca that both hope and fear

> belong to a mind in suspense, to a mind in a state of anxiety through looking into the future. Both are mainly due to projecting our thoughts far ahead of us instead of adapting ourselves to the present. Thus it is that foresight, the greatest blessing humanity has been given, is transformed into a curse. Wild animals run from dangers they actually see, and once they have escaped them worry no more. We however are tormented alike by what is past and what is to come.[17]

The reason why, for Spinoza, these two emotions are of special importance is the crucial role they play in our everyday lives and the contribution they make to maintaining us in a perpetual state of 'bondage'. Hope and fear make possible a secondary, conventional kind of bondage that supplements the original, 'natural' slavery to the passions that ordinarily characterizes the multitude. For hope and fear lie at the foundation of organized, sectarian religion. They keep us in a state of obedient expectation for what ecclesiastics, who know how to manipulate these emotions, hold out as the ultimate reward and punishment.

In the *Theological–Political Treatise* Spinoza begins by alerting his readers, through a kind of natural history of religion, to just those superstitious beliefs and behaviors that clergy, by playing on ordinary human emotions, encourage in their followers. A person guided by fear and hope, the central emotions in a life devoted to the pursuit of temporal advantages, turns, in the face of the vagaries of fortune, to superstitious behaviors calculated to secure the uncertain goods he desires.

If men were able to exercise complete control over all their circumstances, or if continuous good fortune were always their lot, they would never be prey to superstition. But since they are often reduced to such straits as to be without any resource, and their immoderate greed for fortune's fickle favors often makes them the wretched victims of alternating hopes and fears, the result is that, for the most part, their credulity knows no bounds. In critical times they are swayed this way or that by the slightest impulse, especially so when they are wavering between the emotions of hope and fear . . . No one can have lived in this world without realizing that, when fortune smiles at them, the majority of men, even if quite unversed in affairs, are so abounding in wisdom that any advice offered to them is regarded as an affront, whereas in adversity they know not where to turn, begging for advice from any quarter; and then there is no counsel so foolish, absurd or vain which they will not follow. Again even the most trivial of causes are enough to raise their hopes or dash them to the ground. For if, while possessed by fear, they see something happen that calls to mind something good or bad in the past, they believe that this portends a happy or unhappy issue, and this they call a lucky or unlucky omen, even though it may fail them a hundred times. Then again, if they are struck with wonder at some unusual phenomenon, they believe this to be a portent signifying the anger of the gods or of a supreme deity.

Thus, people are led to pray, worship, make votive offerings, sacrifice, and engage in all the various rituals of popular religion, trying to make things go their way.

They regard it as a pious duty to avert the evil by sacrifice and vows, susceptible as they are to superstition and opposed to religion. Thus there is no end to the kind of omens that they imagine, and they read extraordinary things into Nature as if the whole of Nature were a partner in their madness.

The root of it all is the passions of hope and fear, and the fleeting material goods of this world—whose comings and goings are beyond our control—to which those emotions are directed.

We see that it is particularly those who greedily covet fortune's favors who are the readiest victims of superstition of every kind, and it is especially when they are helpless in danger that they implore God's help with prayer and womanish tears. Reason they call blind, because it cannot reveal a sure way to the vanities that they covet, and human wisdom they call vain, while the delusions of the imagination, dreams, and other childish absurdities are taken to be the oracles of God. Indeed, they think that God, spurning the wise, has written his decrees not in man's mind but in the entrails of beasts, or that by divine inspiration and instigation these decrees are foretold by fools, madmen or birds. To such madness are men driven by their fears.[18]

Thus the origins in human nature, according to Spinoza, of superstition.

Unfortunately for those who have a vested interest in the maintenance of such beliefs and behaviors, the emotions are as fleeting as the objects that occasion them, and therefore the superstitions grounded in those emotions are subject to fluctuations. As soon as we get what we want, hope changes to satisfaction and we stop praying. This instability is not good for ambitious and self-serving clergy, who want to see those superstitious actions transformed into more fixed practices that will serve as the groundwork for their institutionalized religion. They thus do their best to rectify the situation and give some permanence to those beliefs and behaviors. Their hope is that people will continue to engage in religious practices even when they are not immediately taken by the passions that originally stimulated the superstitious behavior. Even better, if they can somehow keep the populace in a permanent state of hope and fear, then a certain stability in religious practice will follow. In this way, 'immense efforts have been made to invest religion, true or false, with such pomp and ceremony that it can sustain any shock and constantly evoke the deepest reverence in all its worshippers'.[19] Religious leaders are generally abetted in their purposes by the civil authority, which threatens to punish all deviations from theological orthodoxy as 'sedition'. The result is a state religion that has no rational foundations, a mere 'respect for ecclesiastics' that involves adulation and mysteries but no true worship of God. (There can be no question that Spinoza was thinking of the contemporary situation in the Netherlands, where Calvinist preachers, conspiring with the more conservative class of political leaders, tried to influence state policy and control the social behavior of Dutch citizens.[20])

The sectarian religions of his day are, in Spinoza's eyes, nothing but formalized superstition. They all depend on a false, anthropomorphic conception of God. They portray in their theologies a divine being who 'directs all things to some certain end', God as a goal-oriented planner who then judges how well the course of nature conforms to his purposes. It all begins with a certain naive wonder about the world and ends with enslaved folly.

> [People] find—both in themselves and outside themselves—many means that are very helpful in seeking their own advantage, e.g., eyes for seeing, teeth for chewing, plants and animals for food, the sun for light, the sea for supporting fish . . . Hence, they consider all natural things as means to their own advantage. And knowing that they had found these means, not provided them for themselves, they had reason to believe that there was someone else who had prepared those means for their use. For after they considered things as means, they could not believe that the things had made themselves; but from the means they were accustomed to prepare for themselves, they had to infer that there was a ruler, or a number of rulers of nature, endowed with human freedom, who had taken care of all things for them, and made all things for their use.
>
> And since they had never heard anything about the temperament of these rulers, they had to judge it from their own. Hence, they maintained that the Gods direct all things for the use of men in order to bind men to them and be held by men in the highest honor. So it has happened that each of them has thought up from his own temperament different ways of worshipping God, so that God might love them above all the rest, and direct the whole of Nature according to the needs of their blind desire and insatiable greed. Thus this prejudice was changed into superstition, and struck deep roots in their minds.[21]

In fact, God is nothing but Nature and its laws. And 'Nature has no end set before it . . . All things proceed by a certain eternal necessity of nature.' A judging God who has plans and acts purposively, on the other hand, is a God to be obeyed and placated. And this is a most convenient fiction for opportunistic preachers. They can play more easily on our hopes and fears in the face of such a God. They prescribe ways of acting that are calculated to please that God, that will allow us to avoid being punished by him and earn his rewards. They take advantage of our credulity and institute formal sectarian rites that insure that our conformity will persist even during those times when the emotions that originally sustained our obedience are on the wane. That is why the preachers fulminate against anyone who tries to pull aside the curtain and reveal the truths of Nature.

One who seeks the true causes of miracles, and is eager, like an educated man, to understand natural things, not to wonder at them, like a fool, is generally considered and denounced as an impious heretic by those whom the people honor as interpreters of nature and the Gods. For they know that if ignorance is taken away, then foolish wonder, the only means they have of arguing and defending their authority is also taken away.[22]

If our greatest good and highest virtue is the life of reason, the achievement of a true understanding of the essences of things and of their ultimate dependence on the first principles of Nature, and consequently a proper conception of 'God', then the purposes of such religion are an obstacle to our true happiness and well-being.

The greatest and most powerful 'carrot and stick' combination wielded by ecclesiastics—the one which makes the most compelling and lasting appeal to our hopes and fears—is, of course, the promise of an eternal reward in heaven and the threat of an eternal punishment in hell. Spinoza believes that Catholic priests, Calvinist ministers, and Jewish rabbis all take advantage of our tendency toward superstitious behavior by persuading us that there is an everlasting blessedness to be hoped for and a never-ending torture to be feared after this life. Such doctrines not only are perfectly suited philosophically for their task, but also have tended historically to be quite effective in achieving the desired end. They induce in believers a permanent, lifelong state of hope and fear, and a consequent willingness to do what it takes to meet the conditions for salvation.

Of course, these infinitely intimidating promises and threats can succeed in achieving their desired end—obedience—only if a person also believes that his soul will continue to live, as his persisting *self*, after the death of the body. What is thus essential for religious authorities to succeed in their project of entrapping us is the doctrine of personal immortality! Without the conviction that there is something that awaits *me*, as a disembodied soul, postmortem; if I believe that everything that constitutes *my* happiness and well-being comes to an end when I die, then I shall have no hope for eternal reward or fear of eternal punishment. And without these emotions governing me, there will be no reason for me to give up my autonomy so quickly to an organized religion that promises me a sure route to eternal salvation. Spinoza's project of naturalizing (de-anthropomorphizing) God is an important and effective step in undermining the power that religious authorities have over me. So is his deflationary account of the Bible in the *Theological–Political Treatise*, where he argues that it is but a work of human literature, and not literally the word of God or a source of absolute truth. But equally important is the denial of personal immortality. I believe that Spinoza thought that the best way to free us from a life of hope and fear, a life enslaved by these passions, a life of superstitious behavior and subservience to self-appointed spiritual authorities, is to kill it at its roots and eliminate the foundational beliefs on which these emotions are grounded. Without a belief in immortality, we can focus on our happiness and well-being in *this* life.

There can be no greater threat to the power of the clergy than Spinoza's 'free person'—the individual who lives the life of reason and who is little troubled by the passions. Spinoza claims that such a person 'thinks least of all of death'.[23] This is, in part, because the free person knows the truth about human life, the mind, and nature. Because he does not believe in immortality, he is not anxious about what is going to happen to him after his death.

The importance of the denial of the doctrine of immortality for Spinoza's broader philosophical project can be approached from another, albeit related perspective. It, too, is a contextual perspective in that, while different from that which links it up in a general, somewhat political way to his opinion of organized religion and its influence upon our lives, it is grounded in his ideas on a certain doctrine about reward and punishment central to those religions. It is a somewhat more focused philosophical approach in that it shows how, by denying the immortality of the soul, Spinoza can forestall a certain—and, to his mind, deleterious—view on the value and rewards of virtue. It also serves to bring Spinoza into critical connection with traditional Jewish thinking on a classic philosophical question: the so-called 'problem of evil', that is, the problem of understanding the presence of sin and imperfection in a world allegedly created by an omnipotent, all-knowing, wise, just, and good God. A 'theodicy' (to use the term coined by Leibniz) is the attempt to rationalize or justify God's ways in the face of such apparent imperfections in his creation.

On the face of it, the mere idea of discussing Spinoza's approach to theodicy should appear misguided, if not downright absurd. After all, should not Spinoza reject the whole question as incoherent and grounded in a false or inadequate conception of God and the nature of things? It would seem, in fact, that this particular kind of query into the problem of evil cannot even be raised within his metaphysical and moral system, and that thus it is worthless to investigate anything other than why that is so.

And yet I think there is more to it than that.

For the project of a theodicy even to begin, there are a number of essential ingredients required. First, of course, there is the claim that there is a God and that God is the creator of the world we inhabit. Second, there is the claim that there is evil (whether it be apparent or real) in God's creation. Whether we want to call it 'moral' evil, 'metaphysical' evil, or 'physical' evil, to use the categorization employed by Leibniz, there must nonetheless be some order of imperfection in that world, especially relative to human beings. Sometimes that imperfection will be the sins committed by moral agents. At other times—and this, historically, has been the real focus of theodicy discussions—the imperfection will consist in the suffering of the innocent and the flourishing of the wicked. Birth defects, natural disasters, and undeserved reward and punishment are all undeniable and apparently inexplicable features of the world. In and of itself, this is not a problem. It becomes problematic, and inspires the search for a theodicy, only when taken in conjunction with a number of claims about God, claims that also prevent any kind of simplistic solution to those questions. First, God is omnipotent; that is, God can do whatever he wills to do, and God's will is, at least absolutely speaking, of infinite scope. This prevents one from saying that God cannot do anything about the evils in his creation. Second, God is omniscient; he knows everything, including the alleged defects in his work. This prevents one from saying that God could (and would) do something about the evils in his creation, if only he knew about them; and since he obviously has not done anything about them, he must not know about them.[24] Third, God is benevolent and just; God wills only what is good. This prevents one from resolving the conundrum simply by saying that God knows about the evils, and is capable of preventing them, but simply does not care to do so. How then can we reconcile the existence of evil, pain, suffering, and apparent injustice in the world with the fact that the world was created by a just, wise, good, omniscient, omnipotent, and free God?

It should be clear by now that Spinoza rejects a number of these claims. First of all, for Spinoza, God (or Nature) is not omnipotent in the classical sense intended by more traditional philosophers and theologians. While Spinoza's God is, to be sure, the ultimate and infinite cause of everything that exists, he is not, on the other hand, a free God who acts by will and choice. As Spinoza explicitly notes, God, while free, 'does not produce any effect by freedom of the will'.[25] All aspects of the universe follow necessarily and with absolute determination from the infinite substance—God—and its attributes. Nor is Spinoza's God a good and just being. In fact, God for Spinoza is entirely devoid of any moral characteristics. God is the active, generative, eternal, and infinite aspects of nature and is not a being that is motivated to act by any conception of the good; in fact, Spinoza's God acts for the sake of no ends whatsoever.[26] All ascription to God of 'acting for the sake of some good end', or of a free will moved by a conception of the good, is to succumb to the kind of anthropomorphizing of God that is typical of the organized superstitions that pass for the major sectarian religions. God is decidedly *not* a 'providential' being in the sense of having a plan for creation and managing it so that it realizes that plan.

Without a free, good, and just God, the whole problem of evil does not even get off the ground. Or maybe it would be better to say that the question is answered immediately. There is suffering and disaster in the world because there is no wise and providential God watching over and caring for the world, a world all of whose events are necessitated simply by the laws of nature. So why even discuss Spinoza in the context of theodicy?

Moreover, Spinoza at times seems to evince nothing but contempt for those who would waste their time engaged in trying to resolve the problem of evil with a theodicy (much as Job's friends attempt to explain the rationale behind his suffering).

> See, I ask you, how the matter has turned out in the end! Among so many conveniences in nature they had to find many inconveniences: storms, earthquakes, diseases, etc. These, they maintain, happen because the Gods (whom they judge to be of the same nature as themselves) are angry on account of wrongs done to them by men, or on account of sins committed in their worship. And though their daily experience contradicted this, and though infinitely many examples showed that conveniences and inconveniences happen indiscriminately to the pious and the impious alike, they did not on that account give up their longstanding prejudice. It was easier for them to put this among the other unknown things, whose use they were ignorant of, and so remain in the state of ignorance in which they had been born, than to destroy that whole construction, and think up a new one. So they maintained it as certain that the judgments of the Gods far surpass man's grasp.[27]

Engaging in theodician speculation is the way only to superstition, not enlightenment.

And yet, it is equally clear that Spinoza was not entirely unconcerned with the problem of evil and suffering. What he offers us, however, is not so much a theodicy, but rather a response to a particular kind of attempt at theodicy. In fact, the kind of theodicy that Spinoza is responding to is a very prominent one in medieval Jewish philosophy and even earlier rabbinic texts.

Before turning to this question, we need at the outset to bracket two issues in Spinoza's thought that, while they bear on the question of theodicy, are, relative to the discussion of immortality, only peripheral. First, there is Spinoza's definition of 'good' and 'evil'. Spinoza famously claims that good and evil are 'nothing real in themselves'. Whatever is, simply is; in itself it is neither perfect nor imperfect. Absolutely speaking, there are no 'defects' in nature.

> Perfection and imperfection, therefore, are only modes of thinking, i.e., notions we are accustomed to feign because we compare individuals of the same species or genus to one another . . . We call them imperfect, because they do not affect our Mind as much as those we call perfect, and not because something is lacking in them which is theirs, or because Nature has sinned.[28]

The labels 'good' and 'evil', 'perfect', and 'imperfect' are only relative to our conceptions of things, to how close a thing comes to some ideal model we have set for it; they do not denote anything real about things themselves. 'As far as good and evil are concerned, they also indicate nothing positive in things, considered in themselves, nor are they anything other than modes of thinking, or notions we form because we compare things to one another.' There is also an instrumental understanding of these terms, especially with respect to human beings. By 'good', all that is meant is 'what we know certainly is a means by which we may approach nearer and nearer to the model of human nature that we set before ourselves'. On the other hand, by 'evil', all we should mean is 'what we certainly know prevents us from becoming like that model'.[29] What is good, in other words, is simply what is regarded by some creature as being useful to achieving some end it has set itself; what is evil is simply what that creature regards as inhibiting it from attaining its ends or fulfilling its desires. Nothing is good or evil in itself, but rather only in so far as one judges it to be good or evil; and this judgment can be made only relative to some standard that is itself relative.

The problem, however, is that Spinoza also goes on to speak about the 'true knowledge of good and evil', suggesting of course that one can be correct or mistaken about what is truly good or useful.[30] In fact, Spinoza's moral philosophy requires that there be a certain kind of pursuit—namely, the acquisition of adequate ideas and the third kind of knowledge—that truly *is* our good as rational beings. Good and evil may be relative to some standard or model that we set before ourselves—in this case, a model of a human being—but there is also a specifically, objectively proper model of the human being, i.e. Spinoza's 'free person' or 'virtuous person', that we *ought* to strive to emulate. 'Knowledge of God', he says, 'is the mind's greatest good.'[31] And it is good not just because we believe it to be conducive to our well-being and supportive of our strivings, but because it really is so. To be sure, this 'true knowledge of good and evil' is as much an affect or passion as the merely subjective conception of good and evil, or at least involves an affective component that does its motivating work. But I do not think it can easily be dismissed as 'merely relative' to our conceptions.

The ultimate status of good and evil is a notorious problem in understanding Spinoza's ethical theory, one that defies any simple interpretation.[32] But what is clear is that Spinoza's resolution of the problem of evil does *not* consist in his simply eliminating the reality of good and evil altogether, reducing them to mere modes of our thought.

The second issue that needs at least to be mentioned concerns another dimension of the theodicy problem. Sometimes that problem is framed not as a question as to why, in a world freely created by a good and powerful and all-knowing God, there is sin and suffering and all creatures do not get to enjoy their highest deserved perfection, but rather as a question as to why God created a world distinct from himself in the first place. If God is perfect and self-sufficient, what could possibly move him to create anything outside of his own being? Or, considered as a slightly different question, if God is eternal and immutable—that is, not subject to change of any kind—why would God, after a solitary eternity, all of a sudden engage in an act of creation? For Spinoza, this question cannot even be raised. First, God does not choose to create at all; the world follows necessarily and eternally from the eternal attributes and the infinite modes, and could not possibly have not existed. There was never a time before which it did not exist and then came into being. Second, for Spinoza the world is not, in fact, separate from God. Rather, God just *is* the substance of the universe, the immanent cause—and not a distinct transitive cause —of all that exists.

There is, of course, a long and hallowed tradition for thinking in this way about the relationship between God and creation, both in Jewish and Arabic philosophy and, even earlier, in Greek thought. And it would be a fascinating project to try to illuminate how Spinoza's approach to this aspect of theodicy, as well as his views on the nature of good and evil, relate to the ideas of earlier thinkers.[33] But these issues are technical trees, and what we are really interested in here is the programmatic forest.

When Job is overcome by his sufferings, when he has been robbed of everything that was dear to him, when all finally seems lost, he raises his voice to complain to God about the way he, to all appearances an upright man, has been treated. His friends come and try to offer him consolation, or at least a rationalization of why he has been visited with such disaster. There must be a reason for Job's tribulations, they argue, either because he or his relations have sinned or because God has some other reason that transcends our cognitive powers. One of his companions believes that our judgment about God's justice should not be limited to what we see in this life, where often the righteous suffer and the wicked prosper. If Job is truly innocent, Bildad suggests, then he should consider that he will be rewarded in the long term—not just in this life, which for the righteous is long, but especially in what will come to him after his death.

> It is the wicked whose light is extinguished, from whose fire no flame will rekindle; the light fades in his tent, and his lamp dies down and fails him . . . His roots beneath dry up, and above, his branches wither. His memory vanishes from the face of the earth, and he leaves no name in the world. He is driven from light into darkness and banished from the land of the living. He leaves no issue or offspring among his people, no survivor in his earthly home. (Job 18: 5–20)

The ultimate fate of the wicked, despite their temporary flourishing, is oblivion. The implication is that the righteous person, on the other hand, while he may suffer in this life, should enjoy the knowledge that the fruits and rewards of his virtue will persist long after he is gone from this world. As another companion, Zophar, insists, 'the triumph of the wicked is short-lived, the glee of the godless lasts but a moment. Though he stands high as heaven, and his head touches the clouds, he will be swept away utterly, like his own dung' (Job 20: 5–7).

This early biblical text bears no explicit mention or even implication of an immortal soul or an afterlife. But it does suggest a theodicy that has the following general structure: do not judge God's justice without taking an extended perspective on a person's fate, including their death and what happens afterwards. In the end, everyone receives their just deserts: in the long run, the righteous are rewarded and the wicked punished. When any one of the more robust rabbinic Jewish traditions on immortality is, later, added to this idea—which may initially have been merely a simplistic statement about the length of a person's life or the reputation that will persist after they are gone—there emerges, quite naturally, a particular solution to the problem of evil. The true domain of divine justice is not this world, but the world to come, *olam haba*. As we saw in the survey of rabbinic texts in Chapter 3, it is in the world to come that real reward and punishment are allocated to the righteous and wicked. Good people may suffer in this life, they may undergo pain and misfortune, perhaps because of their few sins; but they will be more than compensated for their sufferings by the rewards that await them in the hereafter. Conversely, the wicked may flourish in this world, usually at the expense of the righteous; but whatever gains they acquire in the here and now are nothing in comparison to the suffering to be inflicted upon them either after their death or at the end of days. When we take all of this into account, we can understand the larger context of the suffering of the virtuous and the innocent, and, more importantly, realize the true justice of God's ways. When we take the long-term perspective, we see how everyone ultimately receives their due, and we will no longer be tempted to question God's goodness, wisdom, and power. There are even figures in the Talmud and the Midrash for whom suffering in this life appears to be a welcome prelude to blessedness in the world to come. Thus, we are told that Rabbi Nehemiah insisted: 'Which is the way which brings a man to the life of the world to come? Sufferings.'[34] This may not be *the* dominant theodicean strain in Jewish thought. Many rabbis, believing that divine justice manifests itself not in the world to come but in the world we live in, stressed the importance of punishment for sin and reward for righteousness in *this* life. Nonetheless, it is a theodicy that holds a powerful attraction for some important Jewish thinkers.

The tenth-century philosopher, and head (or *gaon*) of the rabbinic academy in Babylonia, Saadya ben Joseph, presents this kind of theodicy in particularly clear and systematic terms. If God is just, Saadya asks, why do we see pious persons experiencing pain and misfortune in this life while the impious flourish? Saadya regards his explanation as the only rational one, that is, the only one we could reasonably attribute to a rational and nonarbitrary God. A 'pious' person, he claims, is someone in whose conduct 'the good deeds predominate', while the 'impious' person is someone most of whose deeds are wicked. Some pious people commit a greater number of sins than others (with those sins still constituting only a minority of their actions overall), while some impious persons commit more righteous acts than others. Now there is, Saadya insists, a 'second world' beyond this one, 'the world of compensation'. It comes into being 'only when the entire number of rational beings . . . will have been fulfilled. There [God] will requite all [rational beings] according to their deeds.'[35] But it would be unjust for God, in meting out reward and punishment, not to take into account *all* of a person's actions, both the minority and the majority. Saadya thus argues that God has laid down as a general rule that all individuals will be requited in this world for the minority of their deeds, leaving the majority of their deeds to be requited in the world to come. 'He therefore instituted recompense in this world only for the lesser portions of a person's conduct . . . while the totality of his merits is reserved for a far-off time.'[36] This explains

> why it often happens that a generally virtuous person may be afflicted with many failings, on account of which he deserves to be in torment for the greater part of his life. On the other hand, a generally impious individual may have to his credit many good deeds, for the sake of which he deserves to enjoy well-being for the greater part of his earthly existence.

When all is said and done, everyone gets exactly what they deserve: every person gets some reward and some punishment, either in this world or the next, perfectly proportionate to his or her deeds. Saadya admits that sometimes it happens that a completely blameless person nonetheless suffers in this world. He responds by saying that they will be compensated for their trials in the world to come.[37]

Later medieval Jewish philosophers—and Maimonides and Gersonides are clearly in this camp—agree with Saadya that the true reward for virtue is not freedom from pain or suffering in this life, although a life of true virtue will, because of the nature of virtue, grant one some relief and protection from many of life's vicissitudes.[38] Rather, the virtuous find their real reward in a greater recompense in the world to come, in the life hereafter. To take just the case of Gersonides, he argues in *The Wars of the Lord*, in a part of the work devoted entirely to the question of divine providence, that one should not judge concerning God's justice on the basis only of what one observes in this world, particularly the distribution of good and evil.[39] For what we commonly see is clearly a lack of order and equity in their distribution, with people apparently not receiving their due rewards. Evil happens to the righteous, and good to sinners. 'Hence', he insists, 'the following dilemma necessarily ensues: either God can arrange it that a man receives his due reward but he does not attempt to do so, and this would indeed be evil with respect to God (God forbid), or he cannot so arrange this, which would be an imperfection in God.'[40]

Gersonides says that solution to the conundrum is that 'the *true* reward and punishment do not consist in these benefits and evils that we observe. For the reward and punishment that occur to man insofar as he is a man have to be good and evil that are [truly] human, not good and evil that are not human.'[41] The goods and evils that make up the greater part of this world are material benefits and losses—such as good food and other sensual objects and pleasures—that we share with other creatures. These may not be distributed in accordance with a person's dessert, but by chance and nature. The 'true' human good, on the other hand, consists in 'the acquisition of spiritual happiness'; this alone is tailored to what is a human being's highest and most proper perfection. 'Since human evil consists of the absence of this spiritual happiness, i.e., in its imperfection, it is evident that true reward and punishment in man as man consists of the achievement or lack of achievement of spiritual happiness, not of these sensuous goods or evils that are ordered by the heavenly bodies,'[42] that is, by Nature and not by God.

What this spiritual happiness consists in, for Gersonides, is the acquisition of knowledge and an intellectual union with a higher soul, the Agent Intellect. True human happiness lies in the perfecting of the mind—that is, in the attainments of the acquired intellect—that we saw to be central to Gersonides' account of immortality. In this life, we—or, at least, a small number of people, especially prophets—can enjoy some measure of this perfection. But the demands of the body and the force of empirical circumstances often stand in the way of the achievement and enjoyment of true perfection. Thus, even virtuous people—those who have devoted their lives to the search for true knowledge—are subject to the elements, to the disturbances and imperfections of this world; the righteous sometimes, simply as a matter of fortune, do suffer. Conversely, it is possible for sinners to enjoy, through no merit of their own but only as a result of chance and the ordinary course of nature, some benefits and prosperity. When they die, however, the virtuous are capable of enjoying their highest happiness to the highest degree.

> It is important to realize that each man who has attained this perfection enjoys the happiness resulting from his knowledge after death. We have some idea of this pleasure from the pleasure we derive from the little knowledge we now possess which subdues the animal part of our soul [so that] the intellect is isolated in its activity. This pleasure is not comparable to the other pleasures and has no relation to them at all. All the more so will this pleasure be greater after death; for then all the knowledge that we have acquired in this life will be continuously contemplated and all the things in our minds will be apprehended simultaneously, since after death the obstacle that prevents this kind of cognition, i.e., matter, will have disappeared . . . After death, [the intellect] will apprehend all the knowledge it has acquired during life simultaneously.[43]

The true reward for virtue, for pursuing the life of knowledge and intellectual achievement, will be in the world to come, not in a life free of evil and suffering in this world. Our highest happiness comes only after death. 'The view of our rabbis is that true reward and punishment occur in the world to come and that there is no necessity for reward and punishment in this world to be such that the righteous and the sinner receive material benefits and evils, respectively. They say "The reward of a commandment is not in this world".'[44]

Now when Spinoza denies the personal immortality of the soul, he is, in effect, confronting head-on this whole tradition of theodicy. And he does so for the sake of demonstrating that the true value of virtue is in this life. Human virtue—the striving for and acquisition of understanding and the third kind of knowledge—just *is* happiness. 'Blessedness is not the reward of virtue, but virtue itself.'[45] Our freedom, our physical and psychological well-being, indeed our flourishing are directly dependent upon our knowledge of nature, including our understanding both of the necessity of all things and of our place in the world. Spinoza is thus engaged not only in the moral and very political project of freeing us from bondage to our passions, especially hope and fear, and thereby undermining ecclesiastic manipulation of our lives, but also in the philosophical and equally moral project of forestalling a particular type of theodicy—namely, that practiced by the rabbis of the Talmud, by Saadya, Maimonides, and Gersonides, and by a host of other philosophers, Jewish and Gentile—and persuading people not to look at virtue merely as a burden to be borne for the sake of some alleged otherworldly reward.

Morality, then, and religion, and absolutely everything related to strength of character, they [the multitude] believe to be burdens, which they hope to put down after death, when they also hope to receive a reward for their bondage, that is, for their morality and religion. They are induced to live according to the rule of the divine law (as far as their weakness and lack of character allows) not only by this hope, but also, and especially, by the fear that they may be punished horribly after death.

This is not, Spinoza believes, a very solid foundation or motivation for the pursuit of virtue.

If men did not have this hope and fear, but believed instead that minds die with the body, and that the wretched, exhausted with the burden of morality, cannot look forward to a life to come, they would return to their natural disposition, and would prefer to govern all their actions according to lust, and to obey fortune rather than themselves.

It is, he concludes, a foolish, indeed harmful, way to live a life:

These opinions seem no less absurd to me than if someone, because he does not believe he can nourish his body with good food to eternity, should prefer to fill himself with poisons and other deadly things, or because he sees that the mind is not eternal, *or* immortal, should prefer to be mindless, and to live without reason. These [common beliefs] are so absurd they are hardly worth mentioning.[46]

If there is no life after death, if we do not persist after the corruption of the body and the end of its durational existence, if the doctrine of the immortality of the soul is rejected, then there can be no 'justification' of the ways of 'God or Nature' nor any measuring of the value of virtue by pointing to some ultimate reward to hope for in a 'world to come'. In fact, virtue must be its own reward in this world, as a source of abiding happiness and of freedom from the vicissitudes of chance and fortune. If virtue is the pursuit of knowledge, and if it is knowledge that provides autonomy (and especially a liberation from the bondage of the passions), as well as comfort and consolation in the face of fortune, then the benefits of virtue are enjoyed in this life. Virtue is not a burden, but a blessing; it is, as he says, 'blessedness itself'.

The denial of the immortality of the soul is thus central to Spinoza's entire philosophical project: not just the metaphysics and moral philosophy of the *Ethics*, but also the agenda for political and religious reform in the 'scandalous' *Theological–Political Treatise*.

But these are Spinoza's mature writings, composed in the mid- to late 1660s. The question that initiated this long discussion on immortality, however, was: Why was Spinoza put under a *cherem* in 1656? The ban took place almost ten years before he set aside an early draft manuscript of the *Ethics* to work on the more pressing political and religious questions in the *Treatise*. Is there, first of all, any reason to believe that Spinoza was denying the immortality of the soul in the mid-1650s?

As a matter of fact, there is.[47] First, we have the testimony before the Inquisition in Spain of Brother Tomas Solano that was examined in Chapter 2. The friar alleges that, when he met Spinoza in Amsterdam in late 1658, Spinoza told him that he was expelled from the Talmud Torah congregation because, among other heresies, he was claiming that 'the soul dies with the body' (*las almas morian con los cuerpos*).

He knew both Dr. Prado, a physician, whose first name was Juan but whose Jewish name he did not know, who had studied at Alcala, and a certain de Espinosa, who he thinks was a native of one of the villages of Holland, for he had studied at Leiden and was a good philosopher. These two persons had professed the Law of Moses, and the synagogue had expelled and isolated them because they had reached the point of atheism. And they themselves told the witness that they had been circumcised and that they had observed the law of the Jews, and that they had changed their mind because it seemed to them that the said law was not true and that souls died with their bodies and that there is no God except philosophically. And that is why they were expelled from the synagogue; and, while they regretted the absence of the charity that they used to receive from the synagogue and the communication with other Jews, they were happy to be atheists, since they thought that God exists only philosophically . . . and that souls died with their bodies and that thus they had no need for faith.[48]

Then there is Lucas's account of Spinoza's interrogation by his fellow students. Though more colorful (and, given both Lucas's own narrative needs and the amount of time that passed between the events and their telling, possibly more apocryphal) than Tomas's sworn deposition, this report is not without a significant degree of credibility, especially since Lucas knew Spinoza personally (or so he tells us). The students told Rabbi Mortera that when they asked Spinoza 'How does it appear to you? Does God have a body? Is the soul immortal?', Spinoza replied by claiming that 'the soul is not immortal': 'Whenever Scripture speaks of [the human soul], the word "soul" is used simply to express life, or anything that is living. It would be useless to search for any passage in support of its immortality. As for the contrary view, it may be seen in a hundred places, and nothing is so easy as to prove it.' This, according to Lucas, took place *before* the community issued its ban.

Apparently Spinoza arrived at his views on immortality very early in his philosophical apprenticeship. Spinoza was intellectually gifted, and undoubtedly a precocious student in his youth.[49] He had a solid education within the Jewish community, and by the early to mid-1650s was probably already studying philosophy, Jewish and otherwise.[50] I see no reason for doubting the veracity of Lucas's story, at least as a source of some information on Spinoza's views when he was still a young man, and for thinking that Spinoza did not come to his own answers early on such an important question as the immortality of the soul.

This still leaves a second, equally crucial question unanswered. As we have seen, Judaism's view(s) on the soul and its fate after death are much more ambiguous, more indeterminate than its demand that one believe, for example, that God—a wise and just judge, the free creator of the world—revealed the Law to Moses, a Law still binding on Jews to the present day. There is a good deal of latitude on this metaphysical question, enough for Joseph Albo to proclaim that a belief in immortality is neither a fundamental nor a derivative principle of Jewish law; and even enough for Moses Narboni to deny, without being declared a heretic, that there is anything personal or individual about immortality. It could be that an individual Jew need not believe anything about the immortality of the soul. So even if Spinoza *was* denying the immortality of the soul around the time of his *cherem*—as he would do more systematically in his later philosophical writings—why should this have been (as I believe it was) a particularly aggravating factor in the decision to punish him? Why should his denial of immortality, in fact, have contributed at all to his earning the most vitriolic ban ever issued by the Amsterdam Sephardic community in the seventeenth century?

Because it was simply the wrong issue to pick on in Jewish Amsterdam in the 1650s.

Immortality on the Amstel 7

In 1614 the Portuguese Jews of Amsterdam were finally able to secure land for a community cemetery. They had to go outside the city limits of Amsterdam—whose authorities had already twice denied their request, in 1606 and 1608—to Ouderkerk, a small village just a few miles south of the city. The road to Ouderkerk follows the course of the Amstel River, from which the city originally got its name, Amstelodam. The part of the city in which the Jews tended to reside, Vlooienburg, was right beside the river, and the Portuguese would move their recently departed upstream to Ouderkerk by barge.

On bicycle, the trip from what is now called the Jodenbreestraat—'Jews Broad Street'—to the cemetery takes about a half hour, if the wind is not against you. Heading away from the center of town down the main boulevard that once formed one of the central axes of the Jews' prosperous neighborhood, one passes Rembrandt's house and, at the end of the street, the magnificient synagogue that the expanding Talmud Torah congregation built for itself in 1675. After turning right and crossing to the far side of the Amstel over a bridge, a left turn puts you on a narrow road that hugs the river all the way to Ouderkerk. Spinoza, one of his early biographers tells us, left the city of Amsterdam soon after his eviction from the Sephardic community to live *op de weg naar Ouwerkerk*, 'on the way to Ouderkerk'; he may have been referring to a residence on this road.[1] It is a very scenic ride, and passes some well-apportioned houses that, at one time, may have been 'country homes' for the well-off seeking a respite from the confinements of Amsterdam, especially in the summer. As you come to Ouderkerk, still on the same side of the Amstel, you turn right into the village over a little drawbridge and the Jewish cemetery is there on your left.

The grounds are now in disarray. The lawn and bushes are overgrown, and many of the marble headstones have either fallen over or, if they were laid flat to begin with, become covered with grass and weeds. The engraved inscriptions are worn and often hard to read. But there is still an impressive solemnity to the place, as the hedgerows within the wrought-iron gates provide a dark privacy. It is not hard to imagine why the famous Dutch landscape painter Jacob van Ruisdael came several times to Ouderkerk to paint and sketch the Jewish cemetery. In his two somewhat fantastical paintings, composed in the mid-1650s, there is an air both of abandonment and of spiritual power about the place.[2] Rabbis Mortera, Aboab, and Menasseh ben Israel are buried here. So are Michael and Hannah d'Espinoza. Their son Baruch is not.

What happened to a person after he or she died was a very important issue for the Jews of Amsterdam, perhaps more so than for many other Jewish communities in Europe. Given their personal and communal history and social background, these one-time conversos or descendants of conversos took very seriously the questions surrounding the postmortem fate of the soul.

Many members of Amsterdam's Portuguese Jewish community had relatives, close friends, and business associates still living (at least outwardly) as Catholics in Spain. The situation of these people caught between two religions was as precarious and potentially dangerous as ever. The Inquisition had not slackened in its efforts to root out heresy. It was still on the lookout for crypto-Jews among its 'New Christians', and even the most sincere of the converted had to worry about suspicion and betrayal. The Amsterdam Jews were sensitive to the plight of their brethren in Iberia. One of the community's regulations explicitly forbade its members from sending letters or other types of communication (such as business orders) containing any mention of or reference to the Jewish religion to people in Spain; it was feared that such a letter would jeopardize its recipient, most likely someone of converso descent, by putting them under suspicion of being a secret Judaizer.

Indeed, the concern of the Amsterdammers extended well beyond the safety and well-being of the Iberians in *this* life. They seem to have been worried, as well, about what would become of the souls of their relatives and friends in Spain after they died. These were, after all, people who were committing two of the most serious sins a Jew can commit: denying their Jewishness and, by participating in the Catholic mass, engaging in an activity that in Jewish eyes was considered idolatry. Maimonides concedes that there are many occasions when a Jew, under the threat of death, may violate one or another of the Torah's commandments. In such circumstances—if the law is a minor one, for example, or the transgression occurs in private and not in the presence of ten Jewish males—it is preferable to break Jewish law rather than be killed. Martyrdom is not always a virtue. But if one is called upon to renounce the Torah itself or to violate its central and most important commandments, such as that forbidding murder or the worship of idols, then 'one should sacrifice his life rather than transgress'. Later Sephardic emigrés, thinking about their apostate relatives, would have seen a clear lesson here for those living under the oppressive dominion of the Inquisition:

> In times of a decree—that is, when a wicked king like Nebuchadnezzar or his like will arise and issue a decree against the Jews to nullify their faith or one of the mitzvot—one should sacrifice one's life rather than transgress any of the other mitzvot [i.e., the important ones], whether one is compelled to transgress in the midst of ten Jews or one is compelled to transgress merely in the midst of Gentiles.[3]

Rabbi Joseph Caro, the author of the *Shulchan Arukh* and, like Maimonides, an authority of special importance to Sephardim, claims that it is permitted, even preferable, to sacrifice your life in order to observe the Torah even in minor matters. Even if one is not required to choose death over disobedience, it is nonetheless, he notes, a sanctification of God's name to do so.[4]

The question in the minds of Amsterdam's Jews, then, must have been the following: What will happen to the souls of our apostate relatives and friends? Yes, they are suffering torment now in their denial of the faith. But will they find permanent rest from their torments in the hereafter? The Talmud promises that 'all of Israel will have a share in the world to come'.[5] But the same chapter also notes that certain sinners will be denied a place therein. Have the conversos of Iberia forfeited their right to a place in *olam haba* because of their continued renunciation of the Torah? Do they even belong to 'Israel'? Will they suffer eternal punishment for their sin?

This question was so important to the Amsterdam Sephardic Jews, in fact, that it almost led to a schism within the community.[6] In the early 1630s a number of individuals had taken to proclaiming that every Jew will, as a matter both of right and of fact, eventually enjoy a portion of eternal happiness in the world to come. They took the Talmud's words literally and insisted (apparently very vocally) that no Jew will ever suffer eternal punishment. Even if one has committed the most serious of sins, simply by virtue of being Jewish one is still guaranteed a place in paradise. They were, of course, worried about the theological and eschatological status of their converso relatives in Spain and Portugal. The thesis of the unconditional, ultimate salvation of all Jewish souls would be attractive to marranos and former marranos, since it meant that even those Jews who had once practiced, or who were still practicing Catholicism in the old country would be guaranteed a place in *olam haba*.

Rabbi Mortera was not at all pleased by this. Of course, he did not deny that the Talmud contains the statement that it does. But does it follow that whoever belongs by descent to the nation of Israel, no matter how grave his sins and no matter how long he remains a sinner without repentance, is promised an eventual portion in the world to come—the ultimate reward—and thus will not suffer eternal punishment for his sins? In Mortera's mind, such a view could lead only to wanton licentiousness; there would be nothing to fear, long-term and before God, on account of one's misdeeds. The views of the 'young rebels', he also argued, were contrary to classic rabbinic opinion, which clearly excludes certain types of sinner from *olam haba*.

According to Mortera, when the sages claim that every Israelite will have a portion in the world to come, the term 'Israelite' refers only to a righteous person, not simply to any Jew whatsoever. And someone who has failed to follow the laws of the Torah, and who has openly denied the principles of the faith, is no righteous person and will be eternally punished for his transgressions. There is no guarantee that just because a person has a Jewish soul he can avoid eternal punishment in hell for his sins.[7]

Mortera's response only inflamed the passions of his opponents. In early 1635 his sermons at the Beth Jacob synagogue were being disrupted by 'some young men' who took offense at his claim that 'the wicked who commit grave sins and die without repentance do incur eternal punishment'. These 'immature disciples' were not, it seems, acting on their own. Rabbi Isaac Aboab, of the Beth Israel congregation, supported them in their views, and was probably even their inspiration and instigator (or, as Mortera preferred to put it, their 'corruptor'). Pretty quickly the two rabbis themselves were clashing on the issue, much to the dismay of their respective congregants. The debate was a reflection of the ethnic and intellectual differences between the two most important and powerful rabbis in Amsterdam in the seventeenth century. Rabbi Aboab had been born a 'New Christian' in Portugal in 1605. He had a rather mystic bent, more so than the other rabbis in the community, and a deep interest in kabbalah. In this respect, he could not have been more unlike Mortera, who was inclined toward a rationalistic or philosophical approach to religion. Moreover, unlike Aboab, Mortera was an Ashkenazic Jew, and thus neither he nor his family ever went through the marrano experience. Although he lived out his life among the former conversos of Amsterdam and preached to them in fluent Portuguese, it is easy to imagine his lack of empathy with what the members of his congregation (or their ancestors) had been through, and perhaps his impatience with their loose and unorthodox approach to some Jewish beliefs and practices.[8]

Mortera's opponents asked the leaders of the community to issue an injunction forbidding Mortera from preaching the doctrine of eternal punishment. Such a doctrine, they insisted, came dangerously close to

Christian beliefs on reward and punishment, and would therefore discourage conversos from returning to the Jewish fold.[9]

The matter was too big for the relatively young community to handle by itself, especially since it involved a question of orthodoxy, something on which the community's leaders were perhaps still educating themselves. As on so many other questions, they turned to Venice, and asked the leading rabbis of the older, more established Sephardic community there to rule on the dispute. Mortera and his opponents submitted their respective pleas, with Mortera marshalling a great deal of textual evidence—from the Bible and the Talmud, as well as from Jewish philosophers such as Maimonides—to argue for the doctrine of eternal punishment for unrepentant sinners, even if they are Jews. To the Venetian rabbis, it seemed a very delicate tactical matter. They hesitated to bring it up officially before their Beth Din, in part because they did not want it to seem as though the question of eternal punishment was a difficult one to answer and for which there were good reasons on both sides; this would only confuse lay people. Their initial recommendation was that the lay leaders of the Amsterdam community try to find a way to settle it among themselves, mainly by persuading Aboab to set an example for his younger protégés—if indeed they were simply following his directions—and publicly renounce his opinion. It appears that this approach did not work, and so the Venetians wrote to Aboab himself, in early 1636: 'We were hoping for the day that would bring the message of peace . . . but our expectation has been frustrated. For we were again informed that the conflict persists and that the spokesman of those denying the belief in the eternality of punishment is none other than you, Sir, and that you preach thus openly and publicly.'[10] They appealed to Aboab, in gentle and flattering but firm terms, to be reasonable and abandon an opinion that is explicitly denied by the sages of the Talmud and other rabbinic authorities.

The letter from the Venetians did not have its desired effect. In response, Aboab composed, in 1636, a treatise entitled *Nishmat Chayim* ('The Breath of Life'). In the treatise he directly addresses the question 'Is there eternal punishment of souls or not? And what did our rabbis, of blessed memory, intend by saying "The following have no share in the world to come"?' He insists that the true answers to these questions are to be found in kabbalah, not in philosophy or the Talmud (as Mortera had argued); and that the kabbalistic texts show authoritatively, if not clearly to the uninitiated, that *all* Jewish souls ultimately receive salvation. No matter what sins a Jew may have committed (or continues to commit), he or she will eventually enjoy the eternal bliss that is his or her right as a member of the nation of Israel. The doctrine of eternal punishment is inconsistent with the notion of an infinitely merciful God. All things, we are told, eventually return to God, and this is no less true of the human soul than of anything else. While the Talmud does seem at times to speak of eternal punishment, its words need to be carefully interpreted. For example, when we are told that certain classes of sinners will 'descend to hell [Gehinnom] and are punished there for generation after generation',[11] the phrase 'generation after generation' (*ledorei dorot*) must not be understood to mean 'eternally', but rather only until the coming of the Messiah.[12] When the sages insist that 'the following [sinners] shall have no portion in the world to come', what they mean, Aboab claims, is not that their souls will never be admitted to paradise. The Talmud is in fact saying one of two things: either *olam haba* refers to the period of the general resurrection of bodies, and the claim means only that the bodies of sinners will not be resurrected at that time; or *olam haba* refers, as usual, to the spiritual hereafter, and the claim means that *within* the world to come there will be a separation of the souls of sinners from the souls of the righteous, with the latter enjoying their own special realm in paradise.[13] On neither interpretation of the talmudic passage is it the case that the souls of sinners are permanently excluded from eternal bliss.

Aboab says that many souls will, as a result of their sins, have to go through a painful process of purification before they can be admitted to paradise. What he has in mind, following the tradition of Lurianic kabbalah, is a series of transmigrations, whereby the soul of the sinner will be reincarnated a number of times in different kinds of creatures, slowly working its way back to a human form. This journey will effect a *tikkun*, or healing, for the soul. Mortera had grudgingly admitted the possibility of such a transmigration, or *gilgul*; but he limited it to a maximum of three journeys: 'If in the end integrity is not achieved, the wicked will finally be cut off.'[14] Aboab, on the other hand, claims that it may take as many as a thousand such transformations for a soul to be sufficiently prepared, and that in the end it will always have its desired effect. Moreover, it is a remedy available to *every* Jewish soul. Righteous or sinners, they all still belonged to Israel: 'All Israelites are a single body and their soul is hewn from the place of Unity.' The Messiah will come only when all souls are pure enough for the world to come.[15]

Given the background of the overwhelming majority of the Jews in Amsterdam's Portuguese community, there is no question that many of them were sympathetic to Aboab's views. On the other hand, Venice's rabbis, whom they regarded with great respect, had made their own opinion on this matter quite clear: Mortera was right, Aboab was wrong. Although there is no indication that Aboab ever retracted his views, it would seem that—at least as a practical matter—Mortera prevailed, since in less than three years he was made the chief rabbi when the three original congregations merged into one, with Aboab occupying (at least formally, if not in terms of actual authority) the lowest rank (behind David Pardo and Menasseh ben Israel). In 1642 Aboab left for Brazil to minister to the Amsterdam Jews who settled in Recife. His departure from Amsterdam may have been the result of lingering tensions with Mortera.

The debate over eternal punishment was one of the most serious internal crises faced by the community in the period. It had lasting repercussions for the careers of the rabbis involved and for the organizational structure of Amsterdam's Sephardim. But the episode is also important for showing how important the doctrine of the immortality of the soul was for the Amsterdam Jewish community in the seventeenth century. For despite the deep, even irreconcilable differences between Mortera and Aboab, there is a fundamental assumption that is essential to both of their positions: the soul *is* immortal, in a very personal sense. In Aboab's view, there is an eternal reward guaranteed to every Jewish soul after death. This would obviously require a robust doctrine of individual immortality. Aboab, in fact, argues at length that the annihilation of the soul is—not just in fact, but in principle as well—impossible.[16] He cites numerous authorities, especially the late medieval philosopher Nachmanides, in support of the soul's natural incorruptibility and immortality. Because it is immaterial, the soul is not subject to the decay and disintegration that besets the material body.

On the face of it, Mortera's view of eternal punishment might not seem to require the natural and personal immortality of the soul. Following one reading of Maimonides' doctrine, he could have argued simply that the souls of sinners will be 'cut off', *karet*, and that the punishment of sin is death. The eternal punishment he is arguing for could be understood as nothing but the final nonattainment of happiness. But Mortera makes it perfectly clear that he has something stronger in mind. Sinners will not simply fail to sustain a happy life, but after death their souls will positively suffer eternally for their wrongs. The righteous, on the other hand, will enjoy everlasting bliss. Being 'cut off' or denied a portion in *olam haba* means, for Mortera, an eternal presence in hell for an immortal soul, with Gehinnom organized into various levels for different degrees of sin.

Both sides of the debate were thus strongly committed to a full-bodied doctrine of personal immortality. They differed only in what they understood to be the nature of eternal reward and punishment, not on the basic fact that there was compensation and retribution in the afterlife. One can easily imagine, in fact, that the Dutch Sephardim generally, solicitous as they were about the eternal fate of those members of Israel still compelled to live as Christians in Iberia, were very sensitive on the question of immortality, and would not have been tolerant of one who would deny altogether a future life in the hereafter. The Portuguese Jews of Amsterdam would no doubt respond very seriously to any attempt to deny outright the foundational doctrine upon which the positions of both Aboab and Mortera rested.

As a matter of fact, in the 1620s a heretic of questionable emotional stability had given them just the right opportunity to do so. Uriel da Costa's family had arrived in Amsterdam from Portugal in 1612. The 26-year-old Uriel and his brothers were circumcised, and they began to familiarize themselves with the rituals and observances of regular Jewish life. But Uriel, at least, was deeply dissatisfied with the Judaism he encountered in Amsterdam; it certainly did not meet his expectations of the religion of the Bible, a pure devotion to the Law of Moses. What he found instead, he claims, was a sect of latter-day Pharisees following a rabinically altered religion of meaningless and superfluous rules.[17]

In search of a more 'authentic' Judaism, da Costa moved to Hamburg. In 1616 he composed a set of ten theses attacking, among other things, the validity of the Oral Law (that is, the Talmud) and demonstrating 'the vanity and invalidity of the traditions and ordinances of the Pharisees'.

> It is by itself enough to cause the destruction of the foundation of the Torah if one says we should interpret the ordinances of the Torah according to oral reports and that we must believe in these reports as we believe in the Torah of Moses itself. By holding them to be true, we thereby create changes in the Torah and, in fact, create a new Torah opposing the real one. [But] it is impossible that a verbal Torah exists . . . It would make the word of man equal to that of God to say that we are obliged to keep all the laws of the Talmud just as we are to keep the Torah of Moses.[18]

He was also plagued by some doubts about the immortality of the soul and an eternal life in the hereafter, and sent the work to the rabbis in Venice, for their edification.

Venice responded to da Costa's broadside with a *cherem*, pronounced against him on August 14, 1618, by Rabbi Leon Modena, who had been Rabbi Mortera's teacher. Modena condemned those 'who contradict the words of our sages and who, notwithstanding the gaze of Israel, destroy above all the fences around the Torah, claiming that all the words of our sages are a chaos and calling stupid all those who believe in these words'.[19] Modena's judgment would have great force in Hamburg and Amsterdam, given the mentoring relationship that existed between the Venetian congregation and those communities. Rabbi Modena also took it upon himself to refute da Costa's views and defend the Oral Law in a book, *Mogen ve'Tzina* ('The Shield and the Buckle') ('Strive, O Lord, with those who contend against me: fight with those who oppose me. Take hold of shield and buckle, and rise up for my help'; Psalm 35, line 2), 'for the defense of our sages against a stray and stupid man, wise in his own eyes, whose name is insane'.[20]

Da Costa was also put under a ban in Hamburg. Before returning to Amsterdam a short time afterwards, where he continued to propound his views, he had apparently decided to give more systematic vent to his ideas on the Oral Law and, especially, on immortality. By 1623 he had composed a spirited critique of the Jewish religion, which, when finally published in Amsterdam in 1624, bore the title *Exame das Tradiçoes Phariseas* ('Examination of the Pharisaic Traditions'). Among the objects of his attack are the rite of circumcision and the use of various articles of Jewish ritual, including phylacteries (*tefillin*), prayer shawls (*tallitot*), and the attachment of *mezuzot* (parchment containing an excerpt from the Torah) to doorposts. The single issue which receives the greatest amount of attention, however, is the immortality of the soul.

Da Costa tells the reader that the thesis of the immortality of the soul has caused him a good deal of trouble for quite some time. The doctrine of eternal reward and punishment, in both its Jewish and (earlier in his life) Christian versions, was a source of great anxiety to him, and he apparently left the Catholic religion because the fear of eternal damnation tormented him.[21]

> Certainty eluded me and out of reach seemed the means to attain that eternal life, which I had been indoctrinated to believe in as the ultimate goal of human existence . . . In truth, the most distressful and wretched time in my life was when I believed that eternal bliss or misery awaited man and that according to his works he would earn that bliss or that misery.[22]

Relief came only when he realized the true nature of the soul and, thus, its mortality.

The soul, da Costa claims, is not like 'a damsel housed in our bodies', capable of departing upon death. Rather, the soul is a part of the body. It is a vital spirit in the blood, and is that which is responsible for animating an individual. In this respect, the human soul is no different from the soul of any other living creature. The only distinguishing feature of the human soul is its rationality. 'There is no difference between the soul of an animal and the soul of a human being other than that a man's soul is rational and the beast's is devoid of reason.'[23] The origin of the soul in a person lies in a completely natural process.

There is no special act by God creating the soul as a thing distinct from the body. It is engendered, like any other part of a human being's biological makeup, by procreation.

It follows, da Costa argues, that the human soul is essentially and naturally mortal. Because it is a part of the body, when the body dies so does the soul. 'To the question as to whether the soul of a human being is mortal or immortal, we reply that . . . it must be mortal if it is contained in the blood, as we have ascertained. It is in fact the vital spirit which dies and is extinguished before the human being can expire.'[24] In addition to this philosophical argument for the soul's mortality, da Costa marshals a good deal of evidence from the Jewish textual tradition. Nowhere, da Costa insists in opposition to the exegetical arguments of his opponents, does the Torah explicitly say that the soul is immortal. 'The first proof is an *argumentum ex silentio*: the Law nowhere indicates that the human soul is immortal or that another life, whether of punishment or glory awaits it.' In fact, the entire lesson of the Bible—the message of its stories, moral lessons, and epic events—is that 'once he is dead, nothing remains of a man, neither does he ever return to life'.[25] Nor does the immortality of the soul constitute the proper way to understand the manner in which the human being is created 'in the image of God'. Immortality is essentially a divine, not a human quality, and cannot belong to a creature.[26]

Once the truth about human mortality is accepted, a good number of 'errors and evils' generated by the belief in immortality will disappear. 'Since one absurdity leads to another and one error gives birth to many, this erroneous opinion or, rather, delusion concerning the immortality of the soul has such numerous offspring that it will not be easy to exhibit them all.' Because of this doctrine, people recite endless prayers and supplications for the dead, make useless and wasteful offerings to God, and practice 'countless silly superstitions at funerals'. In expectation of some greater good in the hereafter, people despise the goods and evils of this world. They ignore their material well-being and engage in destructive acts of self-mortification, sometimes going so far as to offer themseves for martyrdom. All of this is not only intrinsically unreasonable, but well beyond the bounds of what the Law demands in worship of God.[27]

The true reward for virtue—and the true punishment for sin—is in *this* life, in the distribution of goods and evils that all human beings experience. The righteous will enjoy a long life, full of days of peace and happiness. The wicked will receive their proper downfall, perhaps not right away but eventually; they will, as the sages say, be 'cut off'. 'It is in this life that the righteous and the wicked receive their just deserts . . . Let no one be so stupid and mad as to believe otherwise.'[28] Da Costa is unmoved by claims about the suffering of the righteous and the flourishing of the wicked. God is essentially good and wise, and governs this world with justice. If an apparently good person suffers, there must be some reason why, although that reason may be hidden from us.

Da Costa's treatise holds back nothing, and he is unforgiving in his indictment of the belief in immortality. Many of his charges about the doctrine will reappear in Spinoza's own thinking on immortality and how it is used by ecclesiastics to manipulate the passions of people.[29] Spinoza may possibly have read da Costa's treatise at some point, although it seems unlikely: the Amsterdam authorities—Jewish and Gentile—did everything they could to try to insure that *no one* had the opportunity to see it. He surely heard about its contents, however.[30]

Before da Costa could publish the work, there appeared in Amsterdam, in 1623, a refutation of his views. The author was Samuel da Silva, a medical doctor living in Hamburg who had managed to get a hold of parts of da Costa's manuscript. Da Silva's book, the *Tratado da Immortalidade da Alma*, focuses (as the title suggests) on the immortality of the soul, and was most likely commissioned by the Amsterdam Jewish authorities, in whose domain da Costa was again living.

Da Silva employs a variety of logical and textual arguments to counter da Costa's theses.[31] He argues that while the body does indeed come from the earth, the soul of an individual is created directly by God. It is put into the body at some time after a person's birth—forty days for a man, eighty days for a woman. The rational soul is substantially attached to the body in this world, giving life to it. But upon a person's death the union is dissolved and the soul 'continues to live, free and separate from the body'. It is, therefore, 'immortal and incorruptible', 'incorporeal and invisible'. No one denies this, da Silva pointedly insists, except 'perhaps some isolated individual whose education was neglected and who, carried away by his passionate adherence to depraved opinions in general, ended up so miserably as to be totally blind to his own soul.'[32]

The soul cannot be material, he argues, since purely rational understanding—the intellectual perception of concepts, which is the proper function of the soul—bears no relationship to the body and the physical images with which it operates. Moreover, because the will naturally aspires to virtue and to free itself from the demands of the body, despising all things material, it cannot itself be a part of the material body. Finally, in an appeal to what he hopes is a shared conception of divine justice, da Silva—adopting just the kind of theodicy that we have seen Spinoza argue against—insists that there *must* be an afterlife for the immortal soul. In *this* life, neither are the good adequately rewarded nor the wicked adequately punished.

> We see that many leave this vale of tears without adequate chastisement or reward for their conduct: indeed, in some instances, the quality of their lives is the opposite of what they deserve. We see some of the best who, far from being rewarded or recompensed, spend their life in miserable penury and thus end their days. Others we see who, not worthy even to have been born, never seem to die and the more world goods they accumulate, the ranker their arrogance and the more ostentatious their life-style grows and until the very end of their long lives they neither respect their fellow men nor fear or even remember God.

If the soul were not immortal, and were there no other realm beyond this one in which true punishment and reward could be distributed, God's justice would be undermined.

> Since God did not see fit to redress the balance during these people's lifetime, He will no doubt do so after their death, for otherwise divine justice would be found lacking and deficient. Consequently, we must perforce admit the existence of a world to come, wherein souls dwell and where God's justice is entirely vindicated, everyone receiving his deserts.[33]

Da Silva's 'refutation' of da Costa's views on the soul is a fairly amateurish job. Many of his arguments are invalid (he claims, for example, that the soul cannot be, like the body, material, for then two bodies would be in the same place at the same time; but surely da Costa meant only that the soul was an element or constituent *in* the body), and the more learned parts of his diatribe are borrowed from others.[34] Still, there can be no doubt that his treatise captures the spirit of reaction against da Costa's attack upon a cherished doctrine, one that the Amsterdam Jews considered to be of the utmost importance.

Alerted by the leaders of the Hamburg congregation, the Amsterdam community was clearly alarmed by the heretic's return to their city. And the seriousness with which they regarded da Costa's denial of immortality is testified by the trouble they went to in sponsoring da Silva's retort. They added their own response, on May 15, 1623, in the form of a *cherem*:

> The *chachamim* [rabbis], in the presence of delegates from the three boards of Elders, held meetings with Uriel in the course of which mild and gentle persuasion was applied to bring him back to the truth. Seeing that through pure obduracy and arrogance he persists in his wickedness and wrong opinions, the delegates from the three boards of elders, together with the boards of wardens and the consent of the *chachamim* ordained he be excluded as a person already excommunicated [i.e., in Venice and Hamburg] and accursed of God, and that . . . no communication with him is henceforth permitted to anyone except his brothers, who are granted eight days to wind up their affairs with him.[35]

As if that was not enough—and this makes it only more clear that the real issue in da Costa's case was his denial of immortality—Rabbi Mortera decided to take things into his own hands and compose a direct response to da Costa's views on the soul.[36] Unfortunately, Mortera's handiwork, a treatise that in extant references bears alternately the titles *Sha'arut ha-Nefesh* ('The Immortality of the Soul') and *Nefesh Adam* ('The Soul of Man'), is long lost. One scholar, however, has been able to reconstruct, on the basis of a number of references to the treatise in Mortera's sermons, the likely content of the 1623–4 work, which Mortera (for some reason) never published.[37]

The treatise, devoted primarily to 'proofs from Scripture and reason for the immortality of the soul' (according to one contemporary description of it[38]), apparently contained a defense of the view that there is a storehouse of souls in heaven, all of which were created by God at the beginning of time. Mortera thereby rejects the view that God creates a soul only on the occasion when it is needed to animate a particular body. It is only after this treasury is empty and all of its souls have been sent into the bodies created to receive them that the Messiah will come. Sometime after that point the bodies of the dead will be resurrected and reunited with their souls, and the latter will be judged for their righteousness or wickedness. And there should be no doubt that the ultimate fate allotted to each soul is an eternal one. Mortera thus, more than ten years before his conflict with Aboab, demonstrates a concern for defending the eternality of punishment. But the heart of the treatise is a discussion of the nature of the 'rational soul' (*hanefesh hasechlit*) itself. The soul, Mortera insists, is 'eternal and immortal', and his presentation contains scriptural and philosophical demonstrations to this effect (although none of them are extant).

In the face of this onslaught—da Silva's vituperative polemic, yet another *cherem*, and Mortera's treatise—da Costa was defiant. He went ahead and published his *Examination of Pharisaic Traditions*—at the same Dutch publisher that produced da Silva's work!—including in it a lengthy response to da Silva's attack. This was too much for the Amsterdam Jewish leaders. As da Costa himself tells the story,

> No sooner had [my book] appeared in print than the senators and rulers of the Jews agreed to lodge a complaint against me before the public magistrate, setting forth that I had published a book to disprove the immortality of the soul, and that with a view to subvert not only the Jewish, but also the Christian religion. Upon this information I was apprehended and sent to prison.[39]

His incarceration ended after ten days, when his brothers bailed him out. Either the municipal magistrates or the Jewish governors had also ordered that all copies of da Costa's book be burned publicly.[40] The community leaders had only one final regret: that, because of the absence of an Inquisition in the Netherlands, they could not condemn da Costa to death.[41]

This was only the beginning of a recurring cycle of offense, punishment, repentance, and reconciliation that would characterize da Costa's relationship with the Amsterdam congregations for the next fifteen years. Eventually, it all became too much for poor Uriel to bear. In 1640, after being stripped, publicly whipped, and forced to lie prostrate at the synagogue's doorway while the entire Talmud Torah congregation walked out over his body, he went home and shot himself in the head.

The message was loud and clear. The Jewish community of Amsterdam would not tolerate anyone denying the immortality of the soul. Those who do attempt to undermine the doctrine, especially in a public and prejudiced manner, will be dealt with severely. And it is clear from da Costa's own testimony above that, at least in his mind (and we have no reason to suspect that he was under any illusions about this), his major offense was his denial of immortality.

But the controversy over da Costa's views on immortality took place in the early 1620s. Spinoza's own *cherem* would not occur for another thirty years. Is there any reason to think that the immortality of the soul remained an important and sensitive issue to the rabbis and lay leaders of the Amsterdam Sephardic community well into the 1650s?

Spinoza was not the only person in the 1650s who was both banned by the community and accused of denying the soul's immortality. We have seen that Juan de Prado, with whom Spinoza kept company after their respective punishments, was likewise said to have claimed in conversation with Brother Tomas Solano in 1658 'that the soul dies with the body'. There can be little doubt that this opinion was one of the reasons behind his ban. In January of that year, in fact, the congregation's governing board, suspecting that Prado—who had apologized in 1656 for the error of his ways and become reconciled with the community—was reverting to his old heresies, started to compile a dossier on him. They took a deposition from one Jacob Monsanto, who alleged that, having mentioned to his teacher Prado his own faith in the doctrine of eternal reward and punishment ('Is it not one of [Maimonides'] thirteen articles?'), Prado replied to the effect that he did not share that belief, given the lack of evidence in favor of an afterlife: 'Up until now, no one has ever come back from the other world to ask for our assistance.'[42] Monsanto's testimony, along with that of others, was sufficient to convince the board that a second *cherem* was in order. Some years later, now living outside Amsterdam and responding to a written attack by his erstwhile friend Isaac Orobio de Castro, Prado asserted that he had never denied the immortality of the soul, but few have found his profession of innocence convincing.[43]

Then there is the case of Prado's friend Daniel Ribera, a convert to Judaism who moved to Amsterdam sometime between 1653 and 1655 and who was teaching in one of its schools. Ribera seems to have been a bit of a troublemaker, and was said to be, like Prado, mocking Jewish rituals. Of great concern to the board was the accusation by one of his students, Isaac Pacheco, that Ribera was proclaiming 'that the soul dies together with the body'.[44] Ribera, too, would probably have received a *cherem* had he not skipped town when he learned that the community's leaders were putting together a file on his opinions and behavior.[45]

This shows that there was no more tolerance for the denial of the immortality of the soul in the period around Spinoza's ban than there was in da Costa's time. Given the makeup and mindset of the community's religious leadership, however, this should not be at all surprising.

In Amsterdam in the seventeenth century, and especially from the time of the union of the three original congregations in 1639 through the expulsion of Spinoza in 1656 and up to the building of the new synagogue in 1675, four rabbis stand out both for their learning and personality and, more importantly, for their authority within and influence upon the community.[46] They were, without question, the spiritual and intellectual leaders of the community. Other rabbis came and went, some merely as visitors, but these four *chachamim* were a relatively continuous[47] and highly prominent (if not always cooperative and amicable) presence among the Amsterdam Sephardim. And it is a most telling fact that every single one of these rabbis wrote a treatise defending the immortality of the soul.

Aboab's *Nishmat Chayim*, from 1636, was composed in different circumstances from the other works, since it was directed not at a denial of the doctrine of immortality but at a fellow rabbi's views on eternal punishment. Aboab defended the immortality of the soul as an essential part of his plan to argue for every Jew's being guaranteed a rightful place in the world to come. Mortera's treatise on immortality was written in 1624. But we also know that the immortality and eschatological fate of the soul was a prominent theme in many of his later sermons. In fact, a homily on the Torah portion *vayelech* is devoted mainly to discussing the nature of the soul, its union with the body, and its immortality.[48]

Rabbi Moses Raphael d'Aguilar, raised and educated in Amsterdam, joined the Amsterdam rabbinate in 1639. He was once Mortera's pupil, and he himself served as a teacher and mentor to many of the community's lay leaders.[49] (He took over teaching Talmud in the community school's sixth level from Menasseh, who had replaced Aboab; the seventh, highest level was taught by Mortera.) Among his many writings d'Aguilar composed his own *Tratado da Immortalidade da Alma*. Like his colleagues, he argues on a rational and scriptual basis that the soul is an immaterial and incorruptible substance that survives the death of the body and that will be the recipient of divine reward and punishment in the afterlife.

And then there is Menasseh ben Israel, the unhappy rabbi. Poor Menasseh felt that he never got the respect that he deserved. He was right. Ranked low in the hierarchy of the community's rabbis, stuck teaching in the elementary school, given fewer rabbinic duties than the others, and provided with the lowest salary, the learned and cosmopolitan Menasseh was treated as a second-class rabbi. He was forced to supplement his income by engaging in mercantile dealings, which he found insulting. 'At present, in complete disregard of my personal dignity, I am engaged in trade . . . What else is there for me to do?'[50] Ironically, he was also the most well-known rabbi in Europe among the non-Jewish world. He had far-flung intellectual and commercial contacts, and was internationally celebrated as a printer and bookseller, as well as the most prominent Jewish apologist of his time.

In 1636 Menasseh published his *De la Resurreccion de los Muertos* ('On the Resurrection of the Dead'). Though the main purpose of the book was to combat those 'Sadducees'—an 'abominably perverse sect'—who denied that the bodies of the dead would be resurrected and reunited with their souls at the end of time, the book's subtitle emphasizes the fact that the work also contains a proof of individual immortality: 'In which, contrary to the Sadducees, is demonstrated the immortality of the soul'. Menasseh's immediate target may have been Uriel da Costa,[51] although the book's scriptural, philosophical, and kabbalistic arguments clearly had an independent import greater than any role they played in a particular polemic. Menasseh, in an argument that follows well-established Jewish and Gentile tradition, endorses the opinion of Rabbi Mosseh:

> What you wanted to know, that is, what is the soul, is something about which the books of the Greek sages have already spoken. All agree: the soul is form, not matter; and thus when the body dies, the soul does not die but stays in its place like an immobile angel, and it enjoys and sees in the light of the world what is the world to come.[52]

In 1651 Menasseh published his own *Nishmat Chayim*. It is a long book on the nature of the soul, its temporary union with the body in this life, and, through its intellectual and spiritual union with God, its immortality. It was Menasseh's first book in Hebrew, and he clearly believed that it would provide him with a reputation in the world of Jewish learning to equal that which he already had among Gentile scholars.[53]

When Spinoza was put under a ban in 1656, all four of these men—each of whom had written substantially on the *immortalidade da alma*—were still the community's rabbis.[54] Despite their differences in background, temperament, knowledge, and intellectual persuasion—Mortera was a philosophical rationalist, Aboab a mystical kabbalist, d'Aguilar a stodgy scholastic, and Menasseh a confirmed Messianist—all of them were deeply committed to a rigorous understanding of personal immortality, and all of them had argued strenuously in writing for their views.

Clearly, part of the importance of the question of immortality for these rabbis lay in the fact that they saw it as intimately connected to other, more obviously central elements of the Jewish faith. As Kasher and Biderman show in their thorough study of the issues surrounding Spinoza's *cherem*, Mortera and Menasseh had a tendency to 'lump' together the three doctrines that appear to have played a role in

Spinoza's ban: the truth of the Torah, the existence of a providential God, and the immortality of the soul.[55] Menasseh, in fact, explicitly saw the doctrine of immortality as fundamental for the other tenets:

> On this belief in the immortality of the soul depend, learned reader, the major foundations and the principles of religion, namely, the existence of God, the divine origin of the Torah and reward and punishment. For if you say that the soul dies with the body, this precludes reward and punishment. And if there are no reward and punishment and divine providence, then the existence of God is precluded. And if God does not exist and there is no reward and punishment, what is the purpose of the divine Torah and the toil of observing the precepts? Therefore, the threefold cord is not quickly broken.[56]

For Menasseh, denying the immortality of the soul is the first step down the slippery slope of denying the Jewish faith. Like Maimonides before them, he, Mortera, Aboab, and d'Aguilar believed the immortality of the soul to be one of the 'grand principles' of Judaism.

We have seen that the denial of personal immortality is an important element in Spinoza's philosophy, and especially his moral thought, his views on religion, and his broader social and political project. It is practically certain that Spinoza was denying the immortality of the soul around the time of his *cherem*, and we have credible reports that this was one of the three opinions for which he was banned—the other two being the denial of a providential God and the rejection of the validity (or 'truth') of the Torah. However, there was still the question—and it was a particularly glaring one, in the light of Jewish tradition and the wide maneuvering room usually provided therein for thinking on metaphysical matters—as to *why* a denial of the immortality of the soul should contribute to one's earning an excommunication. But now that we have seen how seriously the rabbis and leaders of the Amsterdam community took the issue of immortality, it should be fairly clear how Spinoza's expression of his views on the matter would have been a particularly aggravating factor in his case. It may possibly have been, in fact, *the* decisive element in the decision to issue Spinoza the harshest writ of *cherem* in the community's history.

Jewish Amsterdam in the 1650s was simply the wrong place in which to deny the immortality of the soul.

We can now ask, finally, why this was the case. Why would an issue that should have been treated with the toleration ordinarily granted to discussions of *aggadah* have been taken in Amsterdam in the 1650s with the seriousness usually reserved for questions of *halachah*? I am not sure that any clear and definitive answer can be given to this question. Surely, part of the explanation will lie in the particular and highly varied temperaments, backgrounds, education, and intellectual persuasions of the individual rabbis. The rationalistic Mortera clearly had a preference for one particular talmudic tradition on the world to come; perhaps this was something he inherited from his Venetian teacher Leon Modena. The kabbalist Aboab, on the other hand, found the doctrine of the immortality of the soul to be the crowning achievement of the process of mystical union with God's emanations; to know why he granted it such importance would involve a close examination not only of his own writings but also of the strain of kabbalistic tradition to which he was partial and the texts that mattered most to him. It would indeed be an interesting and useful exercise not only to demonstrate *that* the individual rabbis in Amsterdam took the question of immortality very seriously, as I have done, but also to examine *why* this was so in each case. But I believe, in fact, that a more informative answer to the question will have to transcend the biographical details of individuals.

We have already seen, in the discussion of the debate over the eternality of punishment in the 1630s, that at least part of the reason for the Amsterdam Portuguese Jewish community's attitude toward immortality lies in its origins and historical and social background. The immortality of the soul would seem naturally to be an important issue for a group of recent returnees to Judaism who still had relatives living in apostasy in Spain and Portugal, and who were therefore concerned about the eventual fate that awaited the souls of their loved ones. Would those who, under compulsion, publicly reject the Torah nonetheless receive the eternal reward that the Talmud appears to promise to every member of Israel?

Remember, too, that the rabbis of the community (with the exception of Mortera) and many of its former marrano leaders had either been born and raised in Catholic environments, educated in Catholic schools, and imbued from childhood with the dogmas of the Catholic faith, or at least grown up in families where traces of decades (even centuries) of Catholicism colored their approach to Judaism. Catholicism is a highly eschatological religion, and the immortality and eternal fate of the soul is a much more important and central dogma to it than it is to mainstream, rabbinic Judaism. The fifth Lateran Council had proclaimed, in 1513, that the personal immortality of the soul is an article of the faith. It is not surprising, then, that among the features of Jewish belief and practice adopted by the Portuguese in Amsterdam, in addition to their celebration of 'saints' days for Jewish heroes, would be a fairly strong concern for the soul after death and at the last judgment.

Another dimension to answering the question lies in the contemporary political situation of the Jews in seventeenth-century Amsterdam. I have shown that the Portuguese in Amsterdam were very concerned about how they were perceived by their Dutch hosts. Having just recently found refuge in the Netherlands from the torments of the Inquisition, they were not feeling entirely secure about their status. Tolerant as the Republic was, it was still officially a Dutch Reformed society. The Jews knew that the stricter elements among the Calvinists were unhappy about having thriving Jewish communities in their midst—almost as unhappy as they were about having Catholics allowed in the Republic. Thus, the Jews were ever cautious about what went on within the community, lest they upset the municipal authorities, and ever vigilant against heresies that attacked not only Jewish law and tradition, but also Christian (and especially Reformed!) dogma. 'If the Dutch regents who run Amsterdam should see our community as a haven for heretics and atheists,' their thinking probably ran, 'then they would surely come down hard on us.'

Now, what issue could be of greater shared importance to Jewish and Christian minds in seventeenth-century Amsterdam than the immortality of the soul? Upon it rested not only ideas of theology and eschatology, but also (or so it was argued) the claims of ordinary morality. A standard response employed against those who would deny the immortality of the soul—a response strongly mocked by Spinoza—derives from the belief that without that doctrine, and its concomitant claims about eternal reward and punishment, people would have no long-term motivation to behave in ethically responsible ways. The young Spinoza made the rather abstract claim that 'God exists only philosophically', and both he and da Costa denied the continued validity of the Law. But if the Jews of Amsterdam were worried about heterodoxy coming from within the community that would be upsetting to their Christian neighbors, they could not afford to overlook the denial of personal immortality. After all, all three of these views were explicitly cited by the provincial assembly of Holland when, in 1619, it granted to its municipalities the prerogative to decide for themselves whether to admit Jews. The assembly stipulated as a general guideline that all members of the Jewish community must declare, besides their belief that there is 'an omnipotent God the creator . . . [and] that Moses and the prophets revealed the truth under divine inspiration'—that is, that there is a providential God and that the Law is 'true'—the further belief that 'there is a life after death in which good people will receive their recompense and wicked people their punishment'.[57] Surely the Amsterdam Sephardim still had at least one eye on this proclamation in the 1650s.

Da Costa himself perceived rather clearly the important role this shared concern for immortality played in his own case: 'The Jews lodged a complaint against me before the public magistrate, setting forth that I had published a book to disprove the immortality of the soul, and that with a view to subvert not only the Jewish, but also the Christian religion.' It was this that moved the city's magistrate to throw him in gaol. Appealing to da Costa's denial of immortality and its consequences for both the Jewish and Christian faiths was a smart tactical move for the Jews to make if they wanted the Dutch authorities to get involved in what would ordinarily be only an internal affair. Responding forcefully to da Costa's—and Spinoza's—views on the soul was also wise if they wanted to send a signal to the Reformed ministers that they were keeping things clean and proper on matters of mutual concern.

The Dutch, of course, may not have cared very much at all about *what* was going on within their Jewish neighborhoods. Or, at least, the liberal regents running Amsterdam in the 1650s may not have worried much about theological heresy; they had more pressing political and economic matters at hand. But what is of interest here is the 'psychology' of the community that banned Spinoza—what the Jews of Amsterdam themselves saw as important, and what *they* most likely *believed* about what the Dutch saw as important and about how that might affect their own fortunes. No doubt, they saw Spinoza's denial of the immortality of the soul as a threat, a provocation; and they were afraid—rightly or wrongly, it does not matter—that the Dutch would see him the same way.

Conclusion

Aristotle was a man who knew his limits; or, better, he was aware of the limitations necessarily involved in our investigations. The canons of rigor appropriate to one discipline should not automatically be carried over to and applied within another discipline. One should tailor one's goals according to one's field of study. Demonstrative certainty may be possible and desirable in mathematics or the natural sciences, for example, but it should not be sought in the study of human behavior, especially in ethics. Discussions in these social, political, and moral matters are adequate, he insists, 'if they achieve clarity within the limits of the subject matter'.

> Precision cannot be expected in the treatment of all subjects alike, any more than it can be expected in all manufactured articles . . . A well-schooled man is one who searches for that degree of precision in each kind of study which the nature of the subject at hand admits: it is obviously just as foolish to accept arguments of probability from a mathematician as to demand strict demonstrations from an orator.[1]

I am offering these reflections to serve as a kind of *caveat lector*. The reader will naturally want to know what I think I have 'proven' in this book. My response can be only a modest one.

The banning of Baruch Spinoza, a story as ripe with drama and (especially for historians of philosophy and of Judaism) fascination as can be imagined—and, given the dearth of extant information, all we *can* do is imagine—is as good a candidate for overdetermination as there ever has been. We can only speculate on what lay behind the venom directed at Spinoza by the *parnassim* of Talmud Torah; and when we do so, we are confronted with a number of tantalizing and equally plausible possibilities. His *cherem* occurred at a particularly rich juncture in modern European history. On the side streets of Vlooienburg, along the banks of the Houtgracht, the Amsterdam Jewish community intersected with the turbulent politics of the Dutch 'Golden Age', and the intellectual and spiritual ferment of the seventeenth century merged (and clashed!) with centuries of Jewish religious and philosophical thought on the deepest of metaphysical and moral issues. Could there possibly be a single and simple story that will make sense of the most momentous event in the life of one of history's most important and controversial philosophers?

Spinoza denied that the Torah was literally the word of God; he claimed that the Jews were not God's chosen people in any deep and interesting sense; and his naturalistic understanding of God was calculated to discourage the kind of anthropomorphizing of the divine being that is so characteristic of (and essential to) the main sectarian religions. Contemporary witnesses from the time of his *cherem* all tell us that these were his opinions. And they are all opinions that the rabbis and lay leaders of his community would have regarded as highly objectionable. There is no reason to doubt that the public expression of these heretical opinions would have resulted in a *cherem*. I do not deny that they may have played a role in the decision to punish Spinoza. The governors of Spinoza's congregation would have regarded any of these opinions as blasphemous, and would have dealt with a person who expresses them accordingly.

But, as we have seen, there was something special about Spinoza's ban. What I have argued is that there was one opinion in particular that brought out the deepest ire of the *chachamim* and led to the harshest writ of *cherem* ever pronounced by the Portuguese Jews of Amsterdam. In addition to denying the divine and Mosaic authorship of the Pentateuch and saying that 'God exists only philosophically', Spinoza rejected the immortality of the soul. And in Jewish Amsterdam in the mid-1650s, this was just the wrong issue to pick on. Was the denial of the immortality of the soul Spinoza's *only* offense? No. Would not his other opinions have been sufficient to warrant a *cherem*? Yes. But what I hope to have established is that the extreme nature of the ban issued against Spinoza has its roots in this issue dear to the hearts and minds of Amsterdam's Sephardim.

In the early 1950s David Ben-Gurion, who was then the Prime Minister of Israel, lobbied to have the ban against Spinoza lifted. He need not have gone to the trouble. The *cherem* was pronounced by a specific Jewish community against one of its members. And the point of the ban was to exclude that person from the community. It was an act of ostracism. There was, of course, the expectation that other Jewish communities of the time would respect one community's punitive action. But once Spinoza died, the final intent of the *cherem* was fulfilled and its activity terminated. We know that Spinoza himself had no misgivings whatsoever about his break with the community that raised and nurtured him. 'All the better,' he is said to have replied when he learned of the ban; 'they do not force me to do anything that I would not have done of my own accord if I did not dread scandal. But since they want it that way, I enter gladly on the path that is opened to me, with the consolation that my departure will be more innocent than was the exodus of the early Hebrews from Egypt.'[2]

Does the *cherem* mean that there is no portion in the world to come for Spinoza's soul? We know well what Spinoza would say to such a question.

Notes

Chapter 1

1. The Hebrew text is no longer extant, but the Portuguese version is found in the Book of Ordinances (Livro dos acordos de naçao e ascamot), in the Municipal Archives of the City of Amsterdam, Archives of the Portuguese Jewish Community in Amsterdam, 334, no. 19, fo. 408.
2. A fuller treatment of the material in this chapter is found in ch. 6 of my biography of Spinoza, *Spinoza: A Life*. I present the summary here only as an introduction to the study that follows.
3. Originally there were two Portuguese congregations in Amsterdam: Beth Jacob and Neve Shalom. As a result of the events of 1618–19, a third congregation—eventually called Beth Israel—split off from Beth Jacob.
4. That this is the source of the text for Spinoza's *cherem* was first discovered by Salomon; see 'La Vraie Excommunication de Spinoza'. See also Offenberg, 'The Dating of the *Kol Bo*'.
5. For an engaging autobiographical portrait of Modena, one that details, among other things, his gambling addiction, see Cohen (ed.), *The Autobiography of a Seventeenth-Century Venetian Rabbi*.
6. The same text was used by the congregation again in 1712, when David Mendes Henriques and Aaron and Isaac Dias da Fonseca were excommunicated because they were believed to be 'following the sect of the Karaites' and thus denying the validity of the Oral Law; see Kaplan, ' "Karaites" in Early Eighteenth-Century Amsterdam'.
7. That his family was held in high esteem is testified by the fact that his father served in numerous leadership positions in the community, including several terms on the *ma'amad* as one of its *parnassim*. In fact, his final term as *parnas* was in 1649–50, just a few years before his son was banned. See the documents in Vaz Dias and van der Tak, 'Spinoza: Merchant and Autodidact', 130–1.
8. Spinoza's friends, who edited his works and letters for publication immediately after his death, seem to have destroyed all letters that were not of mainly philosophical (as opposed to biographical and personal) interest.

9. See the entry for *cherem* in the *Encyclopaedia Judaica*, as well as the discussion in Katz, *Tradition and Crisis*, 84–6.
10. *Bava Metzia* 59*b*. The verb translated by 'excommunicate' here is ברך. See also Mishnah, *Eduyot* 5: 6.
11. *Mishneh Torah*, 'Hilchot Talmud Torah', ch. 7.
12. Ibid., ch. 6.
13. See *Encyclopaedia Judaica*, 352.
14. Katz, *Tradition and Crisis*, 85.
15. It is a story that has been told many times in several languages. See Bodian, *Hebrews of the Portuguese Nation*; Nadler, *Spinoza: A Life*, ch. 1; Fuks-Mansfield, *De Sefardim in Amsterdam tot 1795*; and Baron, *A Social and Religious History of the Jews*, vol. xv, ch. 63.
16. For a study of this process, and of the religion of these former conversos, see Kaplan, *From Christianity to Judaism*.
17. Wiznitzer, 'The Merger Agreement', 132.
18. In my discussion here I rely greatly on Kaplan's analysis of excommunication in the Amsterdam community in his 'The Social Functions of the *Herem*'.
19. Ibid. 122–4.
20. Municipal Archives of Amsterdam, Archives of the Portuguese Jewish Community, 334, no. 19, fo. 72.
21. All of these cases are mentioned by Kaplan, 'The Social Functions of the *Herem*', 135–8.
22. Ibid. 124.
23. *Encyclopaedia Judaica*, 355.
24. Freudenthal, *Die Lebensgeschichte Spinoza's*, 9–10.
25. Ibid. 42. Meijer claims that, as in Venice, the person who got the job of reading the ban was chosen by lot, and that it may have fallen to Mortera in this case; see *Beeldvorming om Baruch*, 54.
26. Wiznitzer, 'The Merger Agreement', 131–2.
27. Kaplan, 'The Social Functions of the *Herem*', 126–7.
28. Municipal Archives of Amsterdam, Archives of the Portuguese Jewish Community, 334, no. 19, fo. 16.
29. Ibid., fo. 562. On Curiel's case, see Kaplan, 'The Social Functions of the *Herem*', 133–4.
30. The *cherem* indicates that the *ma'mad* made several attempts to get Spinoza to reform his ways, and Lucas relates that Mortera himself went to great lengths to try to persuade him to show some contrition. Pierre

Bayle reports (in an account that cannot be confirmed) that in their efforts to avoid a permanent split, the leaders even went so far as to offer him financial inducements just to keep attending synagogue; see Freudenthal, *Die Lebensgeschichte Spinoza's*, pp. 8 and 40.

31. For the text of Prado's *cherem*, see Revah, *Spinoza et Juan de Prado*, 29–30, 58–9.

Chapter 2

1. Another, third scruple needs to be mentioned at this point, although I hope that the results of my study will answer it in good turn: Is there really anything *new* to be said on the topic of Spinoza's *cherem*? Has it not already been exhausted in the scholarly literature (not to mention the popular imagination)? The standard and, by far, most thorough, treatment of the question is the long article by Kasher and Biderman, 'Why was Spinoza Excommunicated?' They cover a lot of ground, as I note throughout this chapter. But on at least the one crucial issue that interests me in this book, their discussion is fairly thin.
2. See Schwartz, *Rembrandt: His Life, his Paintings.*
3. One need only read through Jonathan Israel's history of the Netherlands in the 17th and 18th centuries—*The Dutch Republic: Its Rise, Greatness and Fall, 1477–1806*—to see how potentially unstable things could be.
4. See Huussen, 'The Legal Position of Sephardi Jews in Holland, *circa* 1600'.
5. Wiznitzer, 'The Merger Agreement', 123–4.
6. Meijer, *Beeldvorming om Baruch*, 57.
7. Ibid. 57–8.
8. The Dutch were quite interested in what was going on in the Jewish community, as evidenced by their visits to the synagogue to watch the Jews at worship. This fact, along with the ordinary and frequent business and social contacts between the Jews and the Dutch, reveals that the Dutch would have had easy and ample opportunity to learn about such a major event in the Jewish community as Spinoza's excommunication, about which the entire congregation must have been talking.
9. See TTP, ch. 16. For a study of Spinoza's defense of democracy, see Smith, *Spinoza, Liberalism and the Question of Jewish Identity*, 130–7.
10. See Nadler, *Spinoza: A Life*, chs. 5–7. On the other hand, Feuer's more extreme thesis—that Spinoza's political views were diametrically

opposed to the essentially monarchistic persuasions of the community's leaders, who tied their fortunes to those of the Calvinist party and the Stadholder—is hard to believe (*Spinoza and the Rise of Liberalism*, ch. 1). First, the Jewish merchants (including the rabbis) had more in common with the republican regents of the mercantile and professional classes who governed Amsterdam than with the Calvinist preachers who so often opposed them. Feuer claims that the *parnassim* would have found common cause with the Orangists in their shared hostility to Catholic Spain (and, after the Brazil debacle, Portugal). But war with Iberia was bad for business, as the Jews knew from experience. Amsterdam's Jews did appreciate the protection that Frederik Hendrik had given them while he was Stadholder; but I think it is going too far to suggest that they preferred on principle a quasi-monarchical state to a republican one. I believe that what they valued, above all else and independently of how it was achieved, was the peace and stability that allowed them to go about their affairs, along with protection from persecution.

11. On the other hand, Yovel's arguments against the importance of political considerations go farther than I would ('Why was Spinoza Excommunicated?', 49–50). While I agree with him that 'it is difficult to imagine that the excommunication took place simply in the name of the ancient Remonstrance from the city magistrates [to enforce orthodoxy within the community]', such political questions must have been in the minds of the community's leaders, as I argue above.
12. Freudenthal, *Die Lebensgeschichte Spinoza's*, 10.
13. 'The Social Functions of the *Herem*', 118–19.
14. See the documents collected and discussed by Revah in *Spinoza et Juan de Prado*.
15. He received at least one *cherem* for his efforts.
16. Mendes, *Memorias do estabelecimento e progresso dos Judeus Portuguezes e Espanhões nesta famosa citade de Amsterdam*, 60–1.
17. Ep. 6, G iv. 36; C 188.
18. Ep. 13.
19. See Vlessing, 'The Jewish Community in Transition: From Acceptance to Emancipation', 205–10.
20. See the documents in Vaz Dias and van der Tak, 'Spinoza: Merchant and Autodidact', 162–3.
21. See Wiznitzer, 'The Merger Agreement'.
22. *Mishneh Torah*, 'Hilchot Talmud Torah', ch. 6.

23. Van der Tak, 'Spinoza's Payments to the Portuguese-Israelitic Community', 190–2.
24. Freudenthal, *Die Lebensgeschichte Spinoza's*, 114.
25. This is suggested, for example, by Revah, 'Aux origines de la rupture Spinozienne: Nouveaux documents', 369; and Levin, *Spinoza*, 180–2.
26. See Nadler, *Spinoza: A Life*, ch. 5.
27. That is, in the home of Franciscus van den Enden, his Latin tutor. Van den Enden was a former Jesuit and a radical democrat (and, according to his numerous enemies, an 'atheist').
28. This is the interpretation favored by van der Tak, 'Spinoza's Payments to the Portuguese-Israelitic Community', 192. He insists that 'even if during the final months preceding his banishment his visits to the synagogue became less frequent, there is no question of his being estranged from his fellow Jews; but that on the contrary the ban must have come quite unexpectedly'. The drop in contributions, then, 'can only be explained as a result of decline in prosperity'.
29. See Vaz Dias and van der Tak, 'Spinoza: Merchant and Autodidact', 191.
30. Kasher and Biderman address the important question of whether Judaism does tolerate, and even recommend, punishment on matters of ideas and not just behavior; see 'Why was Spinoza Excommunicated?', 115–18.
31. Freudenthal, *Die Lebensgeschichte Spinoza's*, 5.
32. Ibid. 7.
33. Revah, *Spinoza et Juan de Prado*, 32–3.
34. The text of Brother Tomas's deposition (Revah, *Spinoza et Juan de Prado*, 32) reads as follows:

> He knew both Dr. Prado, a physician, whose first name was Juan but whose Jewish name he did not know, who had studied at Alcala, and a certain de Espinosa, who he thinks was a native of one of the villages of Holland, for he had studied at Leiden and was a good philosopher. These two persons had professed the Law of Moses, and the synagogue had expelled and isolated them because they had reached the point of atheism. And they themselves told the witness that they had been circumcised and that they had observed the law of the Jews, and that they had changed their mind because it seemed to them that the said law was not true and that souls died with their bodies and that there is no God except philosophically. And that is why they were expelled from the synagogue; and, while they regretted the absence of the charity that they used to receive from the synagogue and the communication with other Jews, they were happy to be atheists, since they thought that God exists

only philosophically . . . and that souls died with their bodies and that thus they had no need for faith.

35. The original text of Maltranilla's testimony is in Revah, *Spinoza et Juan de Prado*, 67.
36. *Memorias do estabelecimento*, 60–1.
37. In what follows, I offer a summary of some of the main points of Spinoza's philosophy. Spinoza scholars will not regard this summary as uncontentious; it is, admittedly, only one plausible (to my mind, the most plausible) reading of his views. I do not offer a longer defense of this reading since that would go beyond my main concern in this book, which is with Spinoza's views on the immortality of the soul. I offer this summary of his other opinions only for the sake of placing his account of the soul in some context.
38. It is also not even the God of Descartes, who was Spinoza's philosophical mentor. As I discuss below, Descartes himself had been accused by his numerous critics of believing in 'only a philosophical God', but the spareness of Spinoza's God goes well beyond anything that Descartes's himself explicitly envisioned.
39. *Ethics*, Ip15s.
40. Ip17s2.
41. Part I, Appendix.
42. Here, then, we have not necessarily an atheism but at least a denial of divine providence. It is a conception of God that, as Kasher and Biderman show, should be 'considered a "heresy" in the theological framework of the notion of Providence' ('Why was Spinoza Excommunicated?', 108).
43. Part I, Appendix, G ii. 78–9; C 440–1.
44. Ip17s1.
45. Although, as Descartes is at pains to insist, in God will and understanding are one and the same; see his letter to Mersenne of May 6, 1630.
46. On God's reason, see e.g. the letter to Hyperaspistes of Aug. 1641, in *Œuvres de Descartes*, iii. 431. On God's 'freedom of indifference', see Sixth Set of Replies, ibid. vii. 432–3.
47. See e.g. Lev. 19: 18: 'You shall love your neighbor as you love yourself.'
48. TTP, ch. 12, G iii. 159; S 206.
49. TTP, ch. 9, G iii. 131; S 175.
50. TTP, ch. 3.
51. TTP, ch. 3, G iii. 56; S 99.

52. As Kasher and Biderman show, these are opinions that the senior rabbis of the Amsterdam congregation would have regarded as 'outright heresies'; see 'Why was Spinoza Excommunicated?', 104–11.
53. *Commentary on the Mishnah, Sanhedrin*, ch. 10 (or ch. 11, according to the Babylonian Talmud).
54. *Mishneh Torah*, 'Hilchot Teshuvah', ch. 3.
55. Mishnah, *Sanhedrin*, ch. 11.
56. Many of Mortera's sermons were published in Amsterdam in 1645 in the collection *Giv'at Sha'ul*. This comes from his homily on the Parshah Tetzave; see Kasher and Biderman, 'Why was Spinoza Excommunicated?', 105.
57. Kasher and Biderman very briefly address these first two questions; see 'Why was Spinoza Excommunicated?', 106–8.
58. See ibid. 106, 108. In fact, Kasher and Biderman convincingly argue that the rabbis of Amsterdam saw these principles—the truth of the Torah, the immortality of the soul, and the existence of a providential God—as connected and together constituting 'the absolute foundations of the faith' (110–11).
59. In fact, as we shall see below, various authoritative figures in the Jewish tradition have argued as much—for example, Joseph Albo.

Chapter 3

1. *Commentary on the Mishnah*, *Sanhedrin*, ch. 10.
2. Such a general discussion of Jewish views on the soul or the afterlife is readily available in other works. For a fuller discussion of these issues, see Charles, *Eschatology*, esp. chs. 1–8; Raphael, *Jewish Views of the Afterlife*; and Olan, *Judaism and Immortality*. See also Finkelstein, 'The Beginnings of the Jewish Doctrine of Immortality' and 'The Jewish Doctrine of Human Immortality'. For an accessible survey, see Gillman, *The Death of Death*.
3. See Charles, *Eschatology*, ch. 1.
4. One scholar sees Enoch's passing as a 'physical translation to heaven', and thus a kind of immortality; see Finkelstein, 'The Beginnings of the Jewish Doctrine of Immortality'.
5. For a rich study of these transformations, see Raphael, *Jewish Views of the Afterlife*, esp. ch. 3.
6. The dating of Job is uncertain, and it may represent, in its thinking, an earlier tradition.

7. The reference to 'his people' here, however, is intentionally vague; Job (or its author) may not be a Jew.
8. This seems, for example, to be Isaiah's view; see 26: 19.
9. At the conclusion of the *megillah* (scroll) of Esther, we are told of the letter of Mordecai and Esther to the members of the Jewish communities of Persia enjoining them to observe the days of Purim, 'as they had decreed for themselves [*nafsham*] and their seed'. *Nefesh* is clearly used here to refer only to the whole person.
10. It is worth noting, however, the episode toward the end of 1 Samuel in which Saul has the woman of En-dor call up Samuel's shade or ghost; the woman, when asked what she sees, replied 'I see an *elohim* [god] coming up from the earth' (28: 13).
11. Raphael, *Jewish Views of the Afterlife*, 42.
12. The standard translation (from the Ethiopic) is Charles, *The Book of Enoch*. All references are to this edition.
13. *The Jewish Wars*, II. 8. xiv.
14. See *Sanhedrin* 11: 1, as well as Maimonides' commentary on this passage in his *Commentary on the Mishnah*.
15. There is, in fact, as becomes clear below, a tendency in rabbinic thinking to conflate the two doctrines of the resurrection of the body and the immortality of the soul.
16. The immateriality of the soul was not a necessary feature of the rabbinic dualism between soul and body; one could hold, for example, that the soul was material, but spun from a type of matter essentially different—finer, rarer, more excellent—than that of the body.
17. *Genesis Rabbah* 100: 7.
18. Ibid. 14: 11.
19. See e.g. *Sanhedrin* 11: 2–3. For some rabbis, the world to come is in fact a *part* of this world, and one enters it during one's lifetime.
20. *Ecclesiastes Rabbah* 3: 17.
21. *Avot* 4: 16.
22. *Berachot* 28*b*.
23. *Leviticus Rabbah* 4: 8.
24. Ibid. 4: 5; see also *Sanhedrin* 91*a*.
25. *Midrash Tanchuma*, 'Beracha' 28*b*.
26. *Berachot* 28*b*.
27. Ibid. 17*a*.
28. *Numbers Rabbah* 13: 2.

29. *Leviticus Rabbah* 18: 1.
30. *Shabbat* 152*b*; 'Throne of Glory' is, in Aramaic, *kisah hakevod*.
31. *Sanhedrin* 11: 1.
32. This is the interpretation of *Sanhedrin* 11: 1 given by Rabbi Joshua; see Tosefta, *Sanhedrin* 13: 2.
33. See the list at *Sanhedrin* 11: 1–4.
34. *Ecclesiastes Rabbah* 3: 18.
35. *Commentary on the Mishnah*, *Sanhedrin*, ch. 10.
36. *Bava Metzia* 59*a*.
37. *Berachot* 57*b*.
38. *Hagigah* 13*a*.
39. *Bava Metzia* 58*b*. See also *Rosh Hashanah* 17*a*.
40. *Rosh Hashanah* 16*b*–17*a*.
41. Although, as I have noted, the Mishnah does say that those who deny the resurrection of the body will have no place in the world to come.
42. Of course, there are always exceptions; such is the nature of rabbinic literature. Thus, to take just one case, in *Leviticus Rabbah* 28: 1 we are told that 'the Sages wanted to store away the Book of Ecclesiastes, for they found in it ideas that leaned towards heresy', in particular, the denial of reward in heaven.
43. *Commentary on the Mishnah*, *Sanhedrin*, ch. 10.
44. *Mishneh Torah*, 'Hilchot Teshuvah', 8: 1.
45. For a discussion of Maimonides' attempt to provide a systematic theology for Judaism, see Kellner, *Dogma in Medieval Jewish Thought*, 10–65. There is a great deal of debate, however, over what Maimonides takes the relationship between these fundamental beliefs and the rest of the principles of Judaism to be. Did he intend them to be 'axioms' or 'dogmas' in the strict sense of those terms? See, in addition to Kellner's discussion on pp. 61–5, Twersky, *Introduction to the Code of Maimonides*, 360 ff.
46. *The Guide of the Perplexed*, Introduction, i. 8–9. See Hartman, *Maimonides: Torah and Philosophical Quest*, 53.
47. Kellner, *Dogma in Medieval Jewish Thought*, 1. See also his sustained defense against introducing dogmatizing into Judaism, *Must a Jew Believe Anything?*
48. In his *Rosh Amanah*; see Kellner, *Dogma in Medieval Jewish Thought*, 179–95.
49. *Sefer ha'Ikkarim*, 134–5.

50. See e.g. the variety of views surveyed in Kellner, *Dogma in Medieval Jewish Thought*.
51. See Hayoun, *La Philosophie et la théologie de Moïse de Narbonne*, 212–13.

Chapter 4

1. Thus, he composed his *Treatise on Resurrection* to appease his critics, who believed that in his discussion of the world to come in the *Commentary on the Mishnah* and elsewhere, the emphasis on the purely spiritual rewards awaiting the soul amounted to a denial of the doctrine of the resurrection of the body.
2. It is odd that there is practically no discussion whatsoever of the way in which Spinoza's views on the eternity of the mind were influenced by his reading of Maimonides and Gersonides. There is, of course, Wolfson's important contribution to our knowledge of the Jewish philosophical background to Spinoza's thought. And he directs us to some crucial parallels between Spinoza and Gersonides and others on the question of immortality, and especially a number of important similarities between Gersonides' account of the acquired intellect and Spinoza's views on knowledge and eternity (see *The Philosophy of Spinoza*, ch. 20). But, as I show in Ch. 5, Wolfson entirely misses the import of Spinoza's account and of his use of Gersonides. The same is true of Tamar Rudavsky's discussion in her book *Time Matters*. She rightly sees that Gersonides' discussion of immortality and the acquired intellect were of great consequence for Spinoza's views on the eternity of the mind; but, like Wolfson, she believes that the comparison with Gersonides shows just how Spinoza *did* try to preserve individuality and personhood for the immortal soul (pp. 175–87).

   In 'A Portrait of Spinoza as a Maimonidean' Warren Zev Harvey does show how Maimonides and Spinoza agree on the fact that 'the ultimate perfection and true happiness of man, and the end he ought to pursue, is intellectual knowledge of true ideas, that is, knowledge of God and the actions which proceed from him', and that 'it is through this intellectual knowledge that he achieves eternity'. 'Spinoza's view', he rightly claims, 'is essentially Maimonides'' (p. 161). But he does not discuss at all the issue of immortality and the eternity of the mind.

   Similarly, Ze'ev Levy's book *Baruch or Benedict: On Some Jewish Aspects of Spinoza's Philosophy*—a work ostensibly devoted to examining 'some important trends of medieval Jewish philosophy on the shaping of Spinoza's thought'—contains no discussion of Spinoza's views on immortality at all; and Gersonides rates barely three mentions in the entire book. This is probably because Levy, while he concedes that many of Spinoza's ideas derive from medieval Jewish philosophy, believes that the Jewish philosophical background is of no use in trying to understand his metaphysics and moral philosophy: 'The Jewish thinkers, except Crescas, exerted little influence on the shaping of Spinoza's general philosophical system; he resorted to them mainly in his Bible criticism in the TPT [*Theological–Political Treatise*]' (p. 20).

Even Seymour Feldman, who, in the introduction and critical apparatus of his translation of Gersonides' *Wars of the Lord*, is so often sensitive to the ways in which various elements of Gersonides' theses and arguments relate to Spinoza's views, does not take any note of the influence Gersonides' account of immortality may have had on Spinoza's views of the eternity of the mind.

3. *The Guide of the Perplexed*, I. 41 (cited by book and chapter).
4. Aristotle's central discussion of substance is found in the *Metaphysics*, book 7.
5. There is some debate, however, over the sense in which forms are immaterial for Aristotle himself; see e.g. Alan Code, 'Aristotle, Searle and the Mind–Body Problem'.
6. This does not, of course, rule out the existence of disembodied forms or souls, such as angels and human souls after death (although explaining such disembodiment of the form is a problem for classical Aristotelian philosophy).
7. *Mishneh Torah*, 'Hilchot Yesodei Hatorah', 4: 7.
8. Ibid. 4: 8.
9. *Commentary on the Mishnah*, 'Eight Chapters', I.
10. Ibid.
11. Ibid.
12. *Mishneh Torah*, 'Hilchot Yesodei Hatorah', 4: 8–9.
13. Ibid. 4: 8.
14. *The Guide of the Perplexed*, I. 41.
15. *Mishneh Torah*, 'Hilchot Yesodei Hatorah', 4: 9.
16. *The Guide of the Perplexed*, III. 8. See also *Treatise on Resurrection*, vii. 36.
17. *Treatise on Resurrection*, ii. 7.
18. *Mishneh Torah*, 'Hilchot Teshuvah', 8: 1.

19. *Commentary on the Mishnah*, *Sanhedrin*, ch. 10.
20. *Mishneh Torah*, 'Hilchot Teshuvah', 8: 1.
21. *Treatise on Resurrection*, ii. 12.
22. Ibid. iv. 24.
23. *Commentary on the Mishnah*, *Sanhedrin*, ch. 10.
24. *Mishneh Torah*, 'Hilchot Teshuvah', 8: 2.
25. *Treatise on Resurrection*, ii. 9.
26. *Commentary on the Mishnah*, *Sanhedrin*, ch. 10.
27. The same criticism was made, in different ways, by Nachmanides, Meir Abulafia of Toledo, and Abraham ben David of Posquières. Rabbi Abraham ben David insists that 'this man's words are in my eyes close to those who claim that there is no resurrection of the body, only of souls. But I swear that this is not the opinion of our sages . . . [who claim] that the dead will rise with their bodies and remain alive' (see his note to 'Hilchot Teshuvah', 8: 2, in the standard Hebrew edition of the *Mishneh Torah*).
28. For discussion of this controversy, see Silver, *Maimonidean Criticism and the Maimonidean Controversy*, and Sarachek, *Faith and Reason: The Conflict over the Rationalism of Maimonides*. Oddly (and, I believe, incorrectly), Finkelstein argues that for Maimonides the doctrine of the resurrection of the body is identical with the doctrine of the immortality of the soul. There is, Finkelstein insists, 'only one dogma; the resurrection of the "shade" is the same as the immortality of the soul'; see 'The Jewish Doctrine of Human Immortality', 9.
29. It is not clear whether Maimonides believes that the world to come is simultaneous with this life, with a person entering it immediately upon death, or arrives only after the end of the Messianic period. For example, in *Mishneh Torah*, 'Hilchot Teshuvah', 8: 8, he claims that 'the world to come exists now . . . it is called the world to come only because human beings will enter into it at a time subsequent to the life of the present world in which we now exist with body and soul, and this existence comes first'. But compare this with 'Hilchot Teshuvah', ch. 9.
30. *The Guide of the Perplexed*, Introduction to Part II, vol. ii, p. 237.
31. This has led Tamar Rudavsky, for one, to insist that there is no personal and individual immortality for Maimonides, and to attribute to him a more Averroist view on the fate of the soul after death; see *Time Matters*, 179.
32. Thus, there is no need to accept Strauss's general theory of esoteric writing in order to make the distinction in Maimonides between the exoteric

and esoteric meanings of his philosophical texts; see Strauss, *Persecution and the Art of Writing and Other Essays.*

33. See Maimonides, Introduction to *The Guide of the Perplexed.*
34. Again, Samuel ben Ali took the lead here.
35. *The Guide of the Perplexed*, III. 54, ii. 635.
36. Ibid.
37. See ibid., III. 51. Maimonides does not elaborate on what such knowledge of God consists in, and with good reason: he is loath to speculate on such matters in writing. In fact, much of Book One of the *Guide* is devoted to showing that knowledge of God is, in principle, beyond human capacity. This is surely one of the 'deliberate contradictions' that Maimonides has introduced into the work.
38. For a discussion of the relationship between the practical and intellectual virtues in Maimonides, see Weiss, *Maimonides' Ethics.*
39. This is the standard Aristotelian account; see *On the Soul* 429^a14 ff., 429^b20, 431^b17–18. See *The Guide of the Perplexed*, I. 68.
40. Ibid. I. 68, i. 163–4.
41. Ibid. I. 70, i. 173–4.
42. *Mishneh Torah*, 'Hilchot Mezuzah', 6: 13.
43. Ibid. 8: 5.
44. See e.g. Sirat, *A History of Jewish Philosophy in the Middle Ages*, 170: 'It seems that if no Maimonidean text states his position [on the individual immortality of the soul] without ambivalence, this was because he inclined towards the solution of non-individual survival, a conclusion he could not postulate openly in writing.' See also Blumberg, 'The Problem of Immortality in Avicenna, Maimonides and St. Thomas Aquinas'; and Finkelstein, 'The Jewish Doctrine of Human Immortality', 31–4. Tamar Rudavsky, in fact, insists that for Maimonides there is no individuality or personal identity for the immortal soul. 'Like the Active Intellect, this soul has no personal features. But given that there are no personal features, it follows that immortal, incorporeal souls cannot be individuated . . . immortal souls are not individuated after death' (*Time Matters*, 179). She argues that Maimonides opts, in fact, for the Averroist view that postmortem 'all immaterial souls form a united whole'.
45. Gersonides explicitly contrasts his own views on the immortality of the soul not only with those of Alexander and Averroes, but also with those of Themistius, a 4th-century Aristotelian commentator.

46. Levi ben Gershom, *The Wars of the Lord*, I. 1 (cited by book, chapter, and section), i. 109. I use the Leipzig edition of the original Hebrew, *Sefer Milchamot Hashem* (1866), along with Feldman's critical apparatus in the back of his translation noting the faulty readings of that edition.
47. Ibid. I. 1–4.
48. Ibid. I. 3, i. 121.
49. Ibid. I. 5.
50. Feldman calls it the 'psychobiological capacity for knowledge'; see ibid. 75. See also Davidson, 'Gersonides on the Material and the Active Intellects', 195–205.
51. Gersonides does not actually use the term 'laws of nature', and it is a somewhat anachronistic phrase to use in this context. However, it does capture part of what it is that the human intellect grasps through the Agent Intellect, i.e., the principles governing the active order of things in nature.
52. *The Wars of the Lord*, V. 2. iv.
53. For Gersonides, then, there are eight primary spheres. There are also secondary spheres associated with each primary sphere to help explain the complexity of its motion. See ibid. V. 3. For a discussion of Gersonides' cosmology, see Goldstein, 'Preliminary Remarks on Levi ben Gershom's Contributions to Cosmology'; Freudenthal, 'Cosmogénie et physique chez Gersonide'; Davidson, 'Gersonides on the Material and Active Intellects'; and Touati, *La Pensée philosophique et théologique de Gersonide*, pt. IV.
54. There are, in fact, fifty separate intellects, corresponding to all the primary and secondary celestial spheres.
55. *The Guide of the Perplexed*, II. 4, ii. 259.
56. See *The Wars of the Lord*, VI. 1. viii; V. 3. viii.
57. Gersonides believes that there is a class of events that escapes this cosmic determinism, namely, the free choices (*bechirot*) of rational agents; see ibid. IV.
58. While there can be no question of the Aristotelian nature of Gersonides' cosmology and epistemology, Feldman points out some striking Plotinian strains in Gersonides' account of the Agent Intellect; see 'Platonic Themes in Gersonides' Doctrine of the Agent Intellect'.
59. *The Wars of the Lord*, II. 2, i. 34–5.
60. Ibid. V. 3. 13, iii. 185.
61. Ibid. V. 3. 13, iii. 188–9. Each of the superior separate intellects has a partial knowledge of this plan, corresponding to the contributing influence that its own sphere exerts on the sublunary realm.

62. Gersonides says that the Agent Intellect is 'the giver of forms' (ibid. I. 6). He is following Maimonides here; see *The Guide of the Perplexed*, II. 12. It is unclear, however, whether these forms 'emanate' from the Agent Intellect directly and immediately, or it generates them through some material intermediary; see *The Wars of the Lord*, v. 5. Davidson argues for the latter; see 'Gersonides on the Material and Active Intellects', 236–8.
63. *The Wars of the Lord*, I. 6, i. 152.
64. Ibid. I. 6, i. 151.
65. Ibid. v. 3. 4, iii. 135.
66. Ibid. v. 3. 9.
67. Ibid. v. 3. 13, iii. 189.
68. Ibid. v. 13. The 'blueprint' analogy is from Feldman's introduction, ibid. i. 82.
69. Since the Agent Intellect emanates from the higher separate intellects, it includes their knowledge of their respective domains as well; see ibid. v. 13.
70. Gersonides uses a Hebrew transliteration of the Greek term *nomos*; ibid. v. 3. 13, iii. 186; *Sefer Milchamot Hashem*, 286.
71. *The Wars of the Lord*, I. 13. See Davidson, 'Gersonides on the Material and Active Intellects', 205–39; and Touati, *La Pensée philosophique et théologique de Gersonide*, pt. VI, ch. 1.
72. Touati compares it to the functioning of the doctrine of the 'vision in God' in Malebranche; see *La Pensée philosophique et théologique de Gersonide*, 425.
73. *The Wars of the Lord*, I. 10, i. 204.
74. See Touati, *La Pensée philosophique et théologique de Gersonide*, 413–23.
75. *The Wars of the Lord*, I. 6, i. 150. Davidson rejects the abstraction model of just how the material intellect, with the aid of the Agent Intellect, is supposed to generate knowledge of forms. He also rejects the emanation model and the literal illumination models. His conclusion, with which I agree, is that Gersonides simply 'leaves us in the dark' on this matter; see 'Gersonides on the Material and Active Intellects', 247.
76. *The Wars of the Lord*, I. 10, i. 205. Gersonides insists that the Agent Intellect operates not on the sensible object or its sensory image; the image itself does not become intelligible. Rather, the Agent Intellect works on the material intellect and 'moves' it by means of the sense image; see ibid. I. 10, i. 206–7.
77. Feldman, 'Gersonides on the Possibility of Conjunction with the Agent Intellect', 117–18.

78. The phrase is Touati's; see *La Pensée philosophique et théologique de Gersonide*, v. 1.
79. *The Wars of the Lord*, I. 10, i. 206. Gersonides is careful to stress, however, that this does not imply that the Agent Intellect itself is known by the material intellect. In fact, we can never fully achieve the kind of science contained in the Agent Intellect; see ibid. I. 6–7.
80. It is also a kind of divine providence, that is, the 'special providence' whereby the intellectually perfected are enabled to navigate successfully through nature's vicissitudes; see ibid. IV.
81. Ibid. I. 11, i. 212.
82. Ibid. I. 13, i. 223.
83. Feldman, in his introduction to book I, ibid. i. 72.
84. Ibid. I. 11, i. 212.
85. Ibid. I. 11, i. 213.
86. See the *Long Commentary on De Anima*, book III, texts 4 and 5. For a useful study, see Ivry, 'Averroës on Intellection and Conjunction'. Averroes' views are notoriously difficult to interpret, and I have relied as much on Gersonides' summary of his views as on my own reading of his text.
87. *The Wars of the Lord*, I. 4, i. 131.
88. Ibid. I. 13, i. 224.
89. Ibid. I. 13, i. 224–5.
90. Ibid. I. 13, i. 224.
91. Gersonides' own views on individuation may pose another problem for distinguishing and personalizing the acquired intellect after death. He insists that 'numerical differentiation accrues to essences as the result of matter; but when essences are construed as abstracted from matter they cannot be conceived as being enumerated at all' (ibid. I. 6, i. 156). Why would not the same principle apply to the abstract body of knowledge that constitutes the acquired intellect? Is matter also necessary for its individuation?
92. Touati appears to have no problem with Gersonides' account on this score. He simply notes that 'each human intellect preserves its individuality in immortality . . . each person is a monad with its own personal apperception' (*La Pensée philosophique et théologique de Gersonide*, 441). But what is lacking is precisely a clear explanation of such apperception!
93. *The Wars of the Lord*, IV. 6, ii. 182–3.
94. See Gersonides' account of providence, ibid. IV.

95. Ibid. I. 13, i. 224–5.
96. Ibid. IV. 6, ii. 197.

Chapter 5

1. Ep. 72.
2. One of the explicit aims of the *Meditations on First Philosophy: Wherein are Demonstrated the Existence of God and the Distinction of Soul from Body*, as enshrined in the work's subtitle, is to establish that the human soul is immortal, although its main purpose is to provide the metaphysical and epistemological foundations for the new mechanistic science.
3. Wolfson's *The Philosophy of Spinoza* is the most exhaustive study of the rich influences on Spinoza's *Ethics.*
4. I offer this summary account of the *Ethics* only to provide context for my discussion of his views on the eternity of the mind. It would digress too much from my aim to argue at length for each and every aspect of this summary, as the interpretation of Spinoza's metaphysics is subject to great scholarly controversy.
5. Ep. 9, G iv. 43–4; C 194–5.
6. Ip17s1.
7. Ip32.
8. But see Curley and Walski, 'Spinoza's Necessitarianism Reconsidered', who argue that while the infinite series of finite events is absolutely necessary as a whole, any single finite event in itself is only 'relatively necessary' (i.e., relative to some antecedent finite events).
9. Ip25c.
10. See Ipp23–8. A good analysis and interpretation of the causal orders of nature, and particularly how the eternal and infinite modes relate to the particular ones, is in Curley, *Spinoza's Metaphysics* and *Behind the Geometrical Method.*
11. Preface to Part Four.
12. Ip29s.
13. But see Cover, 'Spinoza's Extended Substance', who argues that Spinoza's Extension is not necessarily an essence itself but the 'instantiation of an essence'.
14. IIp7s.
15. IVp39.
16. Second Set of Replies, in *Œuvres de Descartes*, vii. 161.

17. There is a fundamental ambiguity in Descartes's definition of substance as 'a thing which exists in such a way as to depend on no other thing for its existence'. Strictly speaking, the term applies only to God; or, as Descartes puts it, the term 'does not apply univocally to God and his creatures'. It does, however, 'apply univocally to mind and to body', since these depend only on God for their existence; see *Principles of Philosophy*, I. 51–2.
18. This has led Curley to claim that Spinoza's view on the nature of the mind is a kind of 'materialism'; see *Behind the Geometrical Method*, 74–8.
19. Second Set of Replies, in *Œuvres de Descartes*, vii. 153.
20. Bennett, *A Study of Spinoza's Ethics*, 357, 372. He adds that 'I don't think that the final three doctrines [of Part Five] can be rescued. The only attempts at complete salvage that I have encountered have been unintelligible to me and poorly related to what Spinoza actually wrote . . . After three centuries of failure to profit from it, the time has come to admit that this part of the *Ethics* has nothing to teach us and is pretty certainly worthless . . . this material is valueless.' Either Bennett is intentionally overstating his case, or he fails to understand the import of the entire work.
21. Curley, *Behind the Geometric Method*, 84.
22. Hampshire, *Spinoza*, 175.
23. Curley, *Behind the Geometric Method*, 84–6.
24. Morrison, 'Spinoza on the Self, Personal Identity and Immortality'.
25. Yovel, *Spinoza and Other Heretics*, i: *The Marrano of Reason*, 170. Yovel, however, goes too far in limiting the eternity of the mind to what can be experienced in this life. See also Moreau, *Spinoza: L'expérience et l'éternité*: 'Il faut faire violence au texte pour y lire au premier plan une doctrine de l'immortalité de l'âme. Cela n'exlut pas une certaine forme d'immortalité dans le système—celle qui correspondrait à une survie de l'entendement sans imagination; mais elle a une signification limitée et spécifique, et il est impossible qu'elle épuise le sens du mot éternité. En tout cas elle ne concerne pas le totalité de l'âme: elle ne peut donc être assimilée à la conception religieuse traditionelle' (p. 535).
26. This form of the distinction between two views on the immortality of the soul is borrowed from Wolfson, *The Philosophy of Spinoza*, ii. 289–90.
27. Donagan, 'Spinoza's Proof of Immortality', 252. See also his *Spinoza*, ch. 10.
28. As I argue in the next chapter, the desire to 'rescue' for Spinoza a 'doctrine of immortality' is misguided, and represents a fundamental misunderstanding of Spinoza's major project.

29. Rudavsky, *Time Matters*, 181, 186.
30. Wolfson, *The Philosophy of Spinoza*, ii. 310–11.
31. Ibid. ii. 295.
32. Ibid. ii. 323. Wolfson has in mind here, in particular, Uriel da Costa. But as we shall see in the next chapter, Spinoza was, in fact, in agreement with da Costa on the question of immortality.
33. Ibid. ii. 295.
34. As Moreau notes, 'Spinoza distingue très rigoureusement ces deux notions'; see *Spinoza: L'expérience et l'éternité*, 534–6.
35. Numerous other authors attribute to Spinoza, as Wolfson does, an account of personal immortality. Some argue that Spinoza simply worked hard to accommodate such a doctrine into his own metaphysical schema and language, to give a Spinozistic spin to it. In his book *The God of Spinoza* Mason seems to take just this position (ch. 10). So does Feldman, who, in his work on Gersonides, insists that for Spinoza 'immortality is individually differentiated' (*The Wars of the Lord*, 76). Other scholars, while noting that Part Five of the *Ethics* speaks only of the *eternity* of the mind, insist that far from wishing to deny the personal immortality of the soul, Spinoza just wanted to stress its persistence outside of time rather than its mere everlastingness in time (Hardin, 'Spinoza on Immortality and Time'); while still others, agreeing that for Spinoza there is personal survival after death, argue on the contrary that in fact the eternity of the mind should be understood as a kind of sempiternity (Kneale, 'Eternity and Sempiternity'; Donagan, 'Spinoza's Proof of Immortality'). Finally, there are those who argue that Spinoza did not want to deny the immortality of the personal soul, but only that these immortal souls would be individuated in the same way as they are individuated in this life, that is, by way of their bodies (Harris, 'Spinoza's Theory of Human Immortality').

    Even Bennett, despite his antipathy to this part of the *Ethics*, tries to understand why Spinoza would cling to a doctrine of immortality. Was he 'terrified of extinction?', he asks. Bennett concludes that 'some passive affects—of fear or hope or excitement—clung stubbornly to the man and overcame his reason' (*A Study of Spinoza's Ethics*, 375).
36. This is not entirely definitive, since the *Short Treatise* exists only in two Dutch manuscripts that were found in the 19th century, neither of which was Spinoza's own manuscript. Spinoza undoubtedly composed the original text in Latin, and what we have are copies of an original Dutch

translation (probably done by one of his friends). We simply do not know for certain if the Latin original used *immortalitas* or *immortalis*, although it is hard to believe that it did not.

37. G i.103; C 141.
38. This is from a 'note' that appears at the beginning of the second part of the treatise; G i. 52; C 96.
39. I would argue that it is the latter, since the language that Spinoza uses in summarizing the main points of Book Two of the *Short Treatise* are very similar to the propositions he will argue for in the *Ethics*: what survives the death of the body is 'an Idea, knowledge, etc. of our body in the thinking thing, as there is now' (G i. 52; C 95).
40. Vp41s.
41. See Moreau, *Spinoza: L'expérience et l'éternité*, 535.
42. Vp23s.
43. Id8.
44. Some commentators have argued that the eternity at stake here *is* just a sempiternity, or what Donagan calls 'omnitemporality'; see Kneale, 'Eternity and Sempiternity', and Donagan, 'Spinoza's Proof of Immortality'. Most, however, have—correctly, I believe—seen that what Spinoza is talking about is a complete atemporality, or timelessness; see Harris, 'Spinoza's Theory of Human Immortality'; Hampshire, *Spinoza*; Moreau, *Spinoza: L'expérience et l'éternité*, 536; Steinberg, 'Spinoza's Theory of the Eternity of the Human Mind'; and Joachim, *A Study of Spinoza Ethics* 298.
45. It is absolutely crucial to see that there are two distinct kinds of eternity; see Moreau, *Spinoza: L'expérience et l'éternité*, 534–9. A failure to distinguish them can lead one into various kinds of misreadings of Spinoza's views on the eternity of the mind (such as is found in Harris, 'Spinoza's Theory of Human Immortality'; and Hardin, 'Spinoza on Immortality and Time').
46. See *Ethics* II, G ii. 99–100; C 460.
47. The determinate study of the various affects in a human being is the subject of Part Three.
48. In fact, this aspect of the mind is eternal *because* the mode of extension of which it is an expression is eternal.
49. IIp13s.
50. Vp13s.
51. The intrinsic complexity of the body is reflected in the variety and multiplicity of ideas that make up the human mind; see IIpp11–13.

52. See Moreau, *Spinoza: L'expérience et l'éternité*, 537–8.
53. It is his failure to recognize this second variety of eternity for the mind that is responsible for Bennett's failure to make sense of Spinoza's views here. Bennett is troubled by the fact that Spinoza believes both that the eternal mind is nothing but the (unchanging) idea of the eternal essense of the body *and* that 'how much of my mind is eternal depends upon some facts about my conduct and my condition'; in other words, that we can *increase* our share of eternity. Since Bennett recognizes only the eternity of the mind as the idea of the unchanging essence of the body, there is (he argues) 'no provision for my increasing how much of my mind is eternal, unless I can change my body's essence, whatever that would mean. But now we are told that how much of my mind is eternal depends on what thinking I do, as though I could work at enlarging the eternal part of my mind' (*A Study of Spinoza's Ethics*, 361–2). In fact, that is *exactly* what Spinoza thinks we can do, by increasing our share of adequate ideas, as I show.
54. See IVpp20–6.
55. IIp29c.
56. This reading of what the second kind of knowledge involves is adopted by Margaret Wilson, 'Spinoza's Theory of Knowledge', 116–119; and Henry Allison, *Benedict de Spinoza*, chapter 4, section 2.
57. Yovel, *Spinoza and Other Heretics*, i: *The Marrano of Reason*, 156. Thus, for Yovel there is no difference in content between the second and third kinds of knowledge: 'No additional information is gained through the third kind of knowledge . . . All the information we need and can possess of the object of our inquiry has already been supplied by *ratio*.' Both kinds of knowledge express 'the same fundamental information' (pp. 165–6).
58. IIp44.
59. See IIp28.
60. IIp40s2.
61. Vp25.
62 G ii. 36–7; C 41.
63 G i. 132; C 230.
64. Vp24.
65. TTP, ch. 4, Giii. 59–60; S 51.
66. IIp46.
67. IIp47.
68. Vp38s.

69. They have been remarked upon in a fairly cursory way by Wolfson; see *The Philosophy of Spinoza*, ch. 20, sect. 3.
70. IIp13c. Morrison offers a good defense of this point in 'Spinoza on the Self, Personal Identity and Immortality'.
71. IIp13.
72. Wolfson, *The Philosophy of Spinoza*, ii. 318.
73. I take this to be the import of IVp35.
74. IVp39s.
75. IIp23.
76. It also makes it hard to see how Donagan can sustain his claim that for Spinoza the eternal mind will have a conscious sense of self. Donagan insists, as well, that memory—which, he agrees, ends with the demise of the body—is not essential for this self-identity; see 'Spinoza's Proof of Immortality'.
77. Vp21.
78. Vp34s.
79. Donagan, 'Spinoza's Proof of Immortality', 251.
80. Ibid. 252. Rudavsky takes a similar tack. Eternal minds, she insists, are to be individuated by the ideas of the body that constitute them.

    On Spinoza's theory of individuation, part of what makes me who I am is that I am affected by other individuals; individuation on this model turns out to be relational, incorporating both material and formal elements . . . [it] is bodies that are the source of identification of persons: The ideas that make up an individual mind acquire their identity by being ideas of a particular body. This identification with both remains embedded in the mind after the 'death of the body'. (*Time Matters*, 185)

    What Rudavsky does not take note of, however, is the fact that such relational elements — the body's causal relations to external bodies — belong to the body only in duration, in its spatial and temporal relationships to other bodies. They necessarily come to an end with the demise of the body and the termination of its durational existence. Thus, they are not available to individuate (the essences of) bodies postmortem.
81. IVp39.
82. This seems to be Hampshire's reading, when he notes that 'insofar as I do attain genuine knowledge, my individuality as a particular thing disappears and my mind becomes so far united with God or Nature conceived under the attribute of Thought' (*Spinoza*, 175).
83. IIp11c.

84. Vp23s.
85. Wolfson, for example, takes note of the precedents in Maimonides and Gersonides for Spinoza's views on the eternity of the mind, but he does not see either how much farther Spinoza goes than his predecessors (since he believes that for Spinoza there is still a personal immortality) nor how his theory is the logical extension of their accounts; see *The Philosophy of Spinoza*, ii. 317–18.

Chapter 6

1. *Phaedrus* 233c.
2. Ibid. 246a–b, 253c–e.
3. This is also, of course, the main lesson of the *Republic*.
4. *Ethics* IV, Preface.
5. IIIp13s.
6. IIIp28.
7. IIIp59s.
8. Vp20s.
9. IVp4.
10. Vp6s.
11. Although Spinoza certainly is critical of the Stoics in important respects; see *Ethics* V, Preface.
12. *Ethics* IV, Appendix, G ii. 276; C 594.
13. Vp42.
14. See Maimonides, *The Guide of the Perplexed*, III. 51. For a discussion of the agreement between Maimonides and Spinoza on this, see Harvey, 'A Portrait of Spinoza as a Maimonidean', 161–2. Harvey notes—rightly, I believe—that 'the view that the knowledge of "the actions" of God *is* knowledge of nature is typically Maimonidean' (p. 162).
15. IVp67.
16. IIIp18s2.
17. Seneca, *Epistulae Morales ad Lucilium*, Letter V.
18. TTP, Preface, G iii. 5–6; S 1–2.
19. TTP, Preface, G iii. 6–7; S 51.
20. One example would be the attempts in the 1650s by the stricter leaders of the Dutch Reformed Church to regulate behavior on the sabbath. For a discussion of the political context of Spinoza's *Theological–Political Treatise*, see Nadler, *Spinoza: A Life*, ch. 10.
21. G ii. 78–9; C 440–1.

22. *Ethics* I, Appendix, G ii. 81; C 443–4.
23. IVp67.
24. Gersonides, in fact, does claim that God's knowledge does not extend to particulars—and especially to the free acts of moral agents; see *The Wars of the Lord*, III.
25. Spinoza does say that God is 'free', but only because God 'exists from the necessity of his nature and acts from the necessity of his nature' (Ip17), not because God is endowed with 'freedom of the will'.
26. I believe that for Spinoza there is, outside of human projects, no teleology or purposiveness, either within nature or for nature as a whole. But see Garrett, 'Teleology in Spinoza and Early Modern Rationalism', for an argument that Spinoza does, in fact, introduce teleology within nature.
27. *Ethics* I, Appendix.
28. *Ethics* IV, Preface, G ii. 207; C 545.
29. Ibid. G ii. 208; C 545.
30. See e.g. IVp14.
31. IVp28.
32. See the discussions by Curley, *Behind the Geometrical Method*, 119–24; and Allison, *Benedict de Spinoza*, 140–4.
33. The place to start, as in all questions about influences upon Spinoza, is Harry Wolfson, in his *The Philosophy of Spinoza*.
34. *Sifre* on Deuteronomy, sect. 32, f. 73*b*.
35. *The Book of Beliefs and Opinions*, Treatise V, ch. 1.
36. Ibid., ch. 2.
37. This, at least, is his claim in the *Book of Beliefs and Opinions*. He offers a more complex account of this problem in his *Commentary on the Book of Job*.
38. For Maimonides on providence, see *The Guide of the Perplexed*, III. 17 and III. 51. There is an apparent ambiguity in Maimonides' account, however, although Touati thinks it is fully resolvable ('Les Deux Théories de Maimonide sur la Providence').
39. This is not Gersonides' only discussion of divine providence and the problem of evil. The topic is also treated in a very similar way in his *Commentary on the Book of Job*. See Touati, *La Pensée philosophique et théologique de Gersonide*, pts. 6 and 7. For a survey of Jewish views on this issue, see Touati, 'La Problème du mal et la providence'.
40. *The Wars of the Lord*, IV. 6, ii. 182.

41. Ibid.
42. Ibid. IV. 6, ii. 183.
43. Ibid. I. 13, i. 224–5.
44. Ibid. IV. 6, ii. 197. As noted above, this is not the only kind of theodicy found in Jewish thought. Many rabbis, believing that divine justice manifests itself in the world we live in, stressed the importance of punishment and reward for sin and righteousness in this life. It has been argued that Gersonides' views, in fact, go against rabbinic tradition; see Kellner, 'Gersonides, Providence and the Rabbinic Tradition'.
45. Vp42.
46. Vp41s.
47. See also the discussion of this question using some of the same sources in Kasher and Biderman, 'Why was Spinoza Excommunicated?', 111–14.
48. Revah, *Spinoza et Juan de Prado*, 64.
49. See Nadler, *Spinoza: A Life*, chs. 4 and 5.
50. I believe he began his Latin and other studies with the Jesuit Franciscus van den Enden around 1654. He may have begun reading Maimonides and Gersonides with Mortera, in the rabbi's yeshiva, even earlier than that; see ibid.

Chapter 7

1. Colerus, in Freudenthal, *Die Lebengeschichte Spinoza's*, 56.
2. One painting is in the Detroit Institute of Arts, and appears on the cover of this book. The other version—a darker and more brooding image—is in the Staatliche Kunstsammlungen, Dresden.
3. *Mishneh Torah*, 'Hilchot Yesodi Hatorah', 5: 3.
4. *Shulchan Arukh*, *Yoreh De'ah*, 157: 1.
5. *Sanhedrin* 11: 1.
6. The event, in fact, undoubtedly contributed to the three congregations' decision in 1638 to merge into one, Talmud Torah, with a ranked cadre of rabbis. The best and most thorough study of the debate over eternal punishment in the 1630s is Altmann's 'Eternality of Punishment'. This article contains both a long discussion of the issues around the debate and the three central texts themselves. I am greatly indebted to Altmann's work here for my summary of the debate.
7. See ibid., Text A, lines 103–6.
8. See ibid. 18.

9. Their argument here was rather disingenuous, as their own belief in eternal salvation was no less 'Christian' than Mortera's position.
10. Ibid. 15.
11. Rosh Hashanah 17*a*.
12. Altmann, 'Eternality of Punishment', Text C, sect. 3, lines 25–33.
13. Ibid., lines 53–156.
14. Ibid., Text A, lines 95–6.
15. Ibid., Text C, sect. 3, lines 1–25.
16. Ibid., sect. 2, lines 9–47.
17. Da Costa himself provides us with this account of his life and beliefs, in his *Exemplar Humanae Vitae*, the text of which is found in Osier, *D'Uriel da Costa à Spinoza*. The story of da Costa's life has been investigated most thoroughly by Revah; see esp. 'Du marranisme au judaisme et au déisme: Uriel da Costa et sa famille'. See also the introduction to da Costa, *Examination of Pharisaic Traditions*, by Salomon and Sassoon.
18. Gebhardt, *Die Schriften des Uriel da Costa*, 59–62.
19. Ibid. 154–5.
20. Modena's text is found in Osier, *D'Uriel da Costa à Spinoza*, 253–92.
21. Gebhardt, *Die Schriften des Uriel da Costa*, 124.
22. Da Costa, *Examination of Pharisaic Traditions*, 343.
23. Ibid. 311.
24. Ibid. 312.
25. Ibid. 316.
26. Ibid. 321.
27. Ibid., Part 2, ch. 3.
28. Ibid. 332.
29. It is clear that Wolfson's thesis that Spinoza composed his views as an effort to combat da Costa's and defend the traditional rabbinic doctrine is entirely untenable (*The Philosophy of Spinoza*, 323–5).
30. The question of da Costa's influence on Spinoza is a contentious one. Revah believes that Spinoza reflected much on da Costa and his ideas; see 'Du marranisme au judaisme et au déisme'. Gebhardt, on the other hand, is more skeptical; see *Die Schriften des Uriel da Costa*, pp. xxxiii–ix. See also the discussions by Yovel, *Spinoza and Other Heretics*, i: *The Marrano of Reason*, 42–51; and Albiac, *La Synagogue vide*, pt. II, ch. 1.
31. An English translation of da Silva's treatise is in da Costa, *Examination of the Pharisaic Traditions*, 429–551. For a discussion of the da Silva–da Costa polemic, see Albiac, *La Synagogue vide*, 293–300.

32. Da Silva, *Treatise on Immortality*, in da Costa, *Examination of the Pharisaic Traditions*, 435.
33. Ibid. 443.
34. From Rabbi Modena, for example; see Salomon and Sassoon's introduction, ibid. 29–32.
35. Gebhardt, *Die Schriften des Uriel da Costa*, 181–3.
36. Saperstein has argued, however, that Mortera's treatise was composed not as a response to da Costa, but rather as a 'discursive and encyclopedic' treatment of an issue of great importance to Mortera, although 'it undoubtedly contained material directly relevant to the da Costa conflict'; see 'Saul Levi Morteira's *Treatise on the Immortality of the Soul*', 140–1.
37. Ibid.
38. By Sabbetai Bass, *Siftei Yeshenim* (Amsterdam, 1680); see Saperstein, 'Saul Levi Morteira's *Treatise on the Immortality of the Soul*', 131.
39. Da Costa, *Exemplar Humanae Vitae*, in *Examination of the Pharisaic Traditions*, 558.
40. At least two copies survived. One of them ended up with the Spanish Grand Inquisitor and was put on the Index in 1632; see Solomon and Sassoon's introduction to da Costa, *Examination of the Pharisaic Tradition*, 17.
41. See ibid. 18 for a quote from a letter that the Amsterdam Jewish leaders wrote to Rabbi Jacob Halevi in Venice.
42. The text of Monsanto's deposition is in Revah, 'Aux origines de la rupture Spinozienne: Nouveaux documents', 395.
43. See e.g. Revah, *Spinoza et Juan de Prado*, 45; and, discussing Prado's response to Monsanto's deposition, 'Aux origines de la rupture Spinozienne: Nouveaux documents', 379.
44. Revah, 'Aux origines de la rupture Spinozienne: Nouveaux documents', 402.
45. On Ribera, see Kaplan, *From Christianity to Judaism*, 142–5.
46. In addition to Mortera, Aboab, d'Aguilar, and Menasseh, David Pardo was also a member of the Amsterdam rabbinate. But from what I can tell he was not a major intellectual presence in the community, as the others were. In 1639, when the original congregations merged, he was made director of funerals and supervisor of the burial grounds at Ouderkerk.
47. Both Rabbi Aboab and Rabbi d'Aguilar did depart for a time (from 1642 to 1654) to lead the congregation of expatriates in Recife, Brazil, while

Menasseh spent the last two years of his life (1655–7) living in England trying to arrange for the readmission of the Jews into that country.

48. See the collection of his sermons first published in Amsterdam in 1645 by his disciples under the title *Giva'at Shaul*; I have used the edition published in Warsaw in 1912. *Vayelech* appears on pp. 288–303. The substance of this sermon has been discussed above in connection with Mortera's 1624 treatise.
49. See Kaplan, *From Christianity to Judaism*, 110–14.
50. Quoted in Roth, *A Life of Menasseh ben Israel*, 53.
51. Or so Albiac argues; see *La Synagogue vide*, 300–25.
52. *De la resurreccion de los muertos*, quoted in Albiac, *La Synagogue vide*, 319.
53. See Roth, *A Life of Menasseh ben Israel*, 97–9. A modern Hebrew edition of the *Nishmat Chayim* was published in Jerusalem in 1995.
54. However, Menasseh was out of the country at the time of Spinoza's *cherem*, working for the readmission of the Jews to England.
55. 'Why was Spinoza Excommunicated', 110–11.
56. Menasseh ben Israel, *Nishmat Chayim*, Introduction.
57. See Huussen, 'The Legal Position of Sephardi Jews in Holland, *circa* 1600'. What is interesting is that while the States did not incorporate into their proclamation many of the restrictive recommendations made in 1619 by the jurist Hugo Grotius, whom they had commissioned to come up with a set of conditions for allowing Jews to settle and practice openly, they apparently did take into account his demand that (as he put it in his *Remonstrantie nopend de ordre dije in de landen van Hollandt ende Westvriesland dijent gestelt op de Joden*) the Jews hold that 'after death there will be another life in which the just are rewarded and the evil punished'; see Meijer, 'Hugo Grotius' *Remonstrantie*'.

Conclusion

1. *Nicomachean Ethics* 1094^{b}.
2. According to Lucas; see Freudenthal, *Die Lebensgeschichte Spinoza's*, 8.

Bibliography

Akkerman, Fokke, *et al.*, *Spinoza. Korte Geschriften* (Amsterdam: Wereldbibliotheek, 1982).

Albiac, Gabriel, *La Synagogue vide* (Paris: Presses Universitaires de France, 1994).

Allison, Henry E., *Benedict de Spinoza: An Introduction* (New Haven: Yale University Press, 1987).

Alquié, Ferdinand, *Le Rationalisme de Spinoza* (Paris: Presses Universitaires de France, 1981).

Altmann, Alexander, 'Eternality of Punishment: A Theological Controversy within the Amsterdam Rabbinate in the Thirties of the Seventeenth Century', *Proceedings of the American Academy for Jewish Research*, 40 (1972), 1–88.

Baer, Yitzhak, *A History of the Jews in Christian Spain* (Philadelphia: Jewish Publication Society, 1966).

Baron, S. W., *A Social and Religious History of the Jews*, vol. xv (New York: Columbia University Press, 1952).

Belinfante, Judith C. E., *et al.*, *The Esnoga: A Monument to Portuguese-Jewish Culture* (Amsterdam: D'Arts, 1991).

Bennett, Jonathan, *A Study of Spinoza's Ethics* (Indianapolis: Hackett, 1984).

Blumberg, Harry, 'The Problem of Immortality in Avicenna, Maimonides and St. Thomas', *Harry Austryn Wolfson Jubilee Volume*, vol. i (Jerusalem: American Academy of Jewish Research, 1965), 165–85.

Bodian, Miriam, 'Amsterdam, Venice, and the Marrano Diaspora in the Seventeenth Century', *Dutch Jewish History*, 2 (1989), 47–66.

—— *Hebrews of the Portuguese Nation: Conversos and Community in Early Modern Amsterdam* (Bloomington: Indiana University Press, 1998).

Bouillier, Francisque, *Histoire de la philosophie Cartésienne*, 2 vols. (Paris, 1868).

Browne, Lewis, *Blessed Spinoza* (New York: Macmillan, 1932).

Brugmans, H., and A. Frank, *Geschiedenis der Joden in Nederland* (Amsterdam: no publisher, 1940).

BRYKMAN, GENEVIÈVE, *La Judéité de Spinoza* (Paris: J. Vrin, 1972).

CARO, JOSEPH, *Shulchan Arukh*, standard edn. with comm. (Vilna, 1911).

CHARLES, R. H., *The Book of Enoch* (London: SPCK, 1917).

—— *Eschatology: The Doctrine of a Future Life in Israel, Judaism, and Christianity* (New York: Schocken Books, 1963).

CODE, ALAN, 'Aristotle, Searle and the Mind–Body Problem', in E. Lepore and R. Van Gulick (eds.), *John Searle and his Critics* (Oxford: Blackwell, 1991).

COHEN, MARK (ed.), *The Autobiography of a Seventeenth-Century Rabbi* (Princeton: Princeton University Press, 1988).

COHEN, ROBERT, '*Memoria para os siglos futuros*: Myth and Memory on the Beginnings of the Amsterdam Sephardi Community', *Jewish History*, 2 (1987), 67–72.

COVER, JAN, 'Spinoza's Extended Substance', in R. Gennaro and C. Hueneman (eds.), *New Essays on the Rationalists* (Oxford: Oxford University Press, 1999).

CURLEY, EDWIN M., *Behind the Geometrical Method: A Reading of Spinoza's Ethics* (Princeton: Princeton University Press, 1988).

—— 'Notes on a Neglected Masterpiece, II: The *Theological–Political Treatise* as a Prolegomenon to the *Ethics*', in J. A. Cover and M. Kulstad (eds.), *Central Themes in Early Modern Philosophy* (Indianapolis: Hackett, 1990).

—— *Spinoza's Metaphysics: An Essay in Interpretation* (Cambridge, Mass.: Harvard University Press, 1969).

—— and GREGORY WALSKI, 'Spinoza's Necessitarianism Reconsidered', in R. Gennaro and C. Hueneman (eds.), *New Essays on the Rationalists* (Oxford: Oxford University Press, 1999).

DA COSTA, URIEL, *Examination of the Pharisaic Traditions*, trans. H. P. Salomon and I. S. D. Sassoon (Leiden: Brill, 1993).

D'ANCONA, J., 'Komst der Marranen in Noord Nederland: De Portugese Gemeenten te Amsterdam tot de Vereniging', in H. Brugmans and A. Frank (eds.), *Geschiedenis der Joden in Nederland* (Amsterdam: no publisher, 1940).

DAVIDSON, HERBERT, 'Gersonides on the Material and Active Intellects', in G. Freudenthal (ed.), *Studies on Gersonides* (Leiden: Brill, 1992).

DE BARRIOS, MIGUEL (DANIEL LEVI), *Triumpho del govierno popular* (Amsterdam, *c.*1683–4).

DE DEUGD, CORNELIUS (ed.), *Spinoza's Political and Theological Thought* (Amsterdam: North Holland, 1984).

DESCARTES, RENÉ, *Œuvres de Descartes*, ed. Charles Adam and Paul Tannery, 11 vols. (Paris: Vrin, 1964–75).

DONAGAN, ALAN, *Spinoza* (Chicago: University of Chicago Press, 1988).

—— 'Spinoza's Proof of Immortality', in M. Grene (ed.), *Spinoza: A Collection of Critical Essays* (Notre Dame, Ind.: University of Notre Dame Press, 1974).

DUNIN-BORKOWSKI, STANISLAUS VON, *Der Junge de Spinoza* (Münster: Aschendorffsche Verlagsbuchhandlung, 1910).

—— *Spinoza*, 4 vols. (Münster: Aschendorff, 1933).

FELDMAN, SEYMOUR, 'Gersonides on the Possibility of Conjunction with the Agent Intellect', *Association for Jewish Studies Review*, 3 (1978), 99–120.

—— 'Platonic Themes in Gersonides' Doctrine of the Agent Intellect', in L. E. Goodman (ed.), *Neoplatonism and Jewish Thought* (Albany: SUNY Press, 1992).

FEUER, LEWIS SAMUEL, *Spinoza and the Rise of Liberalism* (Boston: Beacon Press, 1958).

FINKELSTEIN, LOUIS, 'The Beginnings of the Jewish Doctrine of Immortality', in S. Baron (ed.), *Freedom and Reason: Studies in Philosophy and Jewish Culture* (Chicago: University of Chicago Press, 1951).

—— 'The Jewish Doctrine of Human Immortality', *Harvard Divinity School Bulletin* (30 Mar. 1945), 5–34.

FREUDENTHAL, GAD, 'Cosmogénie et physique chez Gersonide', *Revue des Études Juives*, 145 (1986), 294–314.

FREUDENTHAL, J., *Die Lebensgeschichte Spinoza's in Quellenschriften, Urkunden und Nichtamtlichen Nachrichten* (Leipzig: Verlag Von Veit, 1899).

—— *Spinoza. Sein Leben und Seine Lehre* (Stuttgart: Fr. Frommanns Verlag, 1904).

FRIEDMANN, GEORGES, *Leibniz et Spinoza* (Paris: Gallimard, 1962).

FUKS-MANSFIELD, R. G., *De Sefardim in Amsterdam tot 1795* (Hilversum: Historische Vereniging Holland, 1989).

GANS, MOZES H., *Memorbook: History of Dutch Jewry from the Renaissance to 1940*, trans. Arnold J. Pomerans (Baarn: Bosch & Keuning, 1971).

GARRETT, DON, 'Teleology in Spinoza and Early Modern Rationalism', in R. Gennaro and C. Hueneman (eds.), *New Essays on the Rationalists* (Oxford: Oxford University Press, 1999).

GEBHARDT, CARL 'Juan de Prado', *Chronicon Spinozanum*, 3 (1923), 219–91.

—— (ed.), *Die Schriften des Uriel da Costa* (Amsterdam: Curis Societatis Spinozanae, 1922).

GERSONIDES, *See* Levi ben Gershom.

GILLMAN, NEIL, *The Death of Death* (Woodstock, Vt.: Jewish Lights, 1997).

GOLDSTEIN, BERNARD, 'Preliminary Remarks on Levi ben Gershom's Contribution to Cosmology', *Proceedings of the Israeli Academy of Science and Humanities*, 3 (1969), 239–54.

HAMPSHIRE, STUART, *Spinoza* (Harmondsworth: Penguin, 1951).

HARDIN, C. L., 'Spinoza on Immortality and Time', in R. Shanahan and J. Biro (eds.), *Spinoza: New Perspectives* (Norman: University of Oklahoma Press, 1978).

HARRIS, ERROL, 'Spinoza's Theory of Human Immortality', in M. Mandelbaum and E. Freeman (eds.), *Spinoza: Essays in Interpretation* (La Salle, Ill.: Open Court, 1975).

HARTMAN, DAVID, *Maimonides: Torah and Philosophic Quest* (Philadelphia: Jewish Publication Society, 1976).

HARVEY, WARREN ZEV, 'A Portrait of Spinoza as a Maimonidean', *Journal of the History of Philosophy*, 18 (1980), 151–72.

HAYOUN, M., *La Philosophie et la théologie de Moise de Narbonne* (Tübingen: Mohr, 1989).

HESSING, SIEGFRIED, *Speculum Spinozanum 1677–1977* (London: Routledge & Kegan Paul, 1977).

HUBBELING, H. G., *Spinoza* (Baarn: het Wereldvenster, 1978).

—— 'Spinoza's Life: A Synopsis of the Sources and Some Documents', *Giornale Critico della Filosofia Italiana*, 8 (1977), 390–409.

HUNTER, GRAEME (ed.), *Spinoza: The Enduring Questions* (Toronto: University of Toronto Press, 1994).

HUUSSEN, AREND H., 'The Legal Position of Sephardi Jews in Holland, *circa* 1600', *Dutch Jewish History*, 3 (1993), 19–41.

ISRAEL, JONATHAN, 'The Banning of Spinoza's Works in the Dutch Republic (1670–1678)', in W. van Bunge and W. Klever (eds.), *Disguised and Overt Spinozism around 1670* (Leiden: Brill, 1996).

—— *The Dutch Republic: Its Rise, Greatness, and Fall, 1477–1806* (Oxford: Oxford University Press, 1995).

IVRY, ALFRED, 'Averroës on Intellection and Conjunction', *Journal of the American Oriental Society*, 86 (1966), 76–85.

JOACHIM, H. H., *A Study of Spinoza's Ethics* (Oxford: Clarendon Press, 1901).

—— *Spinoza's Tractatus de Intellectus Emendatione* (Oxford: Clarendon Press, 1901).

KAPLAN, YOSEF, *From Christianity to Judaism: The Story of Isaac Orobio de Castro* (Oxford: Oxford University Press, 1989).

—— '"Karaites" in Early Eighteenth-Century Amsterdam', in D. S. Katz and J. Israel (eds.), *Sceptics, Millenarians and Jews* (Leiden: Brill, 1990).

—— 'The Portuguese Jews in Amsterdam: From Forced Conversion to a Return to Judaism', *Studia Rosenthaliana*, 15 (1981), 37–51.

—— 'The Social Functions of the *Herem* in the Portuguese Jewish Community of Amsterdam in the Seventeenth Century', *Dutch Jewish History*, 1 (1984), 111–55.

KASHER, ASA, and SHLOMO BIDERMAN, 'When was Spinoza Banned?', *Studia Rosenthaliana*, 12 (1978), 108–10.

—— —— 'Why was Spinoza Excommunicated?', in D. S. Katz and J. Israel (eds.), *Sceptics, Millenarians, and Jews* (Leiden: Brill, 1990).

KATZ, JACOB, *Tradition and Crisis* (New York: New York University Press, 1993).

KAYSERLING, M., 'Un conflit dans la communauté hispano-portugaise d'Amsterdam—ses conséquences', *Revue des Études Juives*, 43 (1901), 275–6.

KELLNER, MENACHEM, *Dogma in Medieval Jewish Thought: From Maimonides to Abravanel* (Oxford: Oxford University Press, 1986).

—— 'Gersonides, Providence and the Rabbinic Tradition', *Journal of the American Academy of Religion*, 42 (1974), 673–85.

—— *Must a Jew Believe Anything?* (London: Vallentine & Mitchell, 1998).

KISTEMAKER, RENÉE, and TIRTSAH LEVIE (eds.), *Exodo: Portugezen in Amsterdam, 1600–1680* (Amsterdam: Amsterdams Historisch Museum, 1987).

KNEALE, MARTHA, 'Eternity and Sempiternity', in M. Grene (ed.), *Spinoza: A Collection of Critical Essays* (Notre Dame, Ind.: University of Notre Dame Press, 1979).

KOENEN, H. J., *Geschiedenis der Joden in Nederland* (Utrecht, 1843).

KOLAKOWSKI, LESZEK, *Chrétiens sans église* (Paris: NRF/Éditions Gallimard, 1969).

LAGRÉE, JACQUELINE, 'Louis Meyer et la *Philosophia S. Scripturae Interpres*', *Revue des Sciences Philosophiques et Théologiques*, 71 (1987), 31–43.

LEIBNIZ, GOTTFRIED WILHELM, *Die Philosophischen Schriften von Gottfried Wilhelm Leibniz*, ed. C. I. Gerhardt, 7 vols. (Berlin: Weidmann, 1895–90; repr. Hildesheim: Georg Olms, 1978).

—— *Sämtliche Schriften und Briefe*, Deutsche Akademie der Wissenschaften, multiple vols. in 7 series (Darmstadt, Leipzig, Berlin: Akademie Verlag, 1923).

LEVI BEN GERSHOM (GERSONIDES), *Commentary on the Book of Job*, trans. A. Lassen (New York: Bloch, 1946).

—— *Sefer Milchamot Hashem* (Leipzig, 1866).

—— *The Wars of the Lord*, trans. Seymour Feldman, 3 vols. (Philadelphia: Jewish Publication Society, 1984–99).

LEVIE, TIRTSAH, and HENK ZANTKUYL, *Wonen in Amsterdam in de 17de en 18de Eeuw* (Amsterdam: Amsterdams Historisch Museum, 1980).

LEVIN, DAN, *Spinoza: The Young Thinker who Destroyed the Past* (New York: Weybright & Talley, 1970).

LEVINE, RUTH E., and SUSAN W. MORGENSTERN (eds.), *The Jews in the Age of Rembrandt* (Rockville, Md.: The Judaic Museum of the Jewish Community Center of Greater Washington, 1981–2).

LEVY, ZE'EV, *Baruch or Benedict: On Some Jewish Aspects of Spinoza's Philosophy* (New York: Peter Lang, 1989).

—— 'Sur quelques influences Juives dans le développement philosophique du jeune Spinoza', *Revue des Sciences Philosophiques et Théologiques*, 71 (1987), 67–75.

LIEBERMAN, SAUL, 'Some Aspects of Afterlife in Early Rabbinic Literature', *Harry Austryn Wolfson Jubilee Volume*, vol. ii (Jerusalem: American Academy of Jewish Research, 1965).

MAIMONIDES, *See* Moses ben Maimon.

MASON, RICHARD, *The God of Spinoza* (Cambridge: Cambridge University Press, 1997).

MÉCHOULAN, HENRI, *Amsterdam au temps de Spinoza: argent et liberté* (Paris: Presses Universitaires de France, 1990).

—— *Être Juif à Amsterdam au temps de Spinoza* (Paris: Albin Michel, 1991).

—— 'Le *Herem* à Amsterdam et l'excommunication de Spinoza', *Cahiers Spinoza*, 3 (1980), 117–34.

—— 'Quelques remarques sur le marranisme et la rupture Spinoziste', *Studia Rosenthaliana*, 11 (1977), 113–25.

MEIJER, JAAP, *Beeldvorming om Baruch* (Heemstede: self-published, 1986).

—— 'Hugo Grotius' *Remonstrantie*', *Jewish Social Studies*, 17 (1955), 91–104.

MEINSMA, K. O., *Spinoza et son cercle*, trans. S. Roosenberg and J.-P. Osier (Paris: Vrin, 1983).

MELNICK, RALPH, *From Polemics to Apologetics: Jewish–Christian Rapprochement in Seventeenth Century Amsterdam* (Assen: Van Gorcum, 1981).

MENASSEH BEN ISRAEL, *The Hope of Israel*, ed. Henri Méchoulan and Gérard Nahon (Oxford: Oxford University Press, 1987).

—— *Nishmat Chayim* (Jerusalem: Yedid Hasefrim, 1995).

MENDES, DAVID FRANCO, *Memorias do estabelecimento e progresso dos Judeos Portuguezes e Espanhões nesta famosa citade de Amsterdam*, *Studia Rosenthaliana*, 9 (1975).

MICHMAN, JOZEPH, 'Historiography of the Jews in the Netherlands', *Dutch Jewish History*, 1 (1984), 16–22.

—— HARTOG BEEM, and DAN MICHMAN, *PINCHAS: Geschiedenis van de Joodse Gemeenschap in Nederland* (Antwerp: Kluwer, 1989).

MIGNINI, FILIPPO, 'Données et problèmes de la chronologie spinozienne entre 1656 et 1665', *Revue des Sciences Philosophiques et Théologiques*, 71 (1987), 9–21.

MINKIN, JACOB S. (ed.), *The Teachings of Maimonides* (Northvale, NJ: Jason Aronson, 1987).

MOREAU, PIERRE-FRANÇOIS, *Spinoza: L'expérience et l'éternité* (Paris: Presses Universitaires de France, 1994).

MORRISON, JAMES, 'Spinoza on the Self, Personal Identity and Immortality', in G. Hunter (ed.), *Spinoza: The Enduring Questions* (Toronto: University of Toronto Press, 1994).

MORTERA, SAUL LEVI, *Giva'at Shaul* (Amsterdam, 1645).

—— *Traktaat Betreffende de Waarheid van de Wet van Mozes (Tratado da verdade da lei de Moises)*, ed. H. P. Salomon (Braga, 1988).

—— *Tratado da verdade da lei de Moises* (Coimbra: no publisher, 1988).

MOSES BEN MAIMON (MAIMONIDES), *Commentary on the Mishnah*, 7 vols. (Jerusalem: Mossad Harav Kook, 1963–8).

—— *The Guide of the Perplexed*, trans. Shlomo Pines, 2 vols. (Chicago: University of Chicago Press, 1963).

—— *Mishneh Torah* (New York: Moznaim, 1989).

—— *Mishneh Torah*, standard Warsaw–Vilna edn. with comm.

—— *Treatise on Resurrection*, trans. Fred Rosner (New York: KTAV, 1982).

NADLER, STEVEN, 'Gersonides on Providence: A Jewish Chapter in the History of the General Will', *Journal of the History of Ideas*, 62 (2000), 37–57.

—— *Spinoza: A Life* (Cambridge: Cambridge University Press, 1999).

NAHON, GÉRARD, 'Amsterdam, métropole occidentale des *Sefarades* au XVIIe siècle', *Cahiers Spinoza*, 3 (1980), 15–50.

OFFENBERG, ADRIAEN, 'The Dating of the *Kol Bo*', *Studia Rosenthaliana*, 6 (1972), 86–106.

OLAN, LEVI, *Judaism and Immortality* (New York: Union of American Hebrew Congregations Press, n.d.).

OSIER, JEAN-PIERRE, *D'Uriel da Costa à Spinoza* (Paris: Berg International, 1983).

PEYRERA ABRAHAM, *La certeza del camino* (Amsterdam, 1666).

PIETERSE, WILHELMINA CHRISTINA, *Daniel Levi de Barrios als Geschiedschrijver Van de Portugees-Israelietische Gemeente te Amsterdam in Zijn 'Triumpho del Govierno Popular'* (Amsterdam, 1968).

POLLOCK, FREDERICK, *Spinoza: His Life and Philosophy* (London: Duckworth, 1899).

POPKIN, RICHARD, 'Spinoza, Neoplatonic Kabbalist?', in L. E. Goodman (ed.), *Neoplatonism and Jewish Thought* (Albany: SUNY Press, 1992).

RAPHAEL, SIMCHA PAULL, *Jewish Views of the Afterlife* (Northvale, NJ: Jason Aronson, 1994).

REVAH, I. S., 'Aux origines de la rupture Spinozienne: Nouveaux documents sur l'incroyance dans la communauté judéo-portugaise d'Amsterdam à l'époque de l'excommunication de Spinoza', *Revue des Études Juives*, 123 (1964), 359–43.

—— 'Aux origines de la rupture Spinozienne: Nouvel examen des origines, du déroulement et des conséquences de l'affaire Spinoza–Prado–Ribera', *Annuaire du Collège de France*, 70 (1970), 562–8.

—— 'Du marranisme au judaisme et au déisme: Uriel da Costa et sa famille', *Annuaire du Collège de France*, 67 (1967), 519.

—— 'La Religion d'Uriel da Costa, marrane de Porto', *Revue de l'Histoire des Religions*, 161 (1962), 44–76.

—— *Spinoza et Juan de Prado* (Paris: Mouton, 1959).

ROTH, CECIL, *A Life of Menasseh ben Israel* (Philadelphia: Jewish Publication Society, 1934).

RUDAVSKY, TAMAR, *Time Matters: Time, Creation and Cosmology in Medieval Jewish Thought* (Albany: SUNY Press, 2000).

SAADYA BEN JOSEPH, *The Book of Beliefs and Opinions*, trans. Samuel Rosenblatt (New Haven: Yale University Press, 1948).

—— *Commentary on the Book of Job*, trans. Lenn E. Goodman (New Haven: Yale University Press, 1988).

SALOMON, H. P., 'La Vraie Excommunication de Spinoza', *Forum Litterarum*, 28 (1994), 181–99.

SAPERSTEIN, MARC, 'Saul Levi Morteira's *Treatise on the Immortality of the Soul*', *Studia Rosenthaliana*, 25 (1991), 131–48.

SARACHEK, J., *Faith and Reason: The Conflict over the Rationalism of Maimonides* (Williamsport, Pa.: Bayard, 1935).

SCHWARTZ, GARY, *Rembrandt: His Life, his Paintings* (Harmondsworth: Viking, 1985).

SIEBRAND, H. J., *Spinoza and the Netherlanders* (Assen: Van Gorcum, 1988).

SILVA ROSA, J. S. da, *Geschiedenis der Portugeesche Joden te Amsterdam* (Amsterdam: Menno Hertzberger, 1925).

SILVER, DAVID, *Maimonidean Criticism and the Maimonidean Controversy* (Leiden: Brill, 1965).

SIRAT, COLETTE, *A History of Jewish Philosophy in the Middle Ages* (Cambridge: Cambridge University Press, 1985).

SMITH, STEVEN, *Spinoza, Liberalism and the Question of Jewish Identity* (New Haven: Yale University Press, 1997).

SPINOZA, BARUCH, *The Collected Works of Spinoza*, trans. E. M. Curley (Princeton: Princeton University Press, 1985).

—— *Spinoza Opera*, ed. Carl Gebhardt, 5 vols. (first pub. 1925; Heidelberg: Carl Winters Universitätsverlag, 1972).

—— *Theological–Political Treatise*, trans. Samuel Shirley (Leiden: Brill, 1989).

STEINBERG, DIANE, 'Spinoza's Theory of the Eternity of the Human Mind', *Canadian Journal of Philosophy*, 11 (1981), 35–68.

STRAUSS, LEO, *Persecution and the Art of Writing and Other Essays* (Glencoe, Ill.: Free Press, 1952).

Talmud Bavli (London: Soncino Press, 1994).

TEICHER, J. L., 'Why was Spinoza Banned?', *Menorah Journal*, 45 (1957), 41–60.

TOUATI, CHARLES, *La Pensée philosophique et théologique de Gersonide* (Paris: Les Éditions de Minuit, 1973).

—— 'La Problème du mal et la providence', in C. Touati, *Prophètes, Talmudistes, philosophes* (Paris: Cerf, 1990).

—— 'Les Deux Théories de Maimonide sur la providence', in C. Touati, *Prophètes, Talmudistes, philosophes* (Paris: Cerf, 1990).

TWERSKY, ISIDORE, *Introduction to the Code of Maimonides* (New Haven: Yale University Press, 1980).

VAN BUNGE, WIEP, 'On the Early Reception of the *Tractatus Theologico-Politicus*', *Studia Spinozana*, 5 (1989), 225–51.

VAN DER TAK, W. G., 'Spinoza's Payments to the Portuguese-Israelitic Community; and the Language in which he was Raised', *Studia Rosenthaliana*, 16 (1982), 190–5.

VAZ DIAS, A. M., 'De Scheiding in de Oudste Amsterdamsche Portugeesche Gemeente Beth Jacob', *De Vrijdagavond*, 7 (1939), 387–8.

VAZ DIAS, A. M., *Uriel da Costa: Nieuwe Bijdrage tot diens Levensgeschiedenis* (Leiden: Brill, 1936).

—— and W. G. VAN DER TAK, 'The Firm of Bento y Gabriel de Spinoza', *Studia Rosenthaliana*, 16 (1982), 178–89.

—— —— 'Spinoza: Merchant and Autodidact', *Studia Rosenthaliana*, 16 (1982), 105–71.

VLESSING, ODETTE, 'New Light on the Earliest History of the Amsterdam Portuguese Jews', in *Dutch Jewish History*, vol. iii (Assen: Van Gorcum, 1993).

—— 'Portugese Joden in de Gouden Eeuw', *Opbouw*, 42 (1989), 3–14.

—— 'The Jewish Community in Transition: From Acceptance to Emancipation', *Studia Rosenthaliana*, 30 (1996), 195–211.

WEISS, RAYMOND, *Maimonides' Ethics* (Chicago: University of Chicago Press, 1991).

WILSON, MARGARET, 'Spinoza's Theory of Knowledge', in D. Garrett (ed.), *The Cambridge Companion to Spinoza* (Cambridge: Cambridge University Press, 1996).

WIZNITZER, A., 'The Merger Agreement and the Regulations of Congregation "Talmud Torah" of Amsterdam (1638–39)', *Historia Judaica*, 20–1 (1958–9), 109–32.

WOLF, A. (ed. and trans.), *The Oldest Biography of Spinoza* (first pub. 1927; Port Washington, NY: Kennikat Press, 1970).

WOLFSON, HARRY, *The Philosophy of Spinoza*, 2 vols. (Cambridge, Mass.: Harvard University Press, 1934).

YOVEL, YIRMIYAHU, *Spinoza and Other Heretics*, i: *The Marrano of Reason* (Princeton: Princeton University Press, 1989).

—— 'Why was Spinoza Excommunicated?', *Commentary* (Nov. 1977), 46–52.

Index